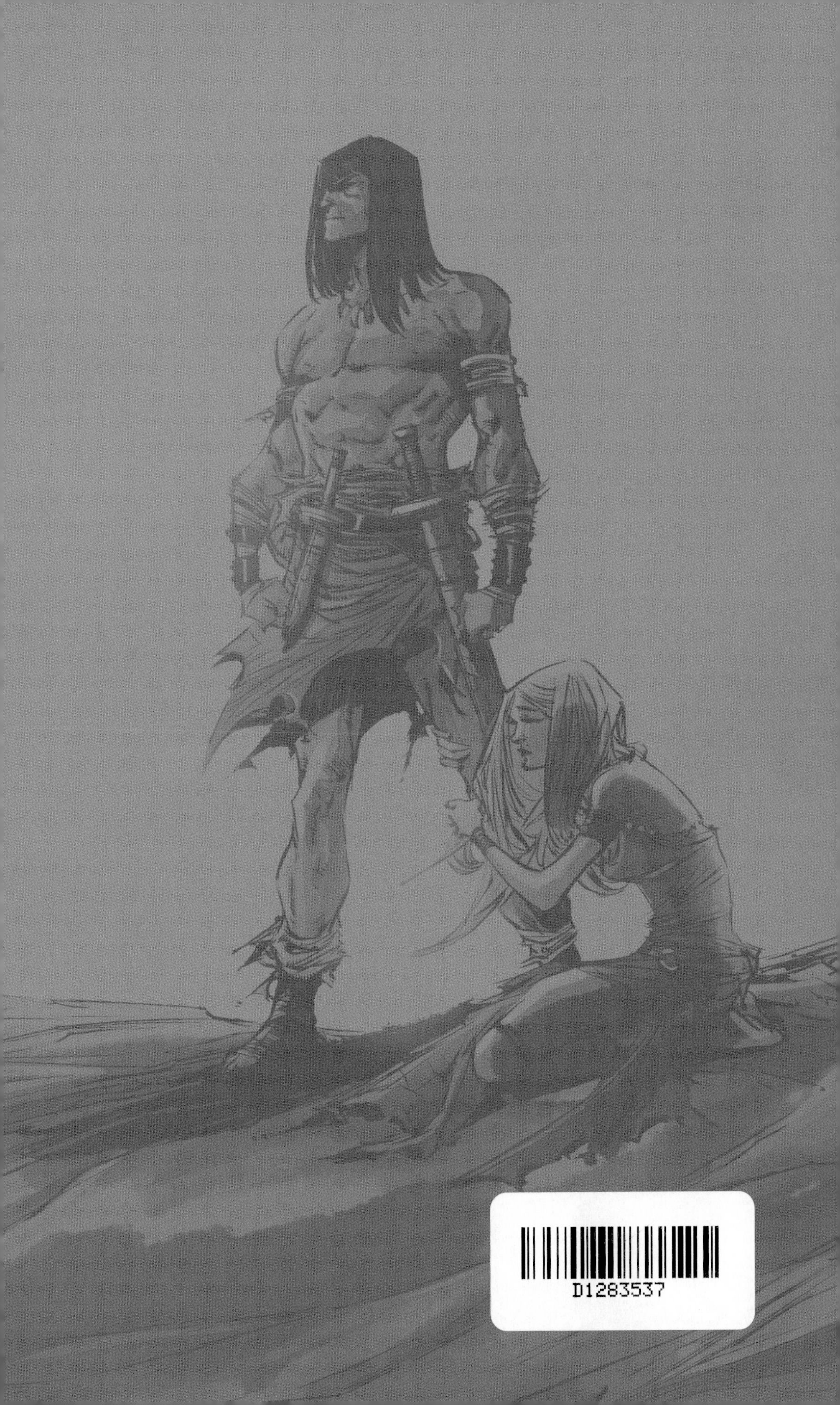

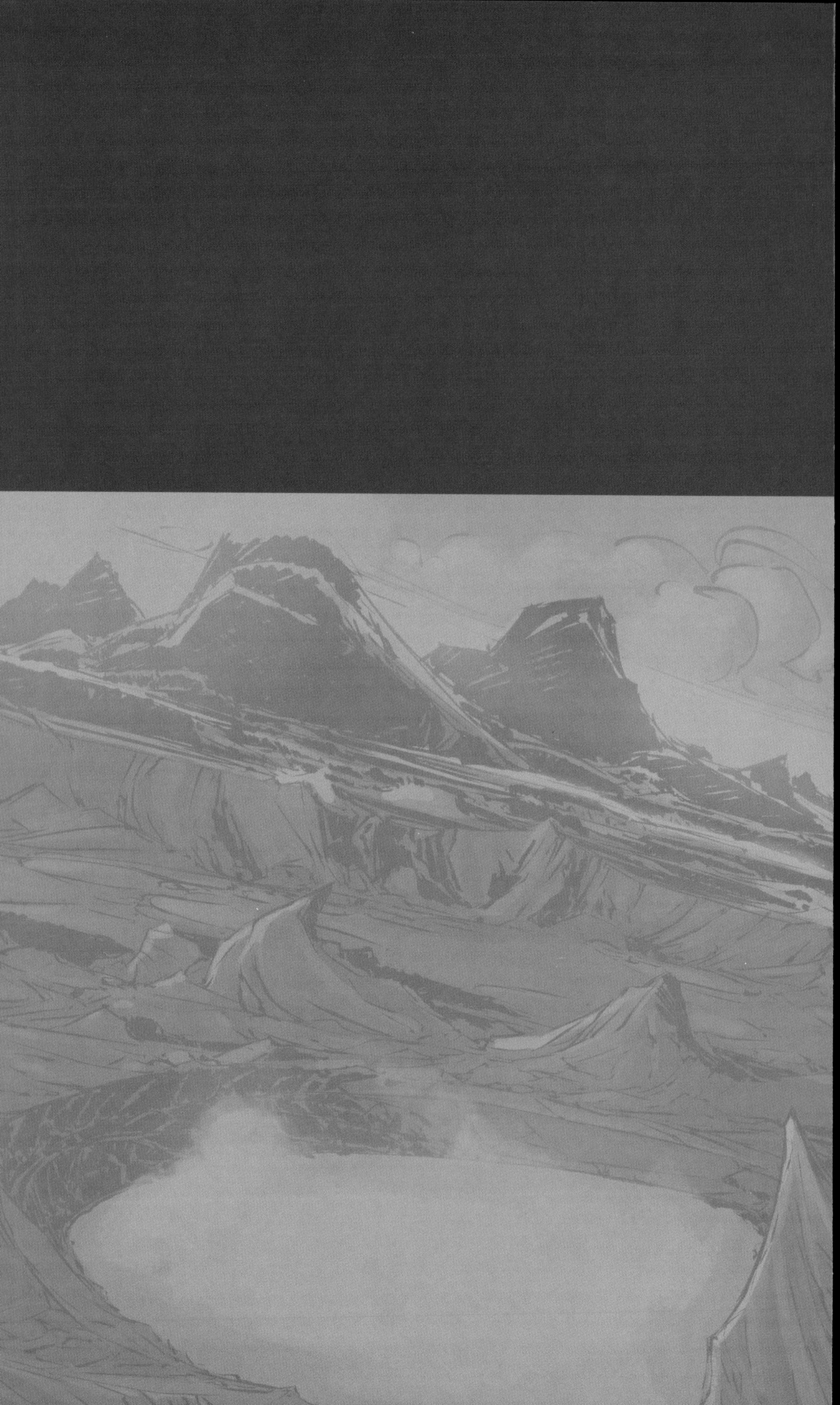

CONAN®

THE DAMNED HORDE

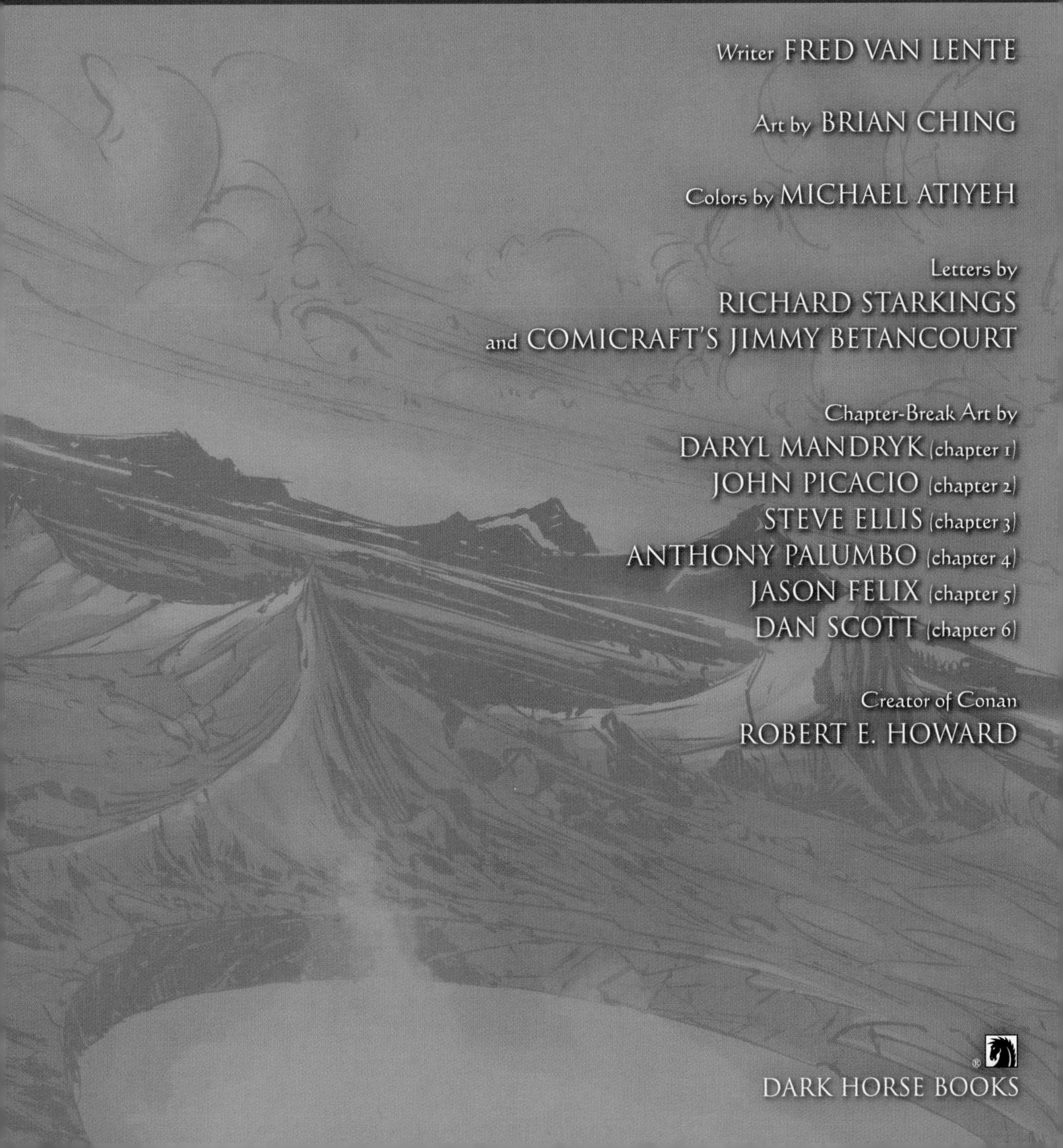

Writer FRED VAN LENTE

Art by BRIAN CHING

Colors by MICHAEL ATIYEH

Letters by
RICHARD STARKINGS
and COMICRAFT'S JIMMY BETANCOURT

Chapter-Break Art by
DARYL MANDRYK (chapter 1)
JOHN PICACIO (chapter 2)
STEVE ELLIS (chapter 3)
ANTHONY PALUMBO (chapter 4)
JASON FELIX (chapter 5)
DAN SCOTT (chapter 6)

Creator of Conan
ROBERT E. HOWARD

DARK HORSE BOOKS

Publisher MIKE RICHARDSON Editor DAVE MARSHALL Assistant Editors ROXY POLK and AARON WALKER Designer KAT LARSON Digital Art Technician CHRISTIANNE GOUDREAU

Special thanks to FREDRIK MALMBERG and JOAKIM ZETTERBERG at CONAN PROPERTIES.

This volume collects issues #7–#12 of the Dark Horse Comics monthly *Conan the Avenger* series.

Published by Dark Horse Books
A division of Dark Horse Comics, Inc.
10956 SE Main Street
Milwaukie, OR 97222

DarkHorse.com

International Licensing: (503) 905-2377
To find a comics shop in your area, call the Comic Shop Locator Service toll-free at 1-888-266-4226

First softcover edition: February 2016
ISBN 978-1-61655-799-7

10 9 8 7 6 5 4 3 2 1

Printed in China

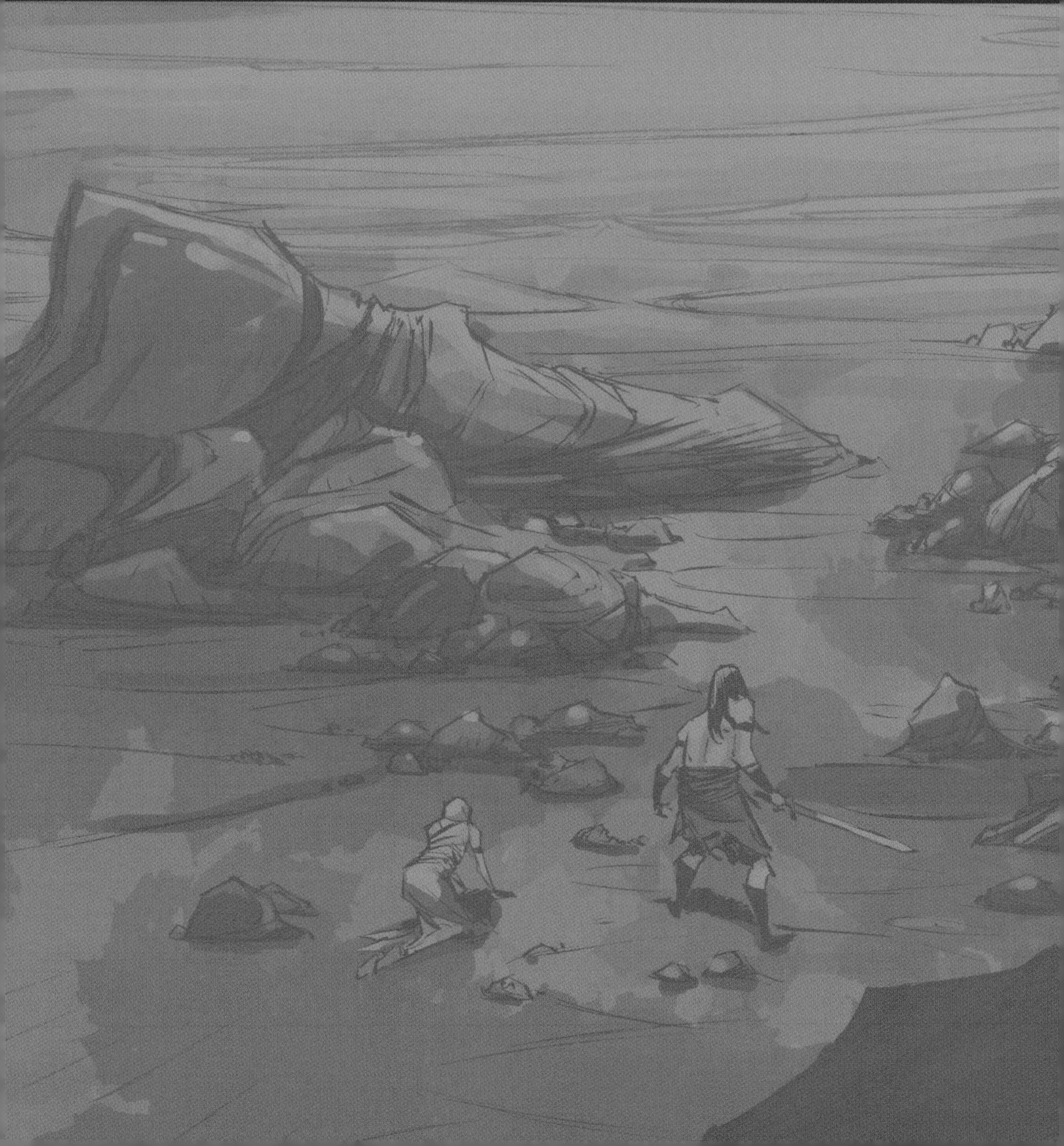

CHAPTER ONE

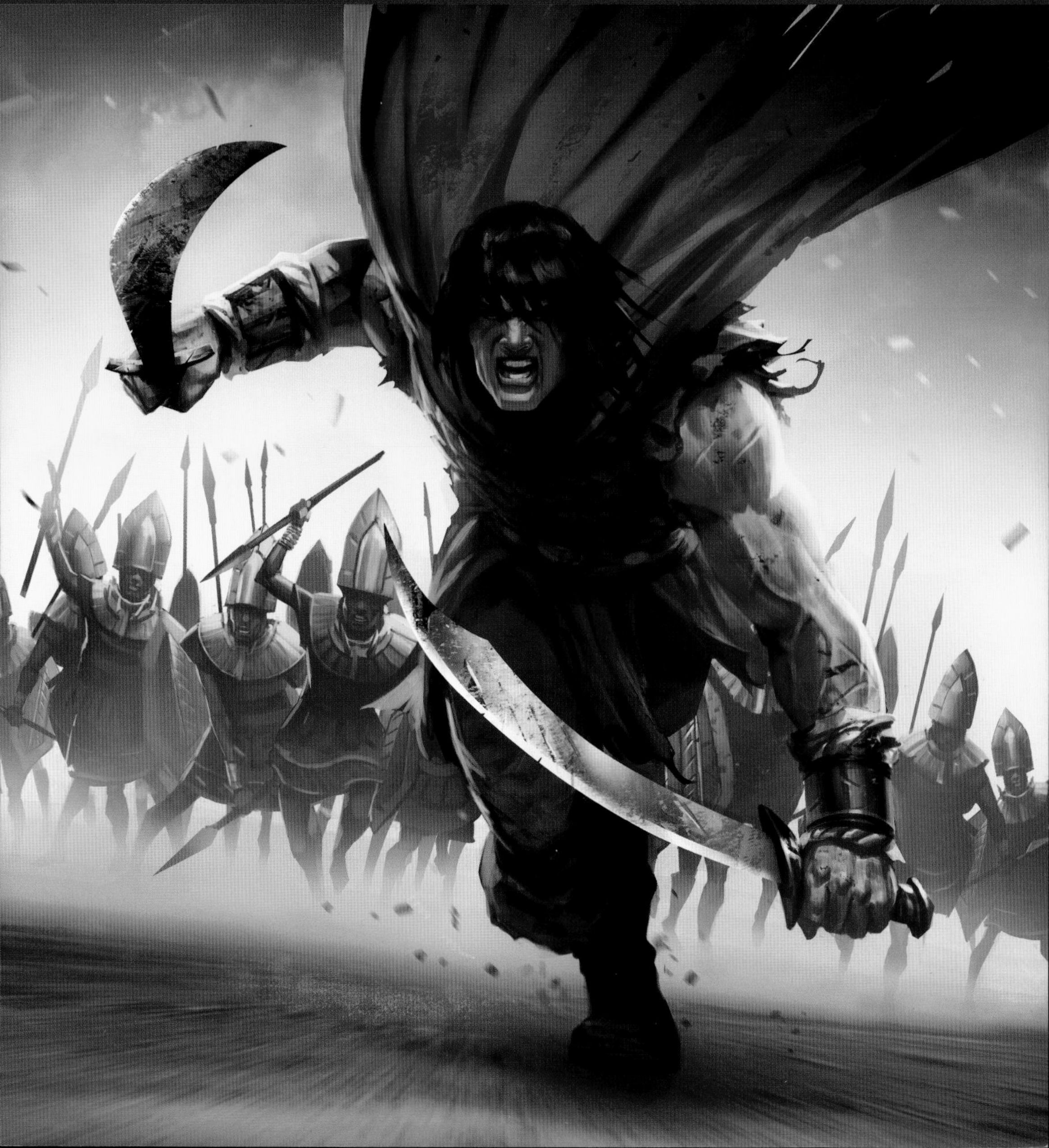

"Have you ever seen so many men who *deserve* to die?"

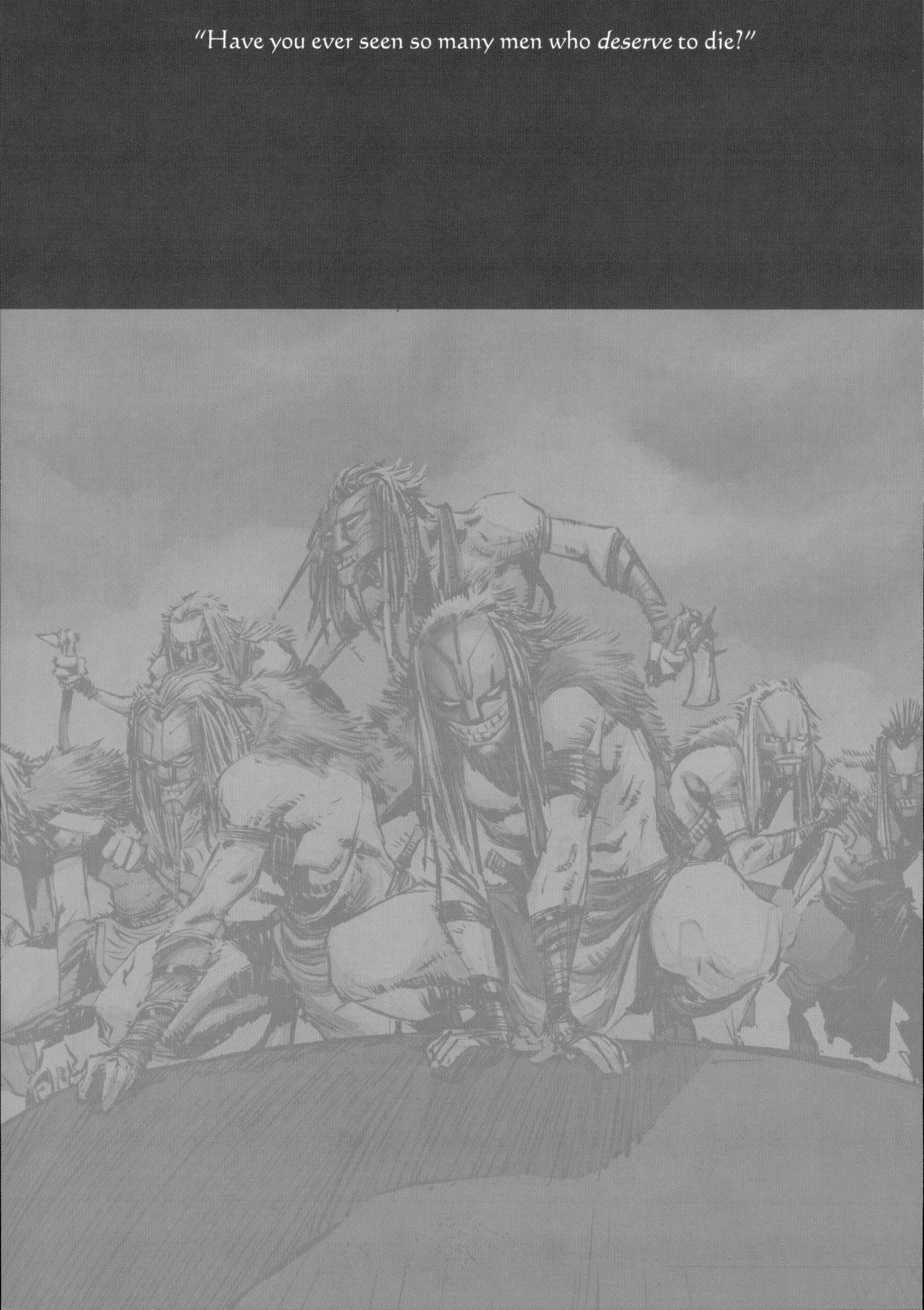

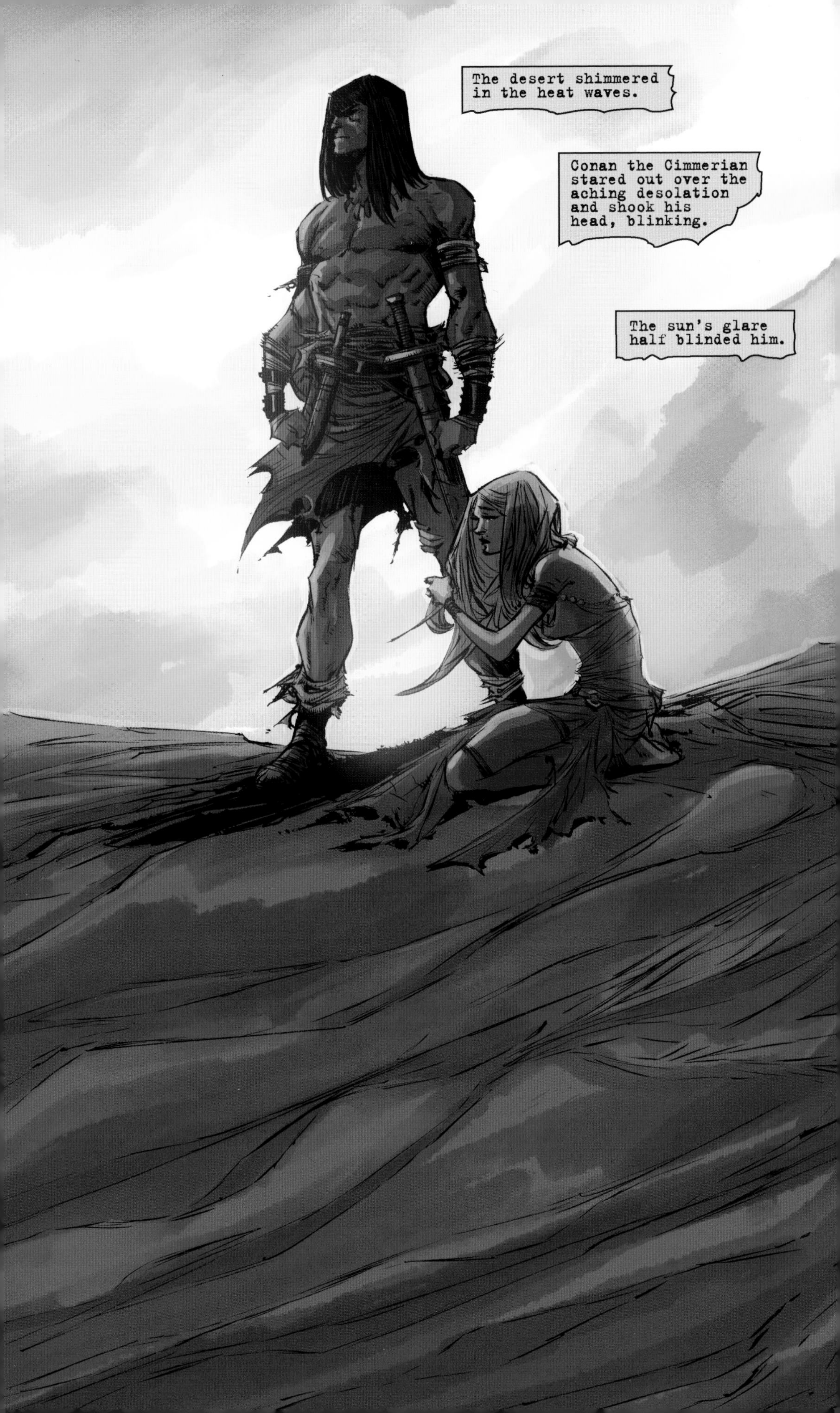
The desert shimmered in the heat waves.
Conan the Cimmerian stared out over the aching desolation and shook his head, blinking.
The sun's glare half blinded him.

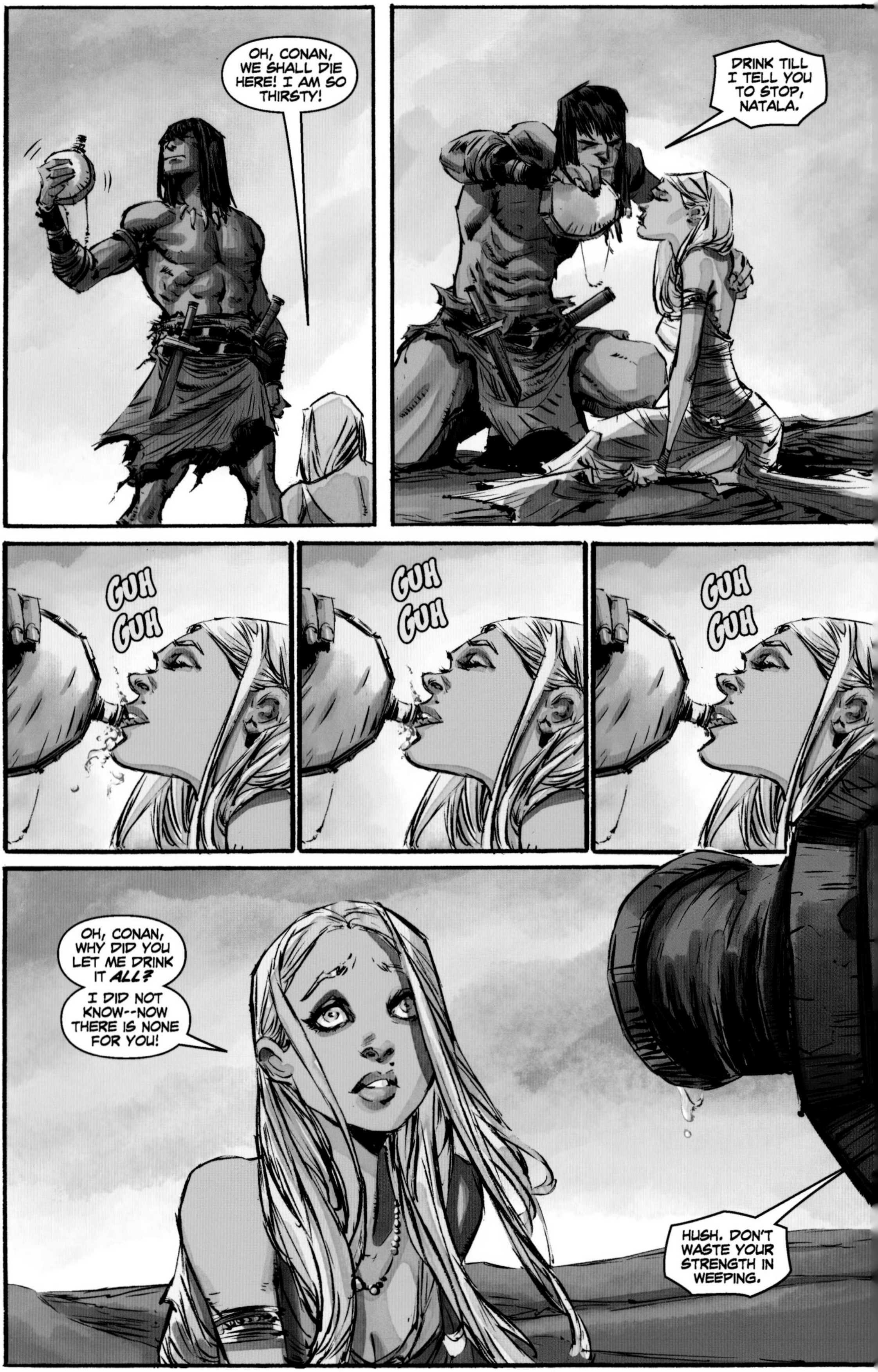

OH, CONAN, WE SHALL DIE HERE! I AM SO THIRSTY!
DRINK TILL I TELL YOU TO STOP, NATALA.
GUH GUH
GUH GUH
GUH GUH
OH, CONAN, WHY DID YOU LET ME DRINK IT ALL?
I DID NOT KNOW--NOW THERE IS NONE FOR YOU!
HUSH. DON'T WASTE YOUR STRENGTH IN WEEPING.

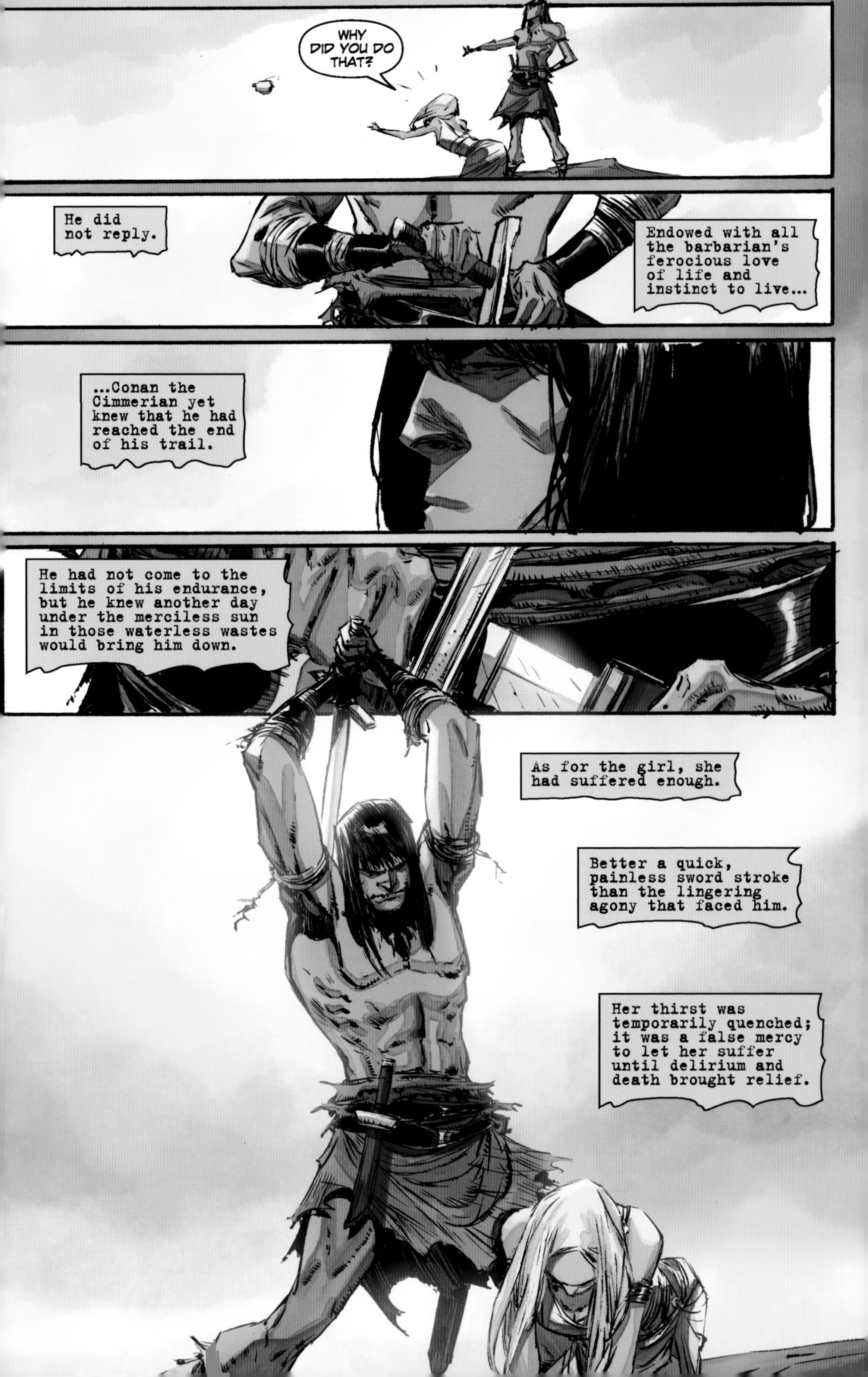
WHY DID YOU DO THAT?
He did not reply.
Endowed with all the barbarian's ferocious love of life and instinct to live...
...Conan the Cimmerian yet knew that he had reached the end of his trail.
He had not come to the limits of his endurance, but he knew another day under the merciless sun in those waterless wastes would bring him down.
As for the girl, she had suffered enough.
Better a quick, painless sword stroke than the lingering agony that faced him.
Her thirst was temporarily quenched; it was a false mercy to let her suffer until delirium and death brought relief.

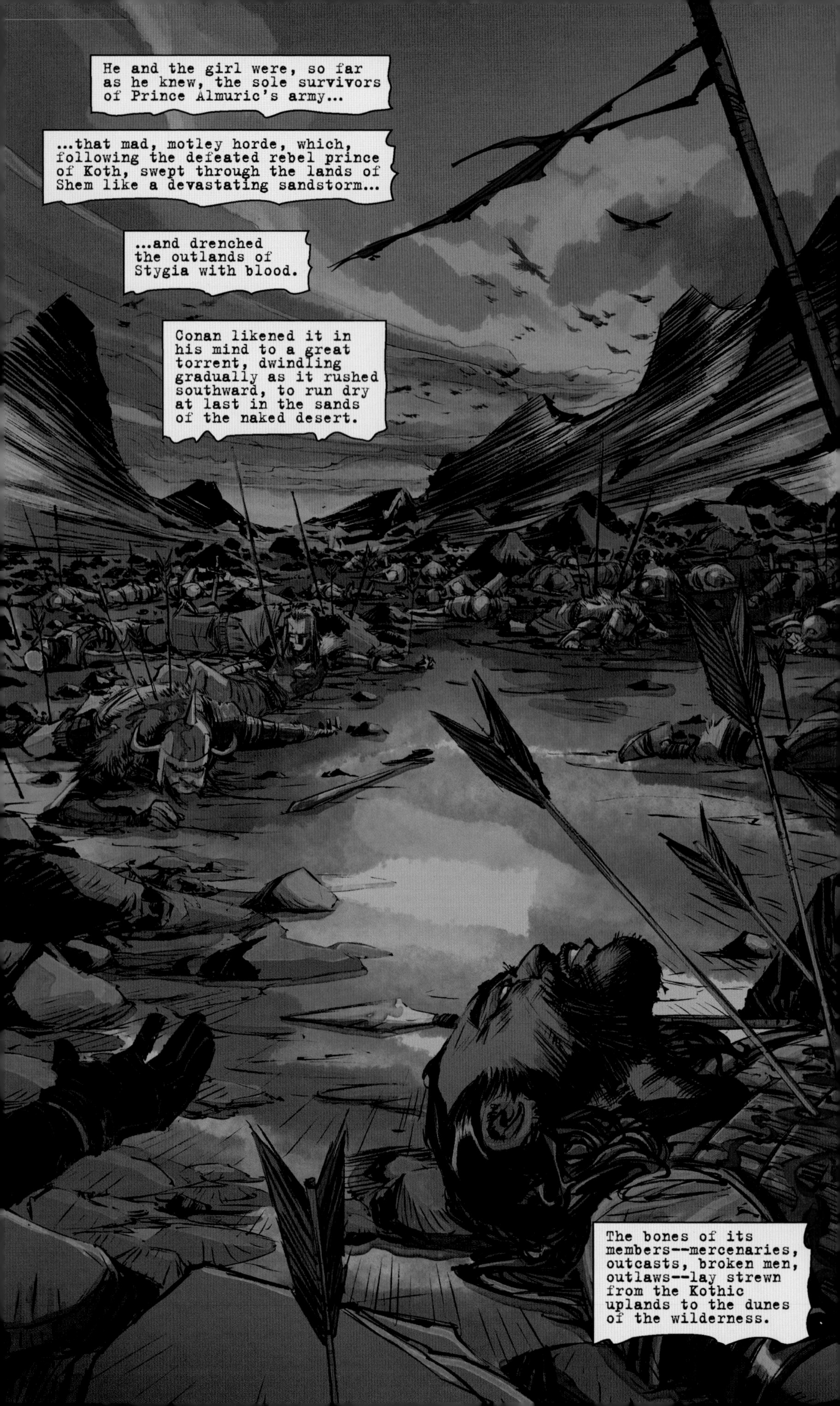
He and the girl were, so far as he knew, the sole survivors of Prince Almuric's army...
...that mad, motley horde, which, following the defeated rebel prince of Koth, swept through the lands of Shem like a devastating sandstorm...
...and drenched the outlands of Stygia with blood.
Conan likened it in his mind to a great torrent, dwindling gradually as it rushed southward, to run dry at last in the sands of the naked desert.
The bones of its members--mercenaries, outcasts, broken men, outlaws--lay strewn from the Kothic uplands to the dunes of the wilderness.

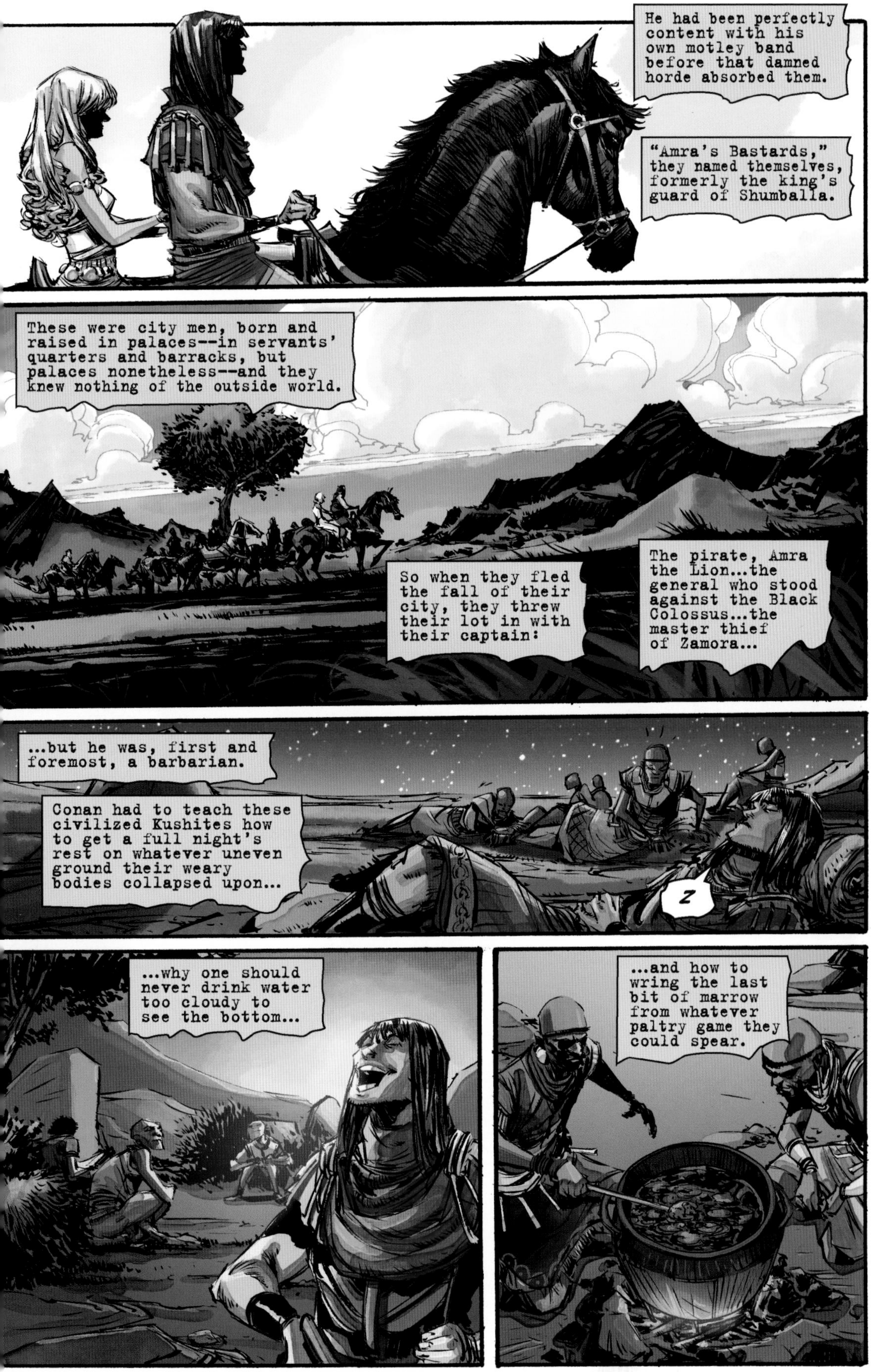
He had been perfectly content with his own motley band before that damned horde absorbed them.
"Amra's Bastards," they named themselves, formerly the king's guard of Shumballa.
These were city men, born and raised in palaces--in servants' quarters and barracks, but palaces nonetheless--and they knew nothing of the outside world.
So when they fled the fall of their city, they threw their lot in with their captain:
The pirate, Amra the Lion...the general who stood against the Black Colossus...the master thief of Zamora...
...but he was, first and foremost, a barbarian.
Conan had to teach these civilized Kushites how to get a full night's rest on whatever uneven ground their weary bodies collapsed upon...
Z
...why one should never drink water too cloudy to see the bottom...
...and how to wring the last bit of marrow from whatever paltry game they could spear.

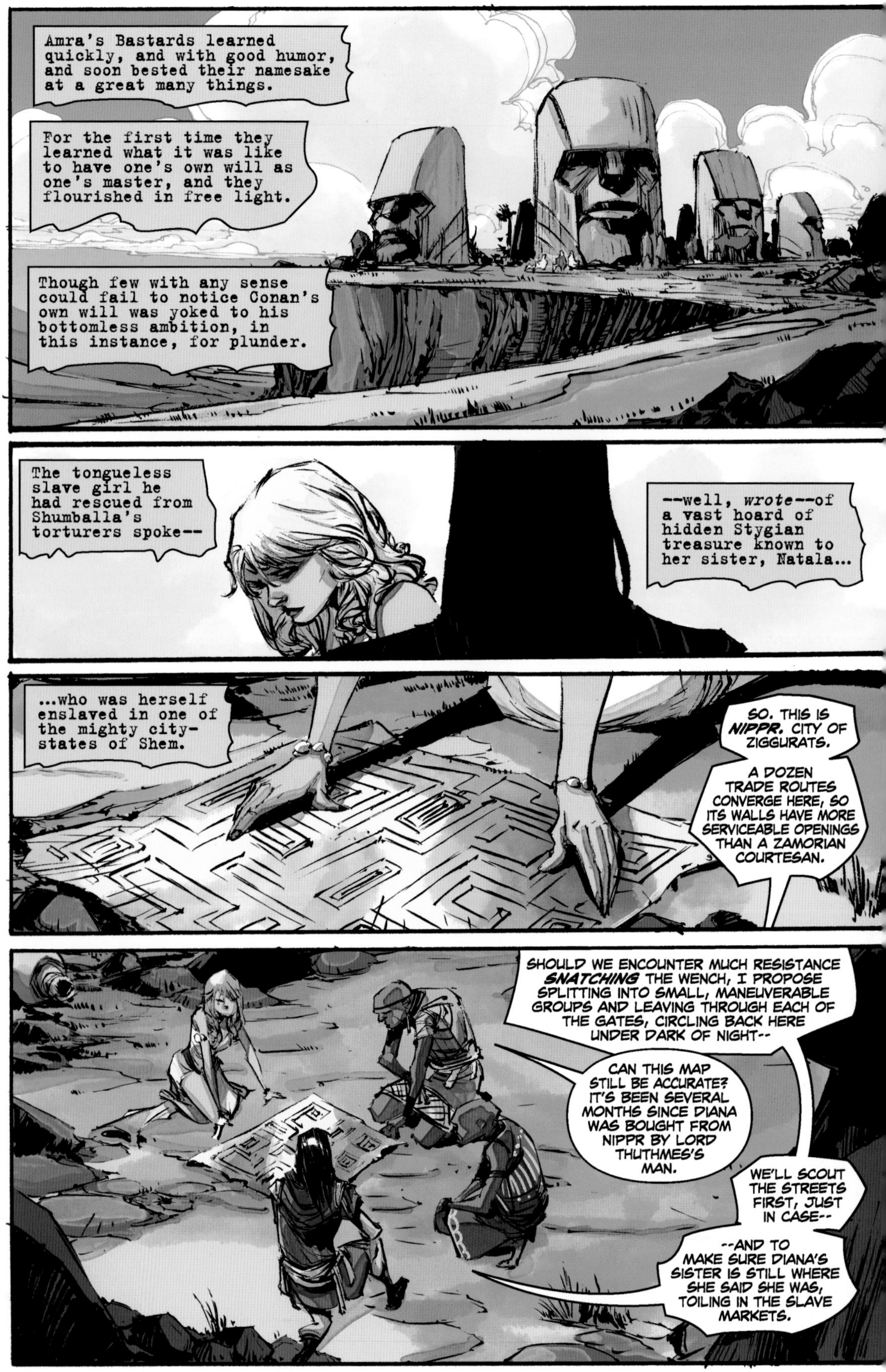
Amra's Bastards learned quickly, and with good humor, and soon bested their namesake at a great many things.
For the first time they learned what it was like to have one's own will as one's master, and they flourished in free light.
Though few with any sense could fail to notice Conan's own will was yoked to his bottomless ambition, in this instance, for plunder.
The tongueless slave girl he had rescued from Shumballa's torturers spoke--
--well, *wrote*--of a vast hoard of hidden Stygian treasure known to her sister, Natala...
...who was herself enslaved in one of the mighty city-states of Shem.
SO. THIS IS ***NIPPR.*** CITY OF ZIGGURATS.
A DOZEN TRADE ROUTES CONVERGE HERE, SO ITS WALLS HAVE MORE SERVICEABLE OPENINGS THAN A ZAMORIAN COURTESAN.
SHOULD WE ENCOUNTER MUCH RESISTANCE ***SNATCHING*** THE WENCH, I PROPOSE SPLITTING INTO SMALL, MANEUVERABLE GROUPS AND LEAVING THROUGH EACH OF THE GATES, CIRCLING BACK HERE UNDER DARK OF NIGHT--
CAN THIS MAP STILL BE ACCURATE? IT'S BEEN SEVERAL MONTHS SINCE DIANA WAS BOUGHT FROM NIPPR BY LORD THUTHMES'S MAN.
WE'LL SCOUT THE STREETS FIRST, JUST IN CASE--
--AND TO MAKE SURE DIANA'S SISTER IS STILL WHERE SHE SAID SHE WAS, TOILING IN THE SLAVE MARKETS.

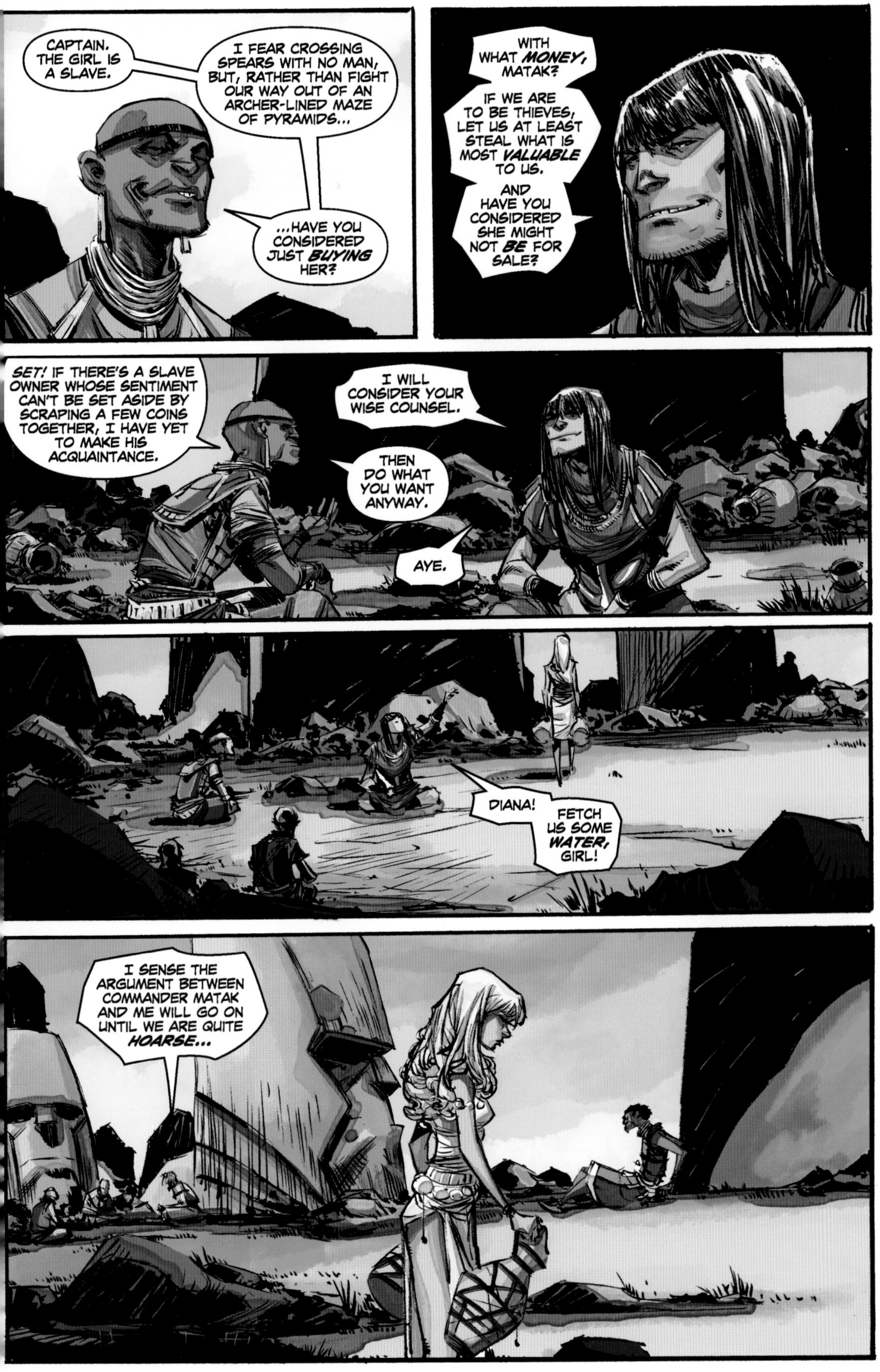
CAPTAIN. THE GIRL IS A SLAVE.
I FEAR CROSSING SPEARS WITH NO MAN, BUT, RATHER THAN FIGHT OUR WAY OUT OF AN ARCHER-LINED MAZE OF PYRAMIDS...
...HAVE YOU CONSIDERED JUST BUYING HER?
WITH WHAT MONEY, MATAK?
IF WE ARE TO BE THIEVES, LET US AT LEAST STEAL WHAT IS MOST VALUABLE TO US.
AND HAVE YOU CONSIDERED SHE MIGHT NOT BE FOR SALE?
SET! IF THERE'S A SLAVE OWNER WHOSE SENTIMENT CAN'T BE SET ASIDE BY SCRAPING A FEW COINS TOGETHER, I HAVE YET TO MAKE HIS ACQUAINTANCE.
I WILL CONSIDER YOUR WISE COUNSEL.
THEN DO WHAT YOU WANT ANYWAY.
AYE.
DIANA!
FETCH US SOME WATER, GIRL!
I SENSE THE ARGUMENT BETWEEN COMMANDER MATAK AND ME WILL GO ON UNTIL WE ARE QUITE HOARSE...

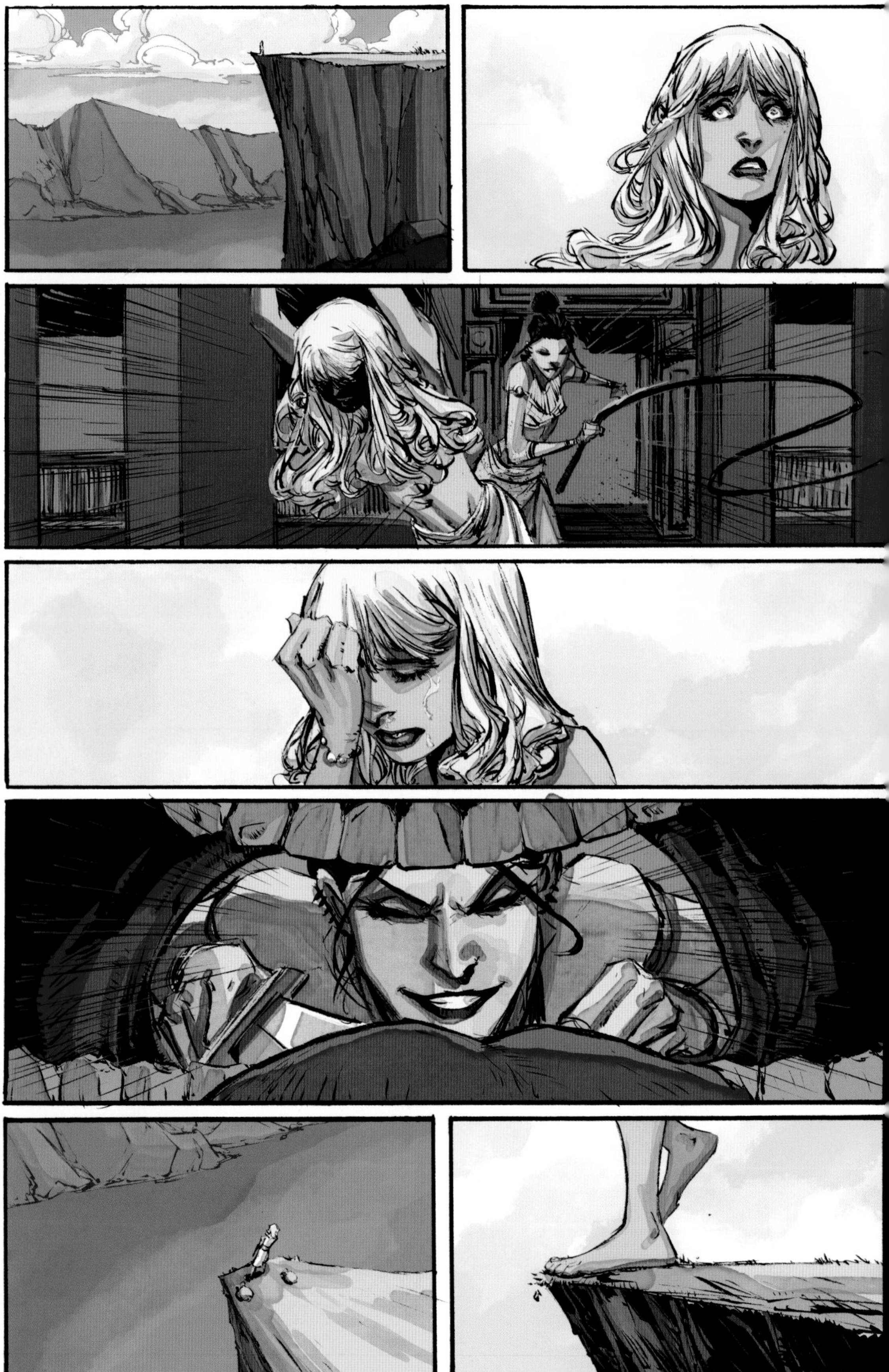

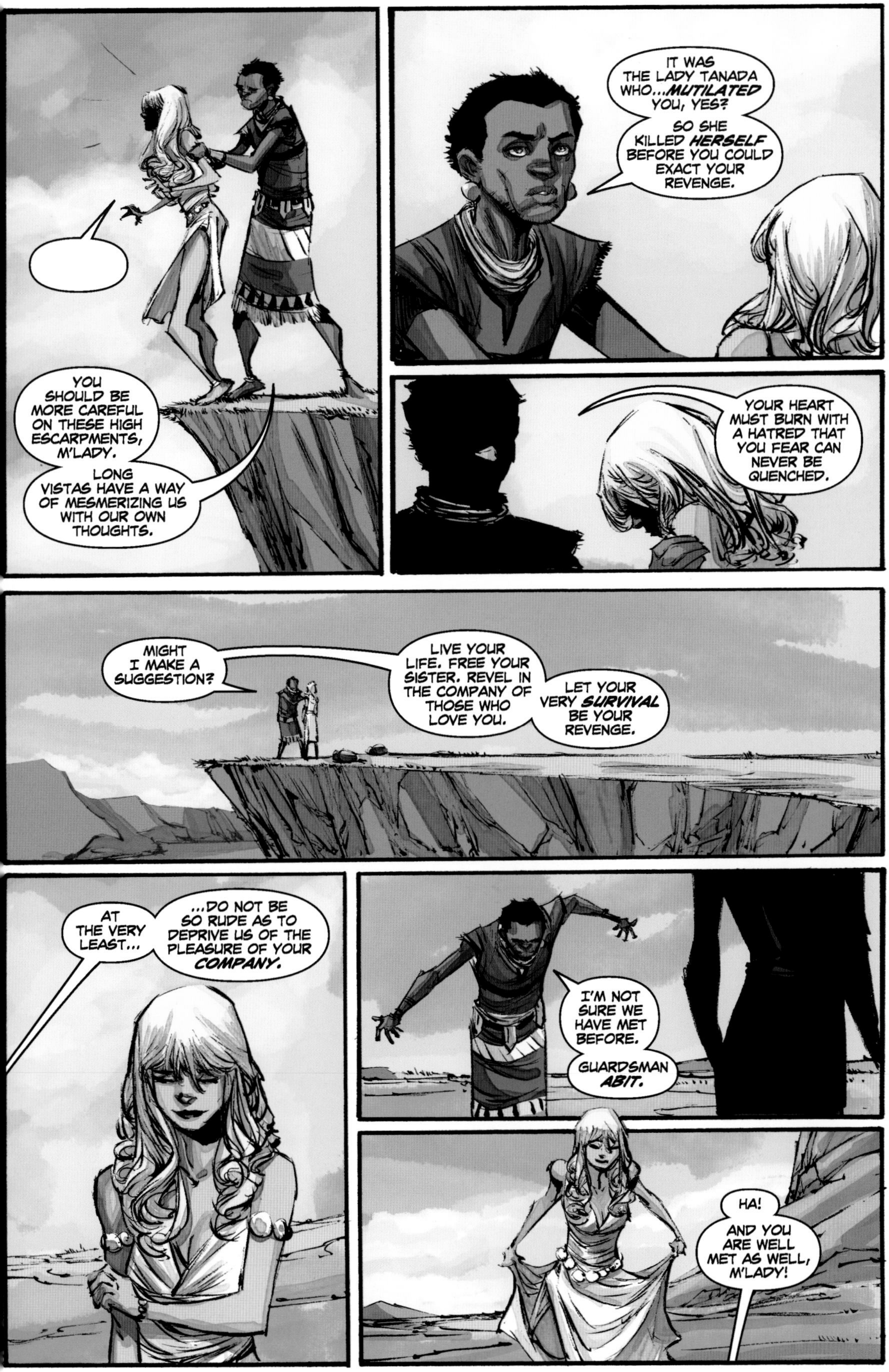
YOU SHOULD BE MORE CAREFUL ON THESE HIGH ESCARPMENTS, M'LADY.
LONG VISTAS HAVE A WAY OF MESMERIZING US WITH OUR OWN THOUGHTS.
IT WAS THE LADY TANADA WHO...MUTILATED YOU, YES?
SO SHE KILLED HERSELF BEFORE YOU COULD EXACT YOUR REVENGE.
YOUR HEART MUST BURN WITH A HATRED THAT YOU FEAR CAN NEVER BE QUENCHED.
MIGHT I MAKE A SUGGESTION?
LIVE YOUR LIFE. FREE YOUR SISTER. REVEL IN THE COMPANY OF THOSE WHO LOVE YOU.
LET YOUR VERY SURVIVAL BE YOUR REVENGE.
AT THE VERY LEAST...
...DO NOT BE SO RUDE AS TO DEPRIVE US OF THE PLEASURE OF YOUR COMPANY.
I'M NOT SURE WE HAVE MET BEFORE.
GUARDSMAN ABIT.
HA!
AND YOU ARE WELL MET AS WELL, M'LADY!

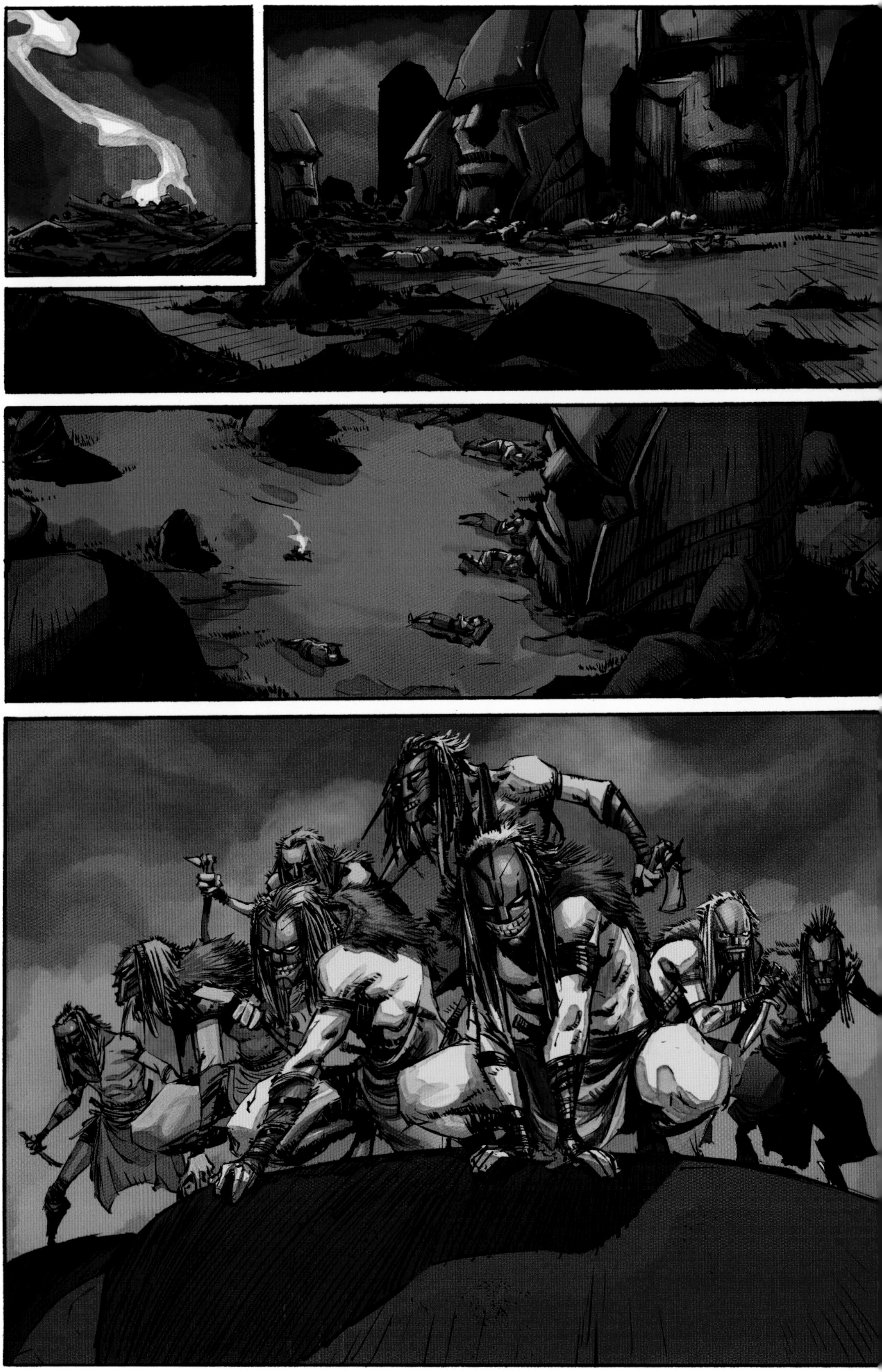

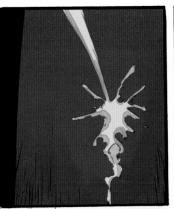

BASTARDS!
TO ARMS!

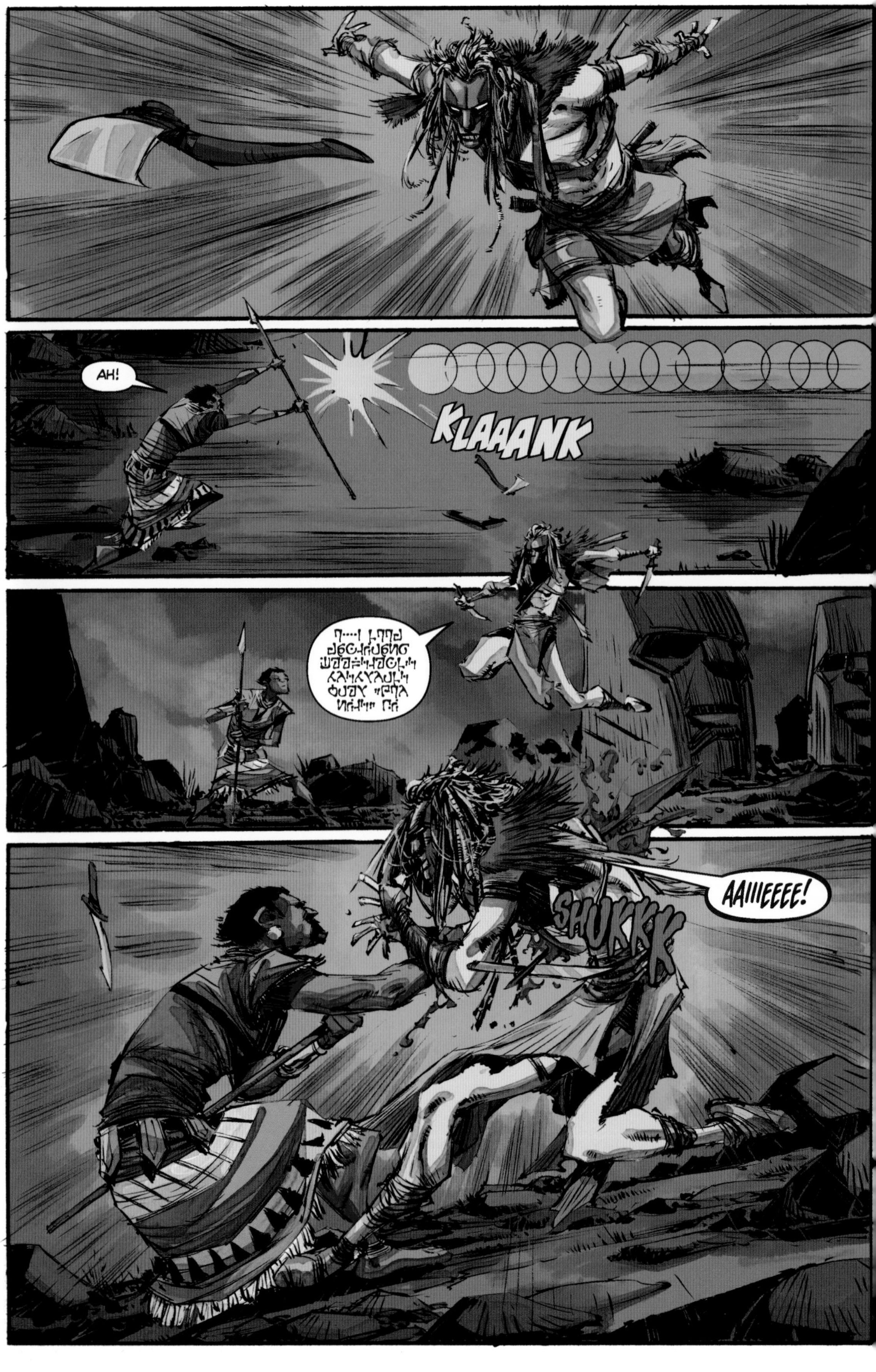
AH!
KLAAANK
AAIIIEEEE!
SHUKKK

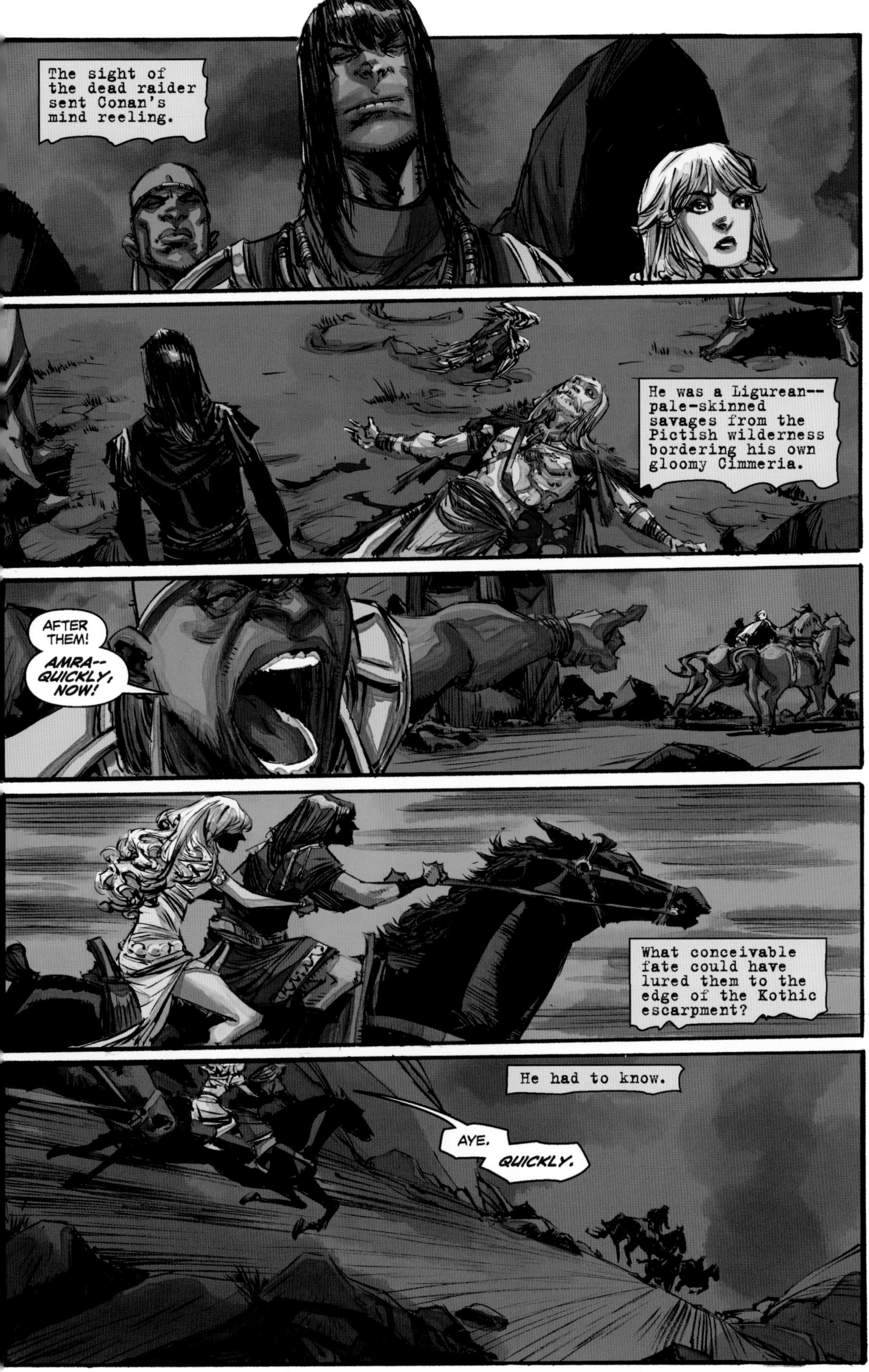

The sight of the dead raider sent Conan's mind reeling.
He was a Ligurean--pale-skinned savages from the Pictish wilderness bordering his own gloomy Cimmeria.
AFTER THEM!
AMRA--QUICKLY, NOW!
What conceivable fate could have lured them to the edge of the Kothic escarpment?
He had to know.
AYE.
QUICKLY.

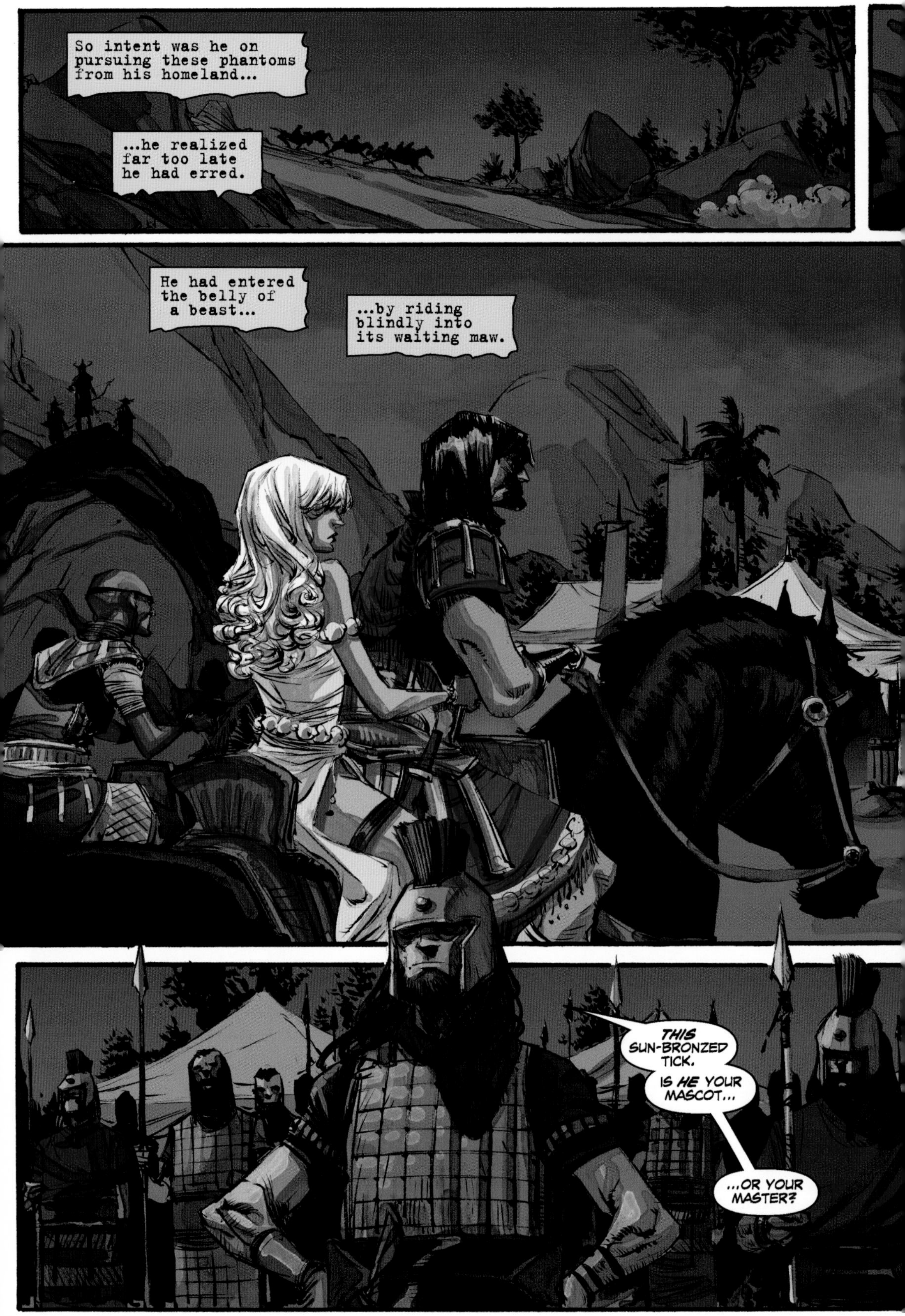

So intent was he on pursuing these phantoms from his homeland...
...he realized far too late he had erred.
He had entered the belly of a beast...
...by riding blindly into its waiting maw.
THIS SUN-BRONZED TICK.
IS HE YOUR MASCOT...
...OR YOUR MASTER?

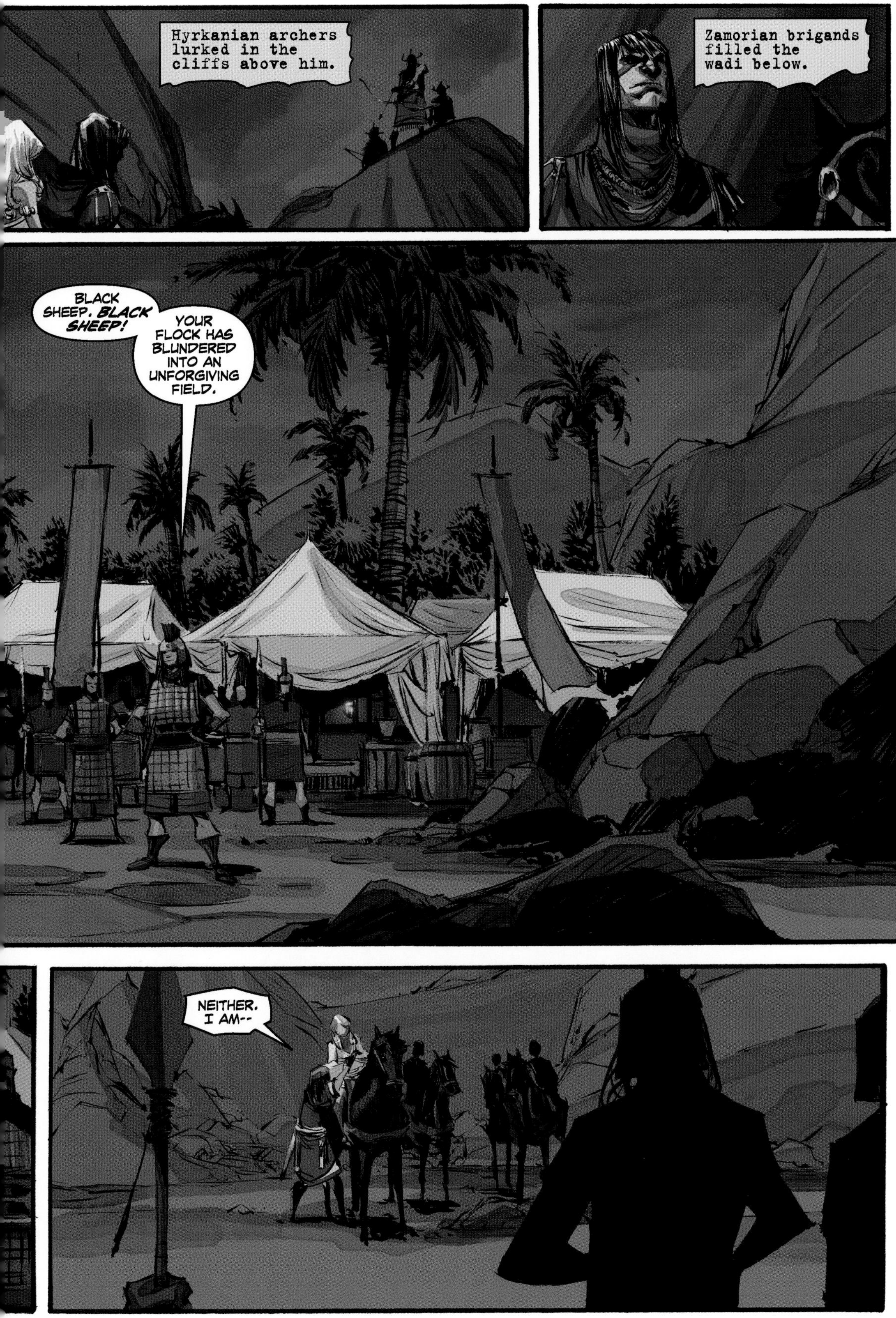
Hyrkanian archers lurked in the cliffs above him.
Zamorian brigands filled the wadi below.
BLACK SHEEP. BLACK SHEEP!
YOUR FLOCK HAS BLUNDERED INTO AN UNFORGIVING FIELD.
NEITHER. I AM--

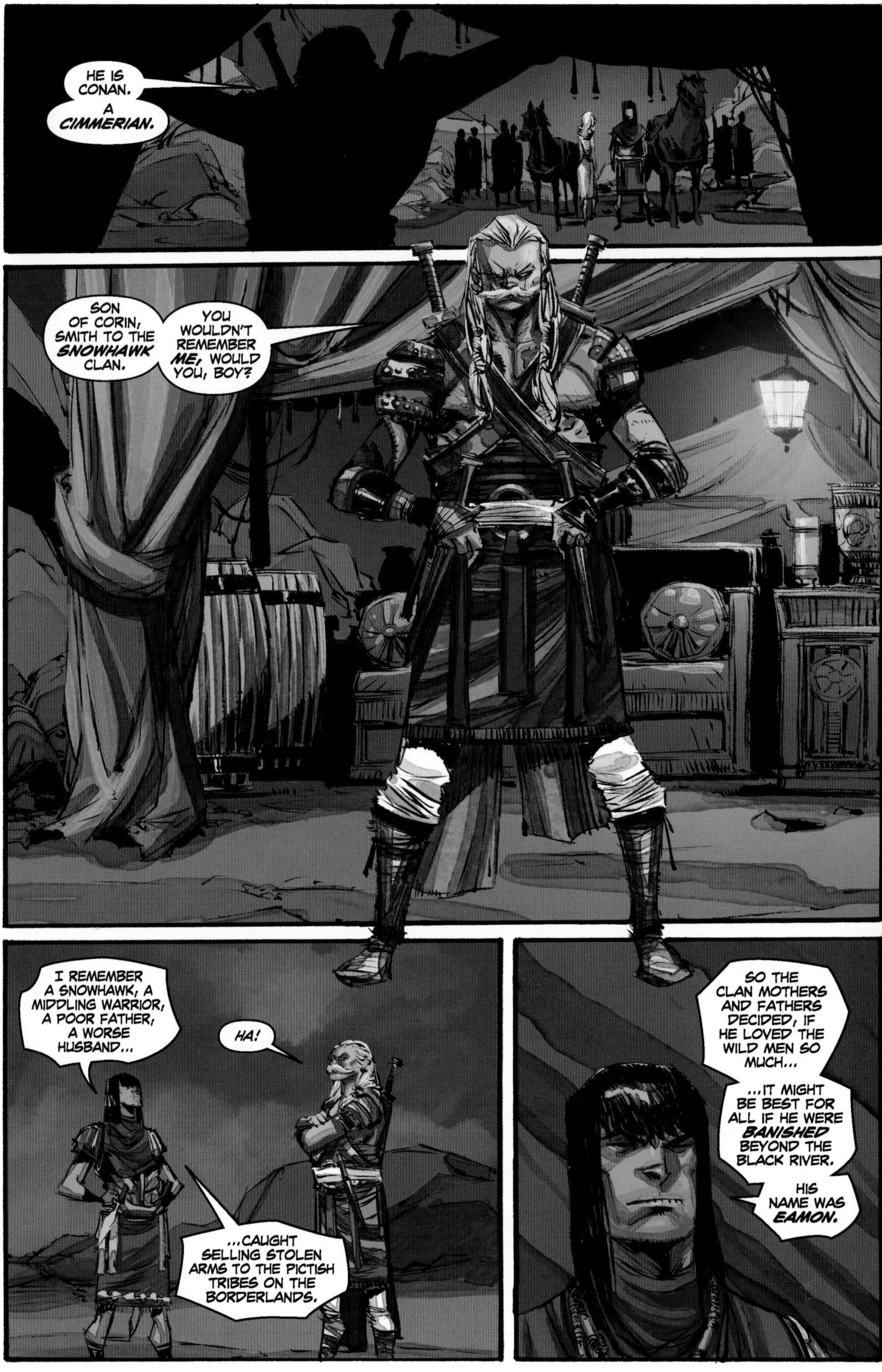
HE IS CONAN.
A CIMMERIAN.
SON OF CORIN, SMITH TO THE SNOWHAWK CLAN.
YOU WOULDN'T REMEMBER ME, WOULD YOU, BOY?
I REMEMBER A SNOWHAWK, A MIDDLING WARRIOR, A POOR FATHER, A WORSE HUSBAND...
HA!
...CAUGHT SELLING STOLEN ARMS TO THE PICTISH TRIBES ON THE BORDERLANDS.
SO THE CLAN MOTHERS AND FATHERS DECIDED, IF HE LOVED THE WILD MEN SO MUCH...
...IT MIGHT BE BEST FOR ALL IF HE WERE BANISHED BEYOND THE BLACK RIVER.
HIS NAME WAS EAMON.

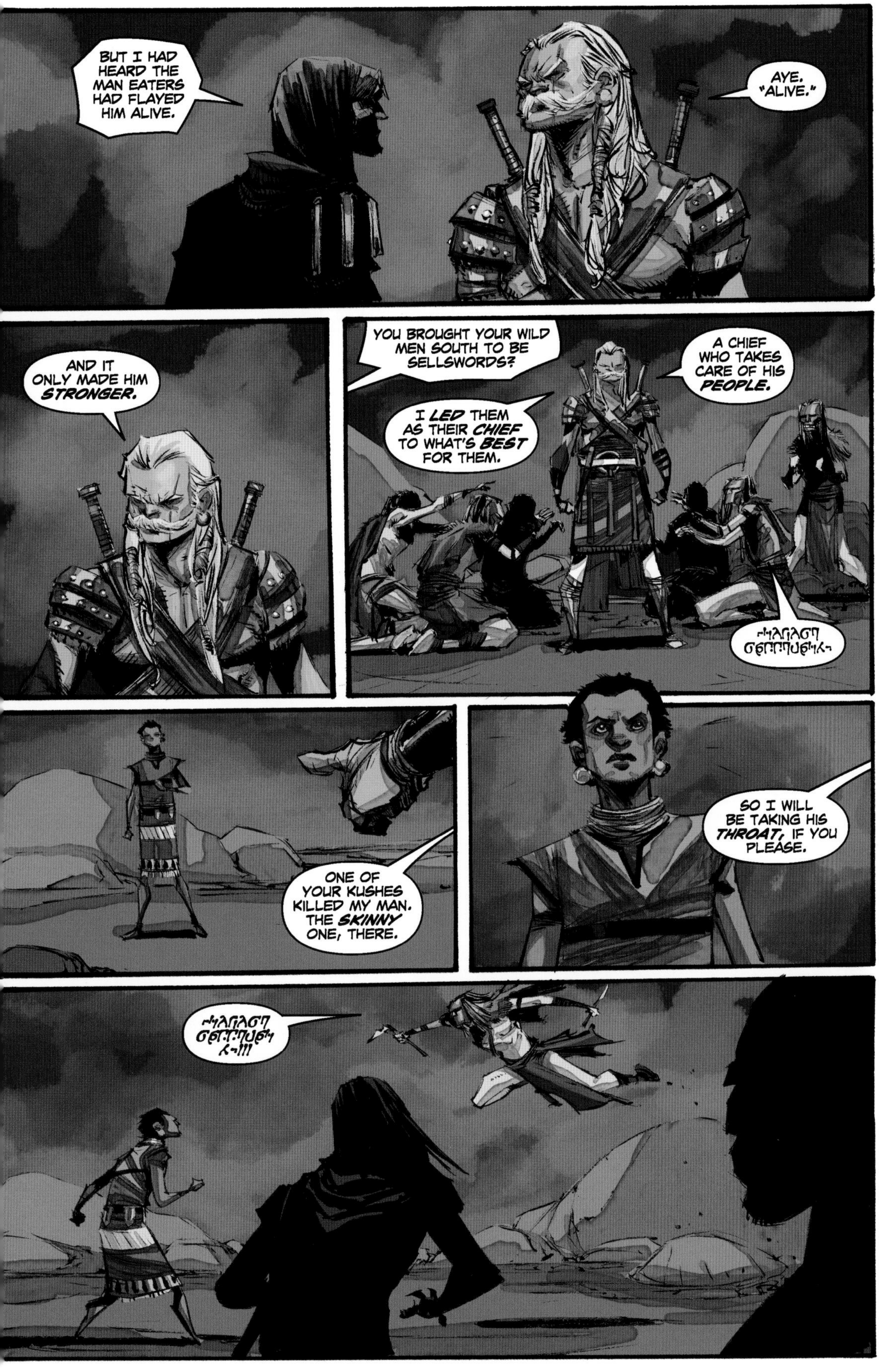
BUT I HAD HEARD THE MAN EATERS HAD FLAYED HIM ALIVE.
AYE. "ALIVE."
AND IT ONLY MADE HIM STRONGER.
YOU BROUGHT YOUR WILD MEN SOUTH TO BE SELLSWORDS?
I LED THEM AS THEIR CHIEF TO WHAT'S BEST FOR THEM.
A CHIEF WHO TAKES CARE OF HIS PEOPLE.
ONE OF YOUR KUSHES KILLED MY MAN. THE SKINNY ONE, THERE.
SO I WILL BE TAKING HIS THROAT, IF YOU PLEASE.

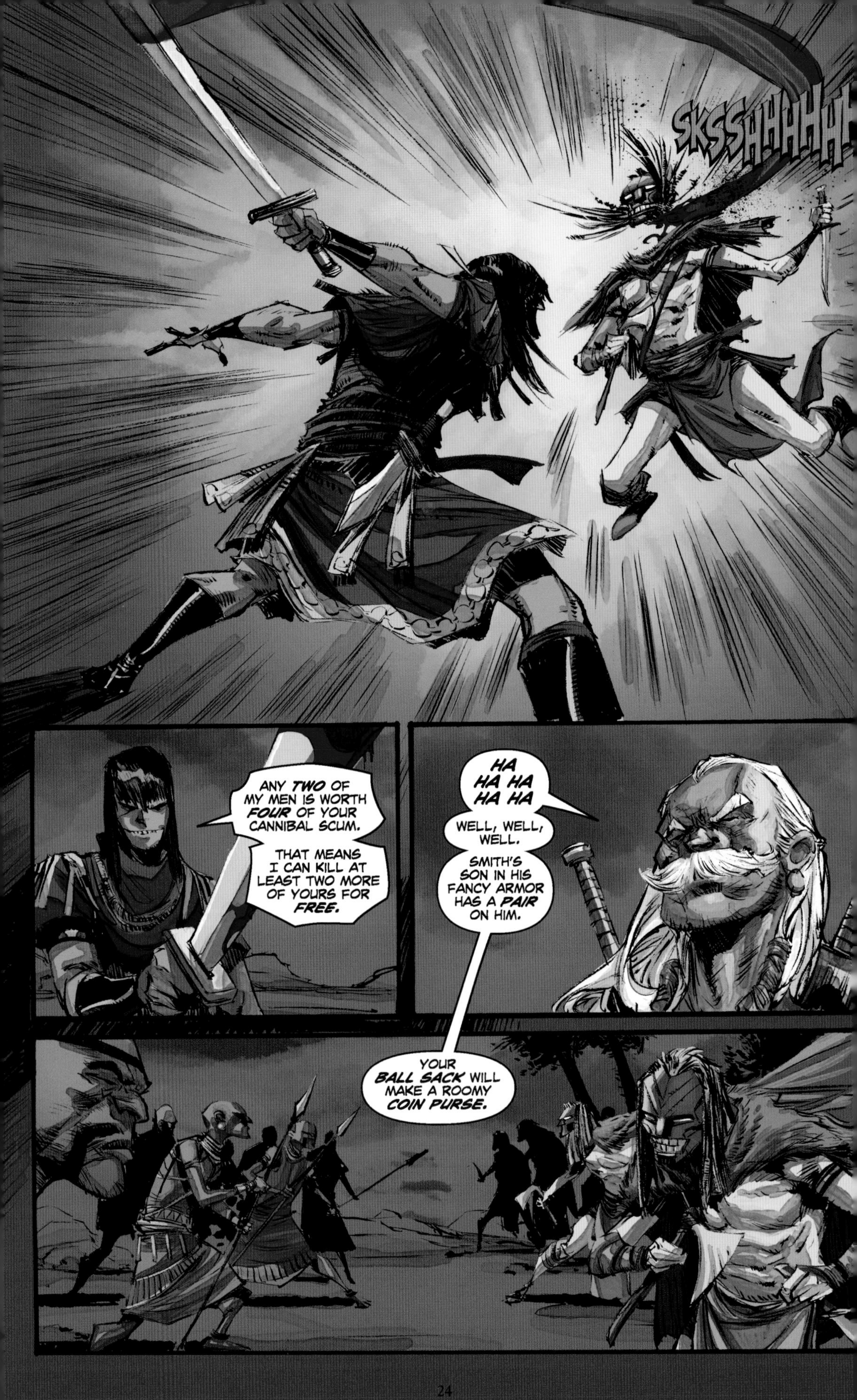
SKSSHHHHH
ANY TWO OF MY MEN IS WORTH FOUR OF YOUR CANNIBAL SCUM.
THAT MEANS I CAN KILL AT LEAST TWO MORE OF YOURS FOR FREE.
HA HA HA HA HA
WELL, WELL, WELL.
SMITH'S SON IN HIS FANCY ARMOR HAS A PAIR ON HIM.
YOUR BALL SACK WILL MAKE A ROOMY COIN PURSE.

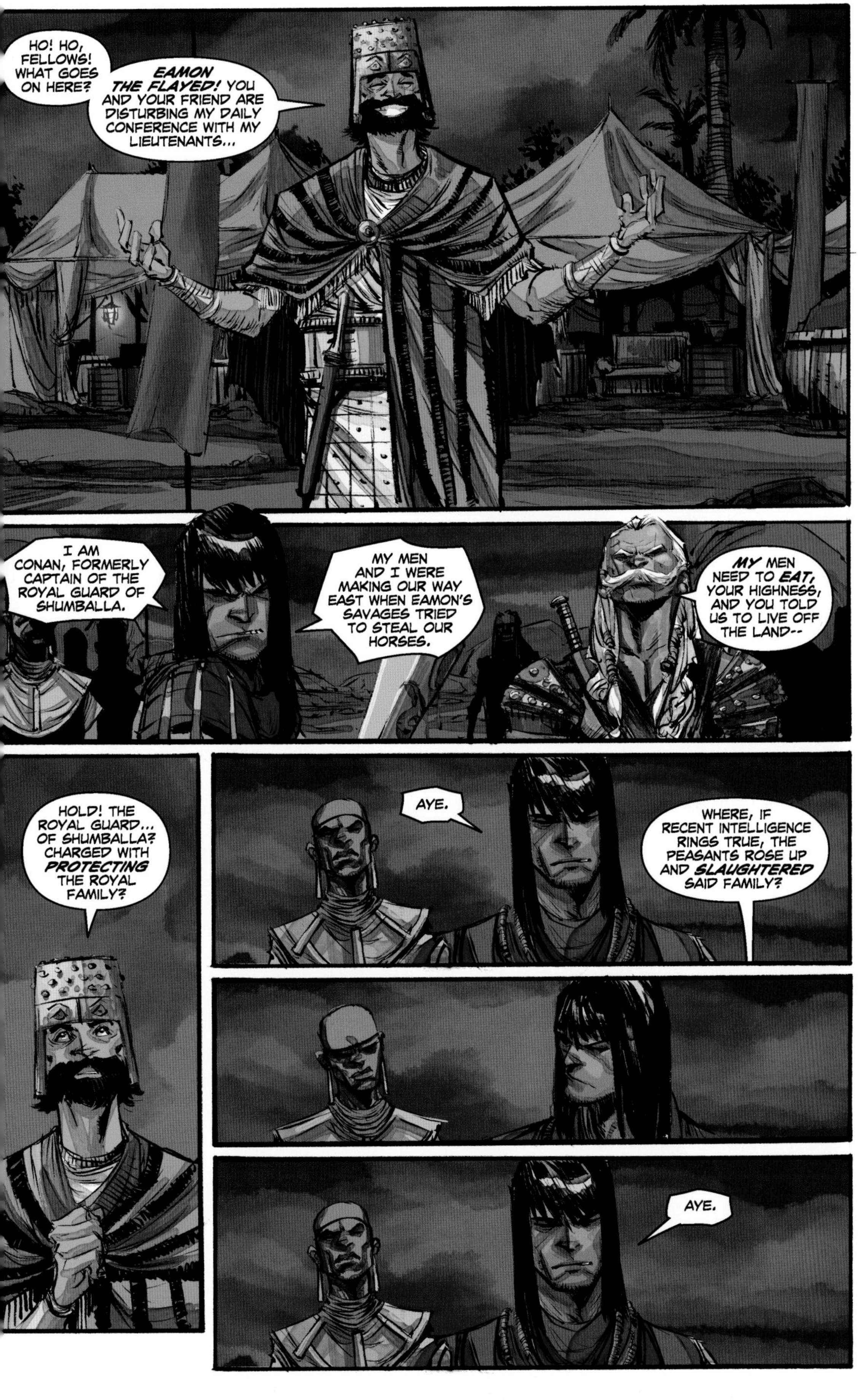
HO! HO, FELLOWS! WHAT GOES ON HERE?
EAMON THE FLAYED! YOU AND YOUR FRIEND ARE DISTURBING MY DAILY CONFERENCE WITH MY LIEUTENANTS...
I AM CONAN, FORMERLY CAPTAIN OF THE ROYAL GUARD OF SHUMBALLA.
MY MEN AND I WERE MAKING OUR WAY EAST WHEN EAMON'S SAVAGES TRIED TO STEAL OUR HORSES.
MY MEN NEED TO EAT, YOUR HIGHNESS, AND YOU TOLD US TO LIVE OFF THE LAND--
HOLD! THE ROYAL GUARD... OF SHUMBALLA? CHARGED WITH PROTECTING THE ROYAL FAMILY?
AYE.
WHERE, IF RECENT INTELLIGENCE RINGS TRUE, THE PEASANTS ROSE UP AND SLAUGHTERED SAID FAMILY?
AYE.

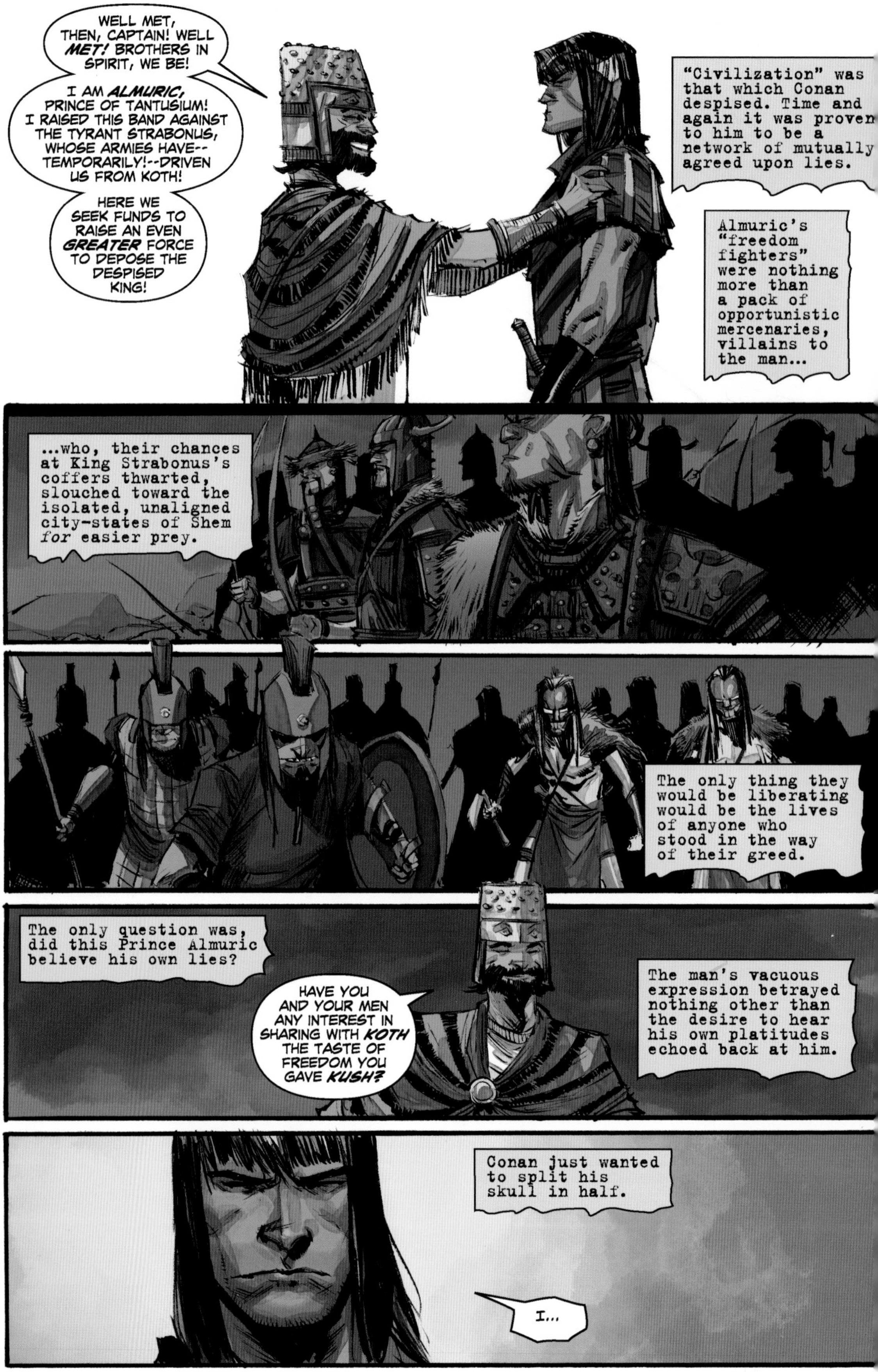
WELL MET, THEN, CAPTAIN! WELL MET! BROTHERS IN SPIRIT, WE BE!
I AM ALMURIC, PRINCE OF TANTUSIUM! I RAISED THIS BAND AGAINST THE TYRANT STRABONUS, WHOSE ARMIES HAVE--TEMPORARILY!--DRIVEN US FROM KOTH!
HERE WE SEEK FUNDS TO RAISE AN EVEN GREATER FORCE TO DEPOSE THE DESPISED KING!
"Civilization" was that which Conan despised. Time and again it was proven to him to be a network of mutually agreed upon lies.
Almuric's "freedom fighters" were nothing more than a pack of opportunistic mercenaries, villains to the man...
...who, their chances at King Strabonus's coffers thwarted, slouched toward the isolated, unaligned city-states of Shem for easier prey.
The only thing they would be liberating would be the lives of anyone who stood in the way of their greed.
The only question was, did this Prince Almuric believe his own lies?
HAVE YOU AND YOUR MEN ANY INTEREST IN SHARING WITH KOTH THE TASTE OF FREEDOM YOU GAVE KUSH?
The man's vacuous expression betrayed nothing other than the desire to hear his own platitudes echoed back at him.
Conan just wanted to split his skull in half.
I...

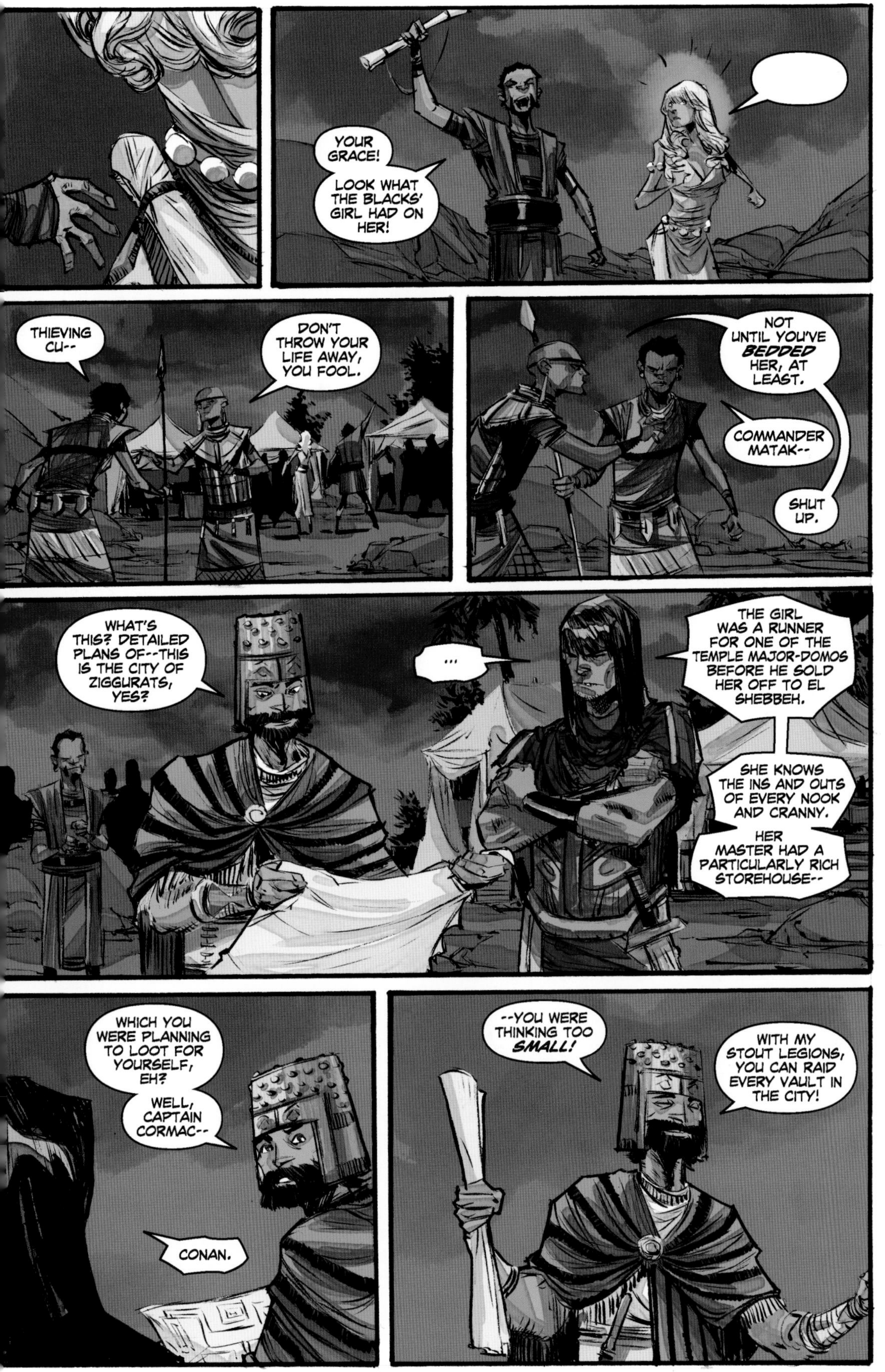
YOUR GRACE!
LOOK WHAT THE BLACKS' GIRL HAD ON HER!
THIEVING CU--
DON'T THROW YOUR LIFE AWAY, YOU FOOL.
NOT UNTIL YOU'VE BEDDED HER, AT LEAST.
COMMANDER MATAK--
SHUT UP.
WHAT'S THIS? DETAILED PLANS OF--THIS IS THE CITY OF ZIGGURATS, YES?
...
THE GIRL WAS A RUNNER FOR ONE OF THE TEMPLE MAJOR-DOMOS BEFORE HE SOLD HER OFF TO EL SHEBBEH.
SHE KNOWS THE INS AND OUTS OF EVERY NOOK AND CRANNY.
HER MASTER HAD A PARTICULARLY RICH STOREHOUSE--
WHICH YOU WERE PLANNING TO LOOT FOR YOURSELF, EH?
WELL, CAPTAIN CORMAC--
CONAN.
--YOU WERE THINKING TOO SMALL!
WITH MY STOUT LEGIONS, YOU CAN RAID EVERY VAULT IN THE CITY!

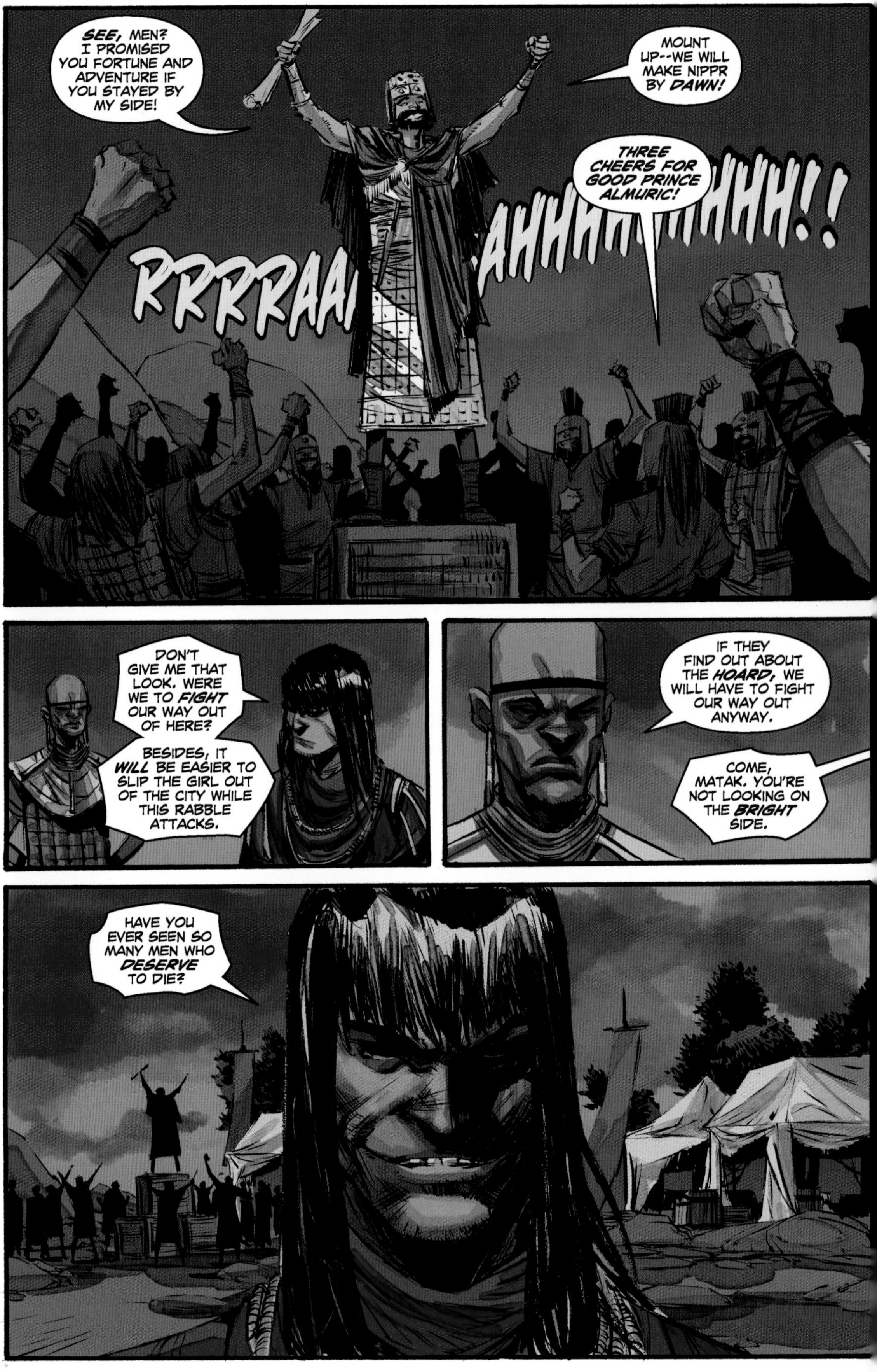
SEE, MEN? I PROMISED YOU FORTUNE AND ADVENTURE IF YOU STAYED BY MY SIDE!
MOUNT UP--WE WILL MAKE NIPPR BY DAWN!
RRRRAAHHHHHHHHH!!
THREE CHEERS FOR GOOD PRINCE ALMURIC!
DON'T GIVE ME THAT LOOK. WERE WE TO FIGHT OUR WAY OUT OF HERE?
BESIDES, IT WILL BE EASIER TO SLIP THE GIRL OUT OF THE CITY WHILE THIS RABBLE ATTACKS.
IF THEY FIND OUT ABOUT THE HOARD, WE WILL HAVE TO FIGHT OUR WAY OUT ANYWAY.
COME, MATAK. YOU'RE NOT LOOKING ON THE BRIGHT SIDE.
HAVE YOU EVER SEEN SO MANY MEN WHO DESERVE TO DIE?

CHAPTER TWO

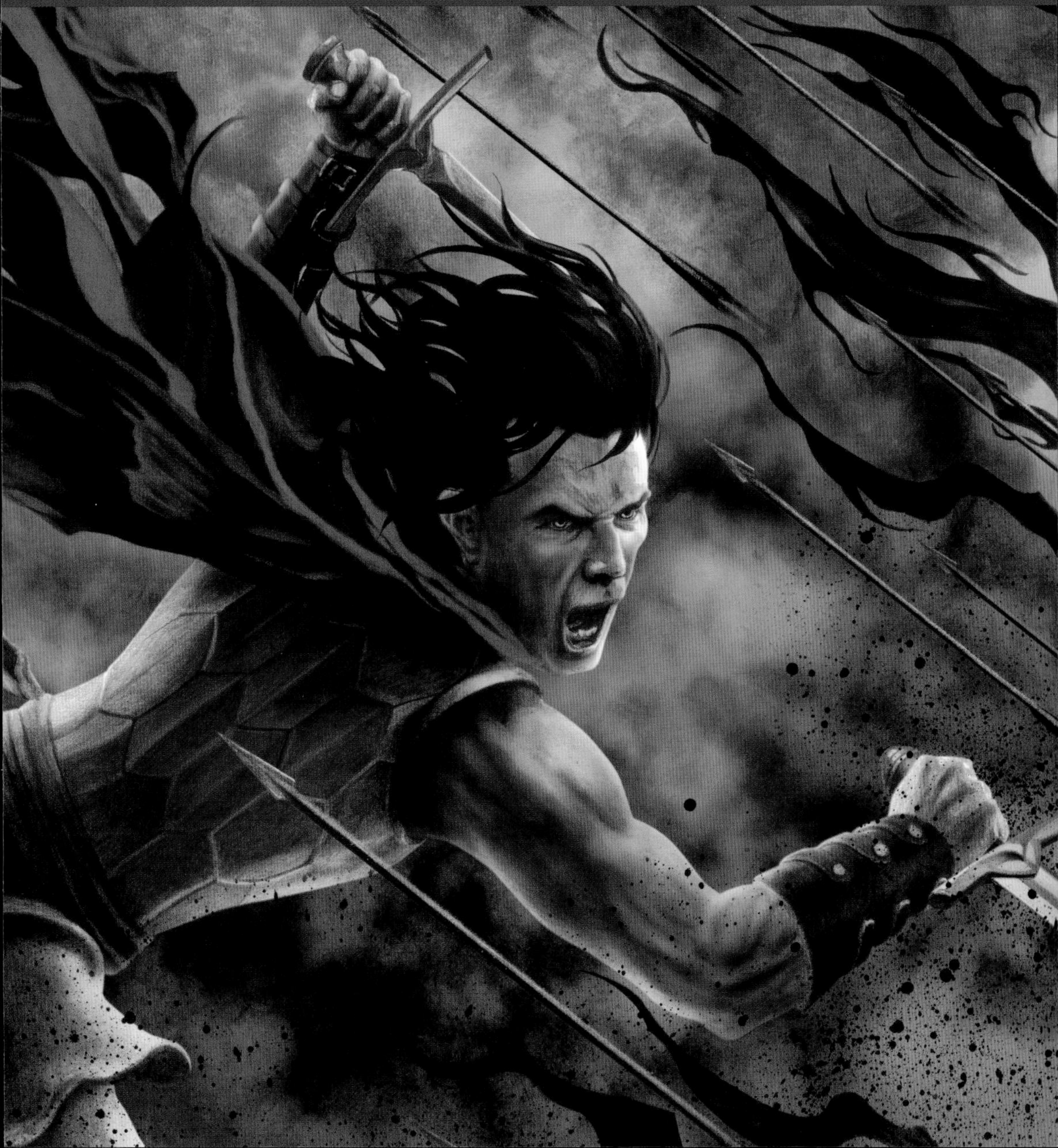

"I said name your *business,* Norther. Not how your mother called you for a beating."

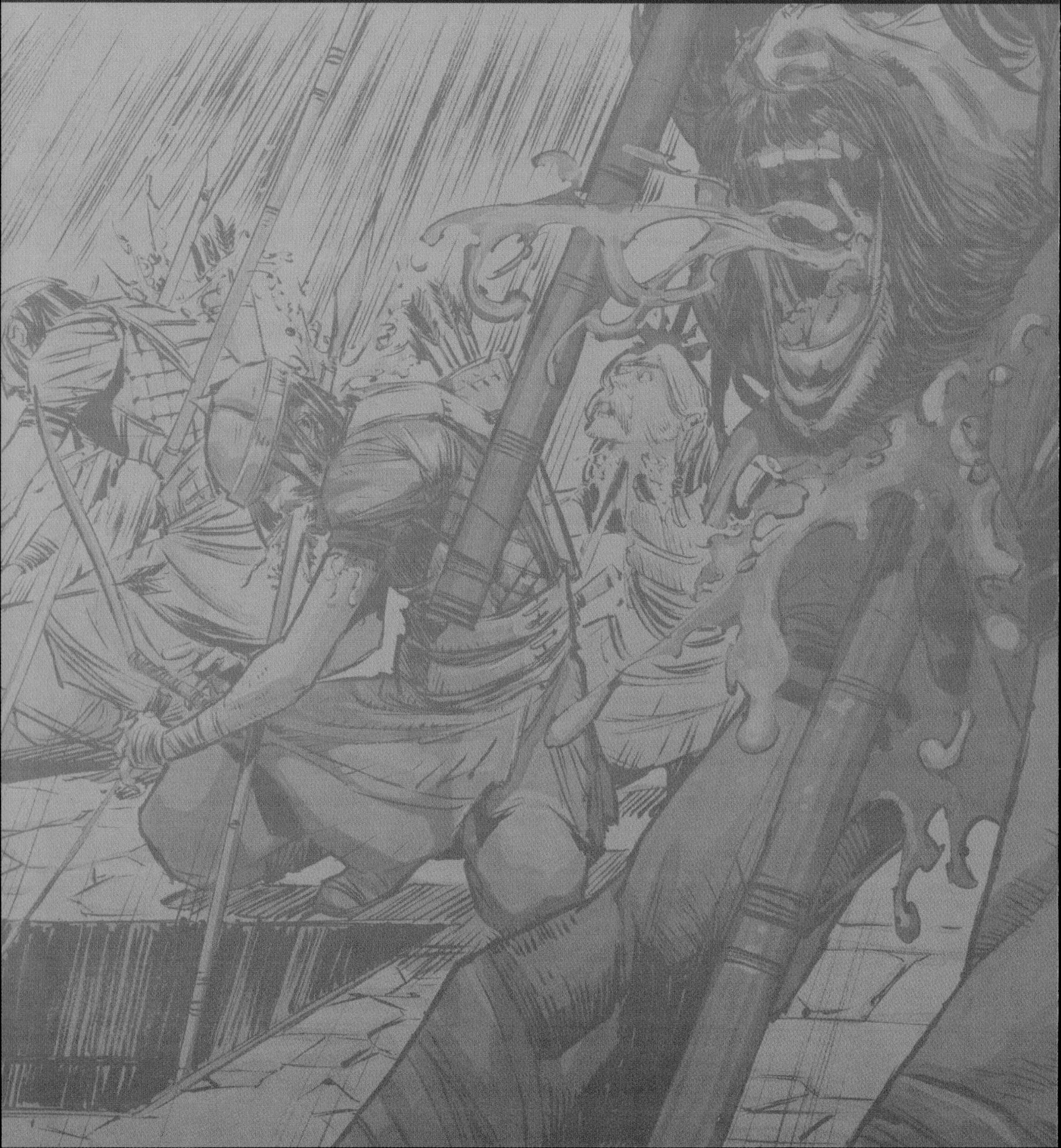

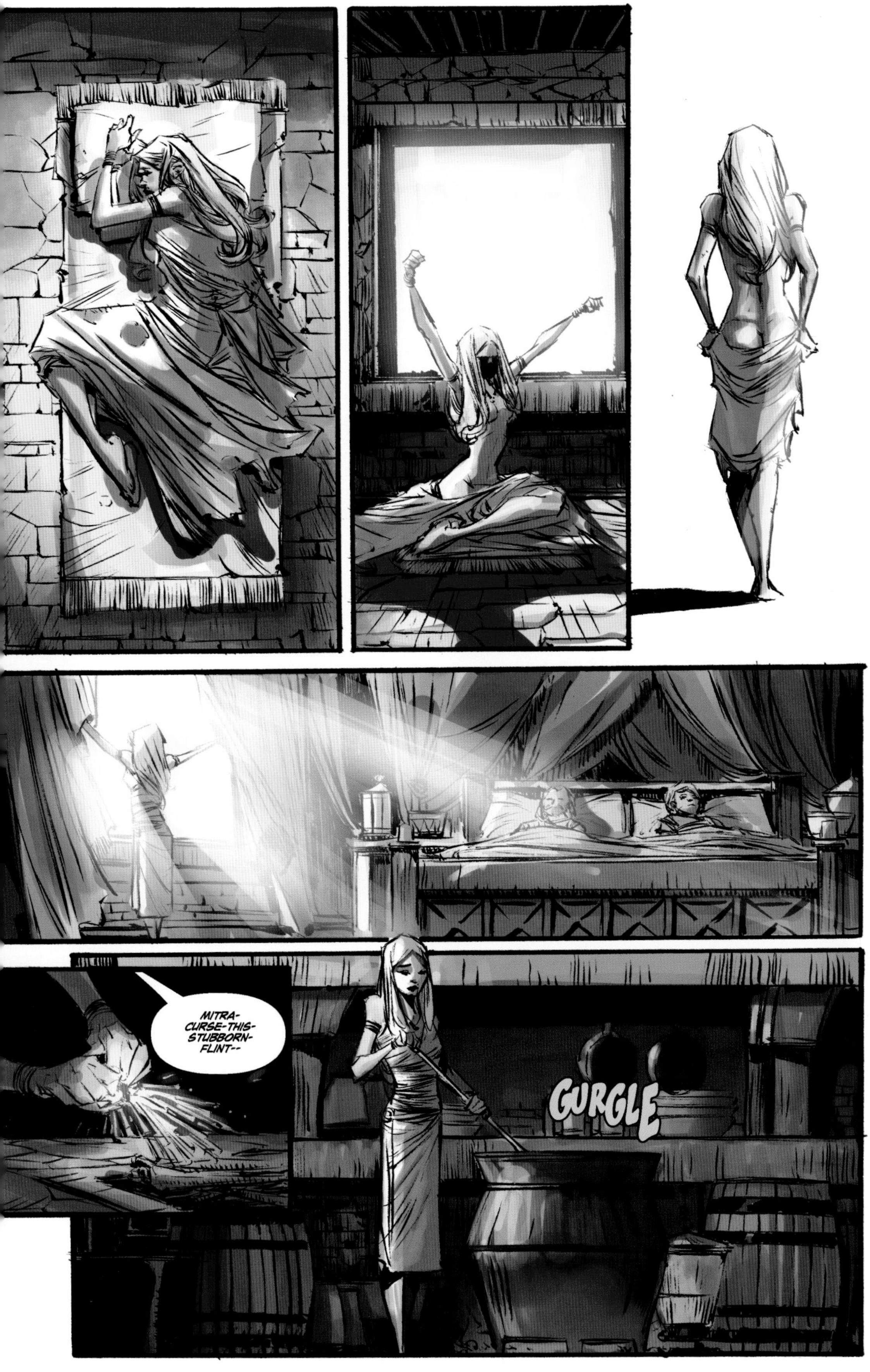
MITRA-CURSE-THIS-STUBBORN-FLINT--
GURGLE

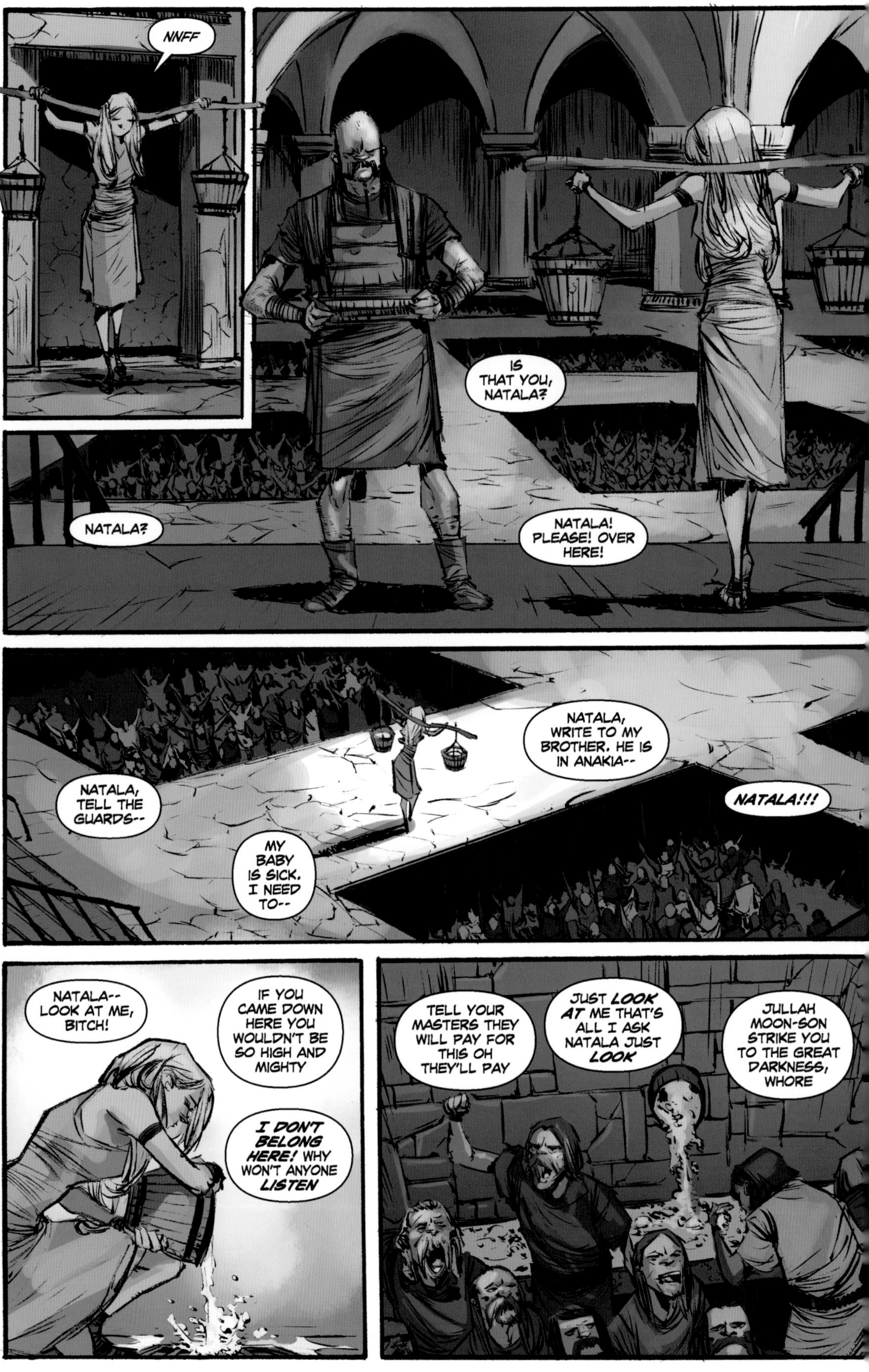
NNFF
IS THAT YOU, NATALA?
NATALA?
NATALA! PLEASE! OVER HERE!
NATALA, TELL THE GUARDS--
MY BABY IS SICK. I NEED TO--
NATALA, WRITE TO MY BROTHER. HE IS IN ANAKIA--
NATALA!!!
NATALA-- LOOK AT ME, BITCH!
IF YOU CAME DOWN HERE YOU WOULDN'T BE SO HIGH AND MIGHTY
I DON'T BELONG HERE! WHY WON'T ANYONE LISTEN
TELL YOUR MASTERS THEY WILL PAY FOR THIS OH THEY'LL PAY
JUST LOOK AT ME THAT'S ALL I ASK NATALA JUST LOOK
JULLAH MOON-SON STRIKE YOU TO THE GREAT DARKNESS, WHORE

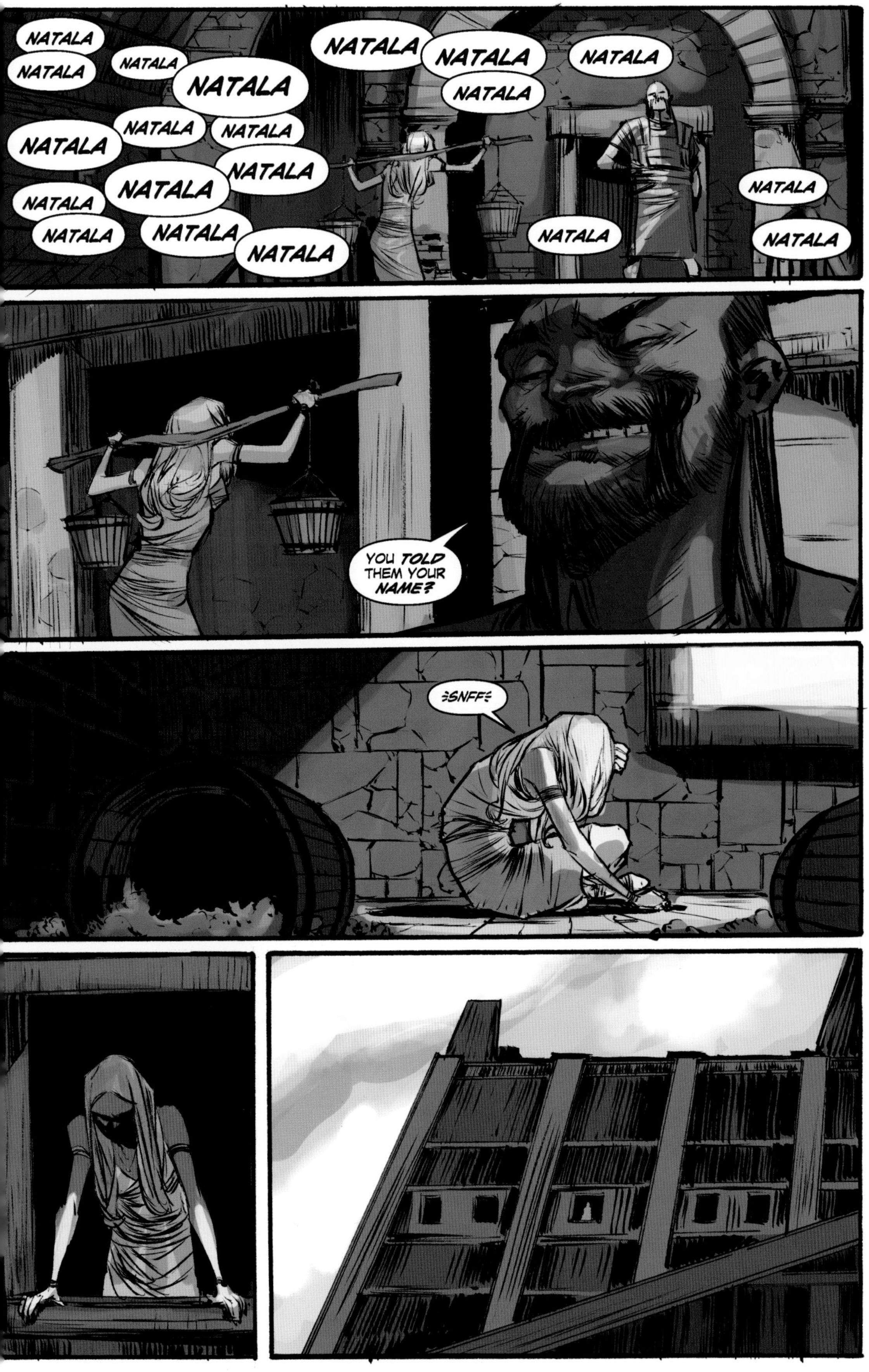
NATALA
NATALA
NATALA
NATALA
NATALA
NATALA
NATALA
NATALA
NATALA
NATALA
NATALA
NATALA
NATALA
NATALA
NATALA
NATALA
NATALA
NATALA
NATALA
NATALA
YOU *TOLD* THEM YOUR *NAME?*
SNFF

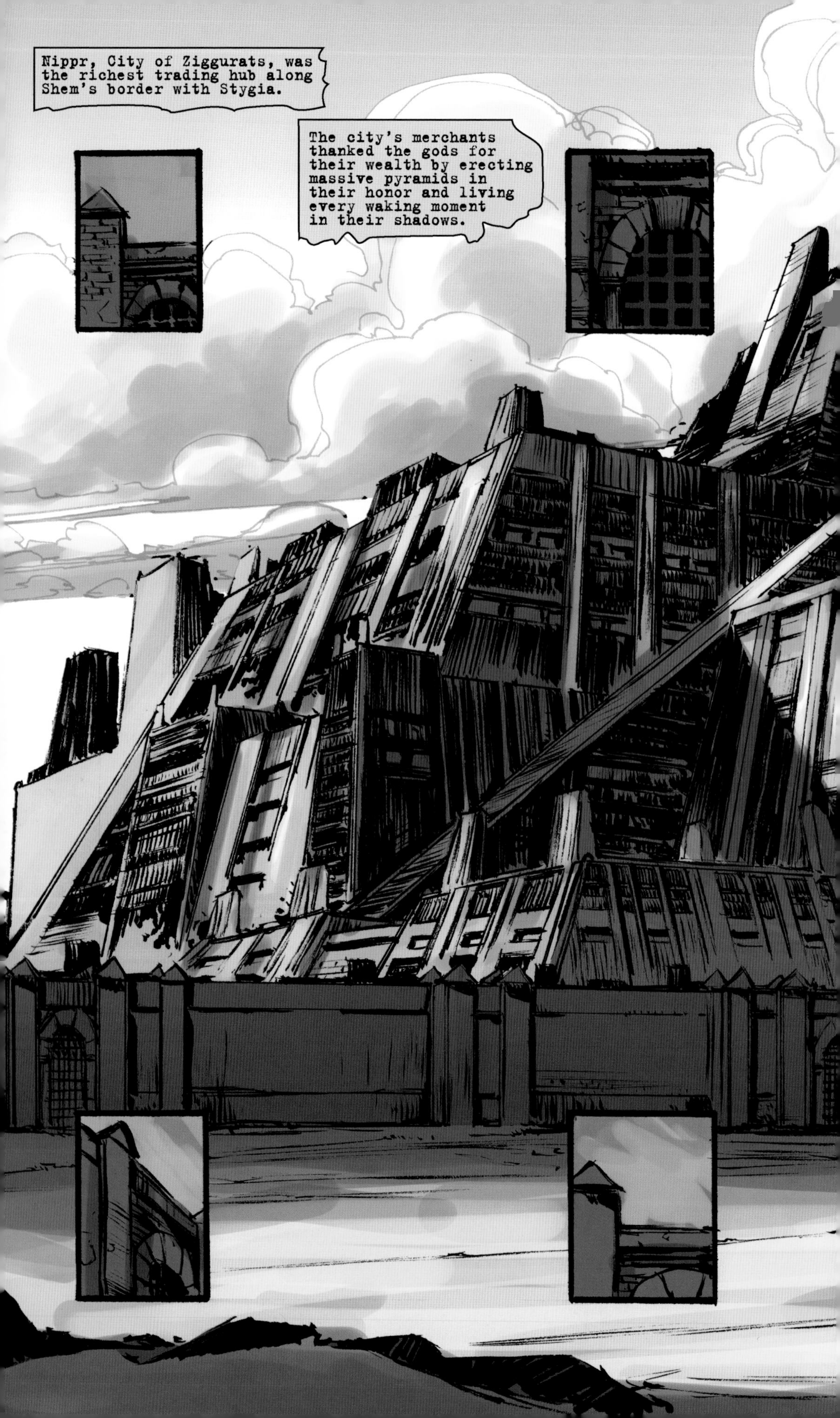
Nippr, City of Ziggurats, was the richest trading hub along Shem's border with Stygia.
The city's merchants thanked the gods for their wealth by erecting massive pyramids in their honor and living every waking moment in their shadows.

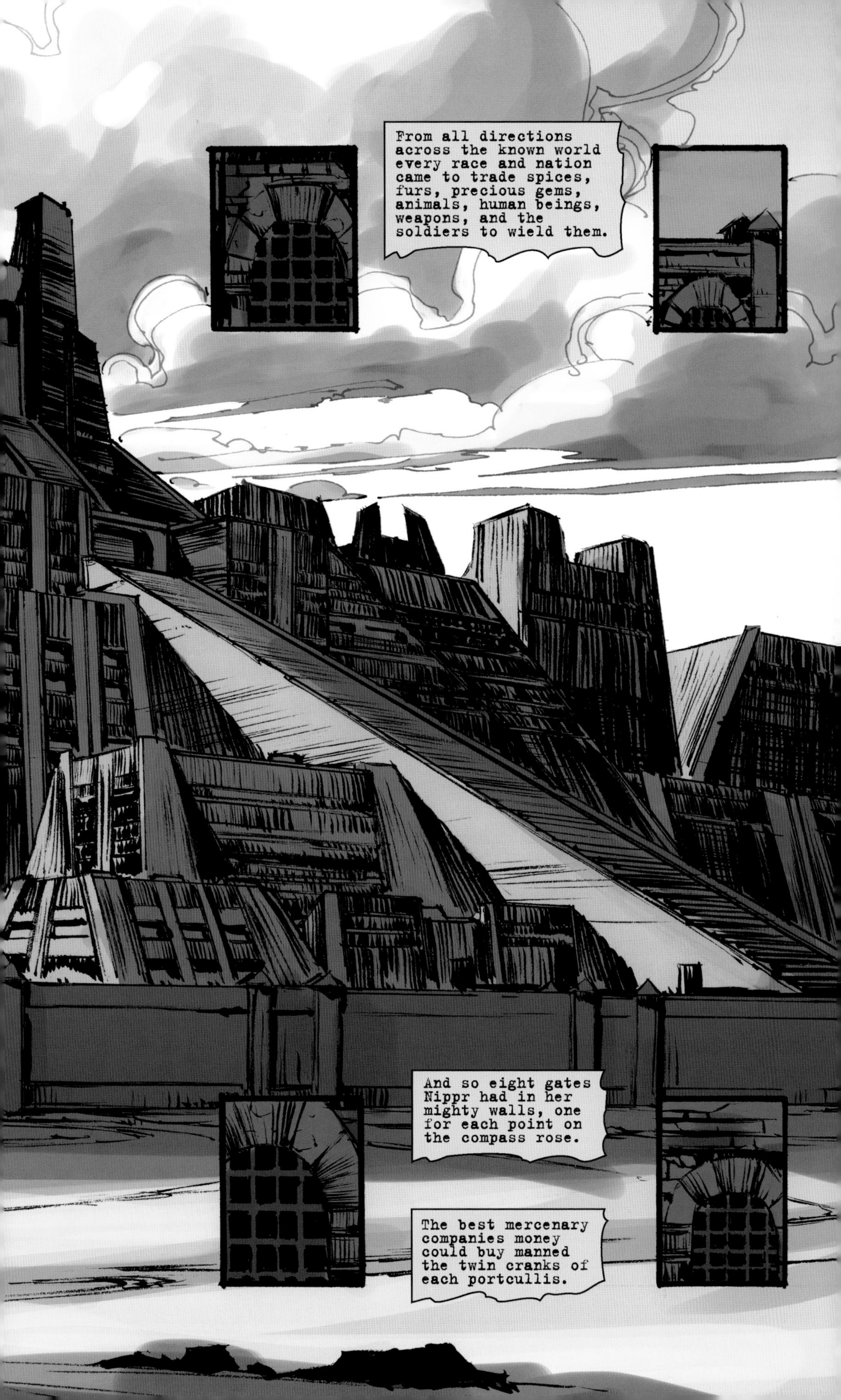
From all directions across the known world every race and nation came to trade spices, furs, precious gems, animals, human beings, weapons, and the soldiers to wield them.
And so eight gates Nippr had in her mighty walls, one for each point on the compass rose.
The best mercenary companies money could buy manned the twin cranks of each portcullis.

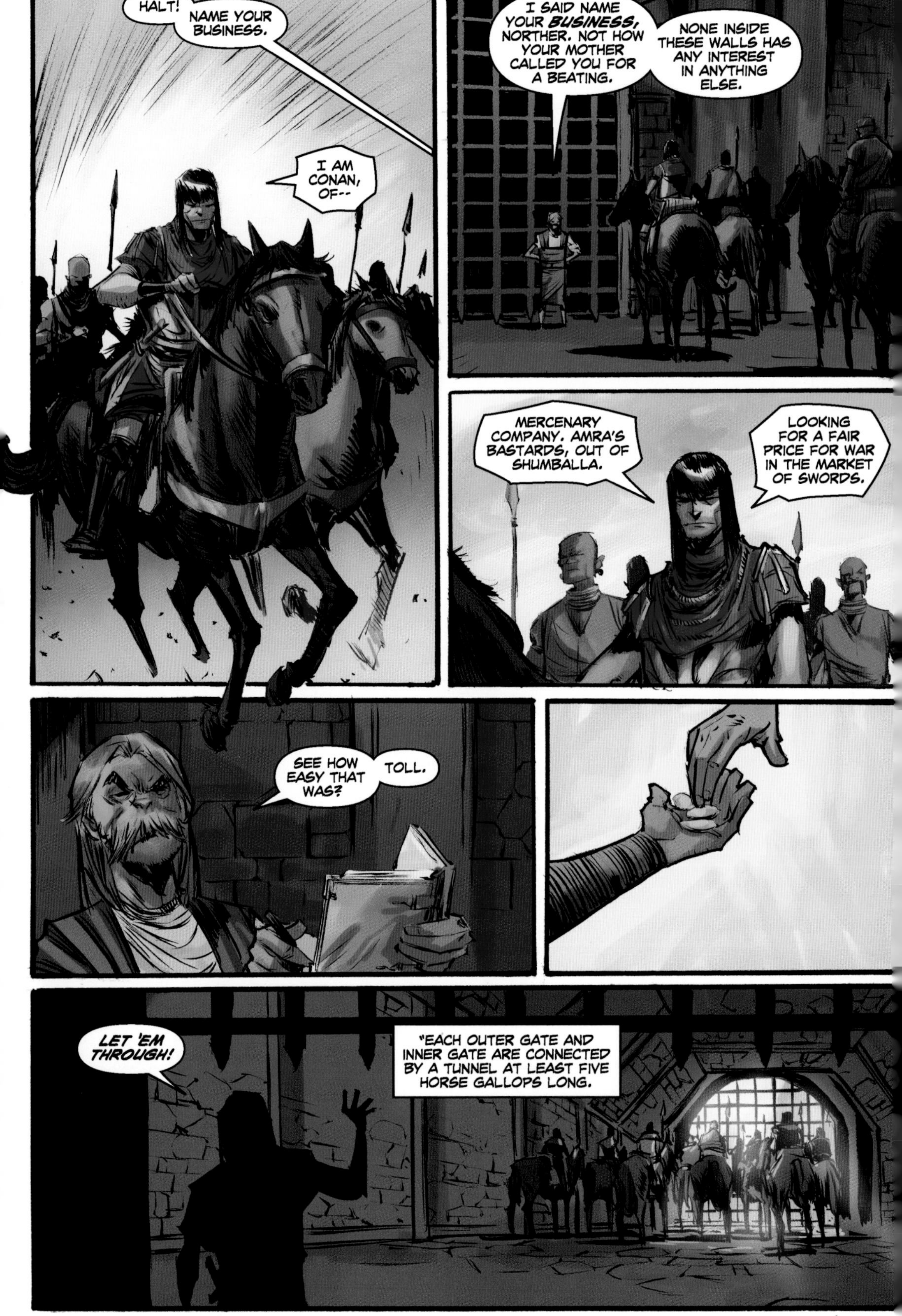
HALT!
NAME YOUR BUSINESS.
I AM CONAN, OF--
I SAID NAME YOUR BUSINESS, NORTHER. NOT HOW YOUR MOTHER CALLED YOU FOR A BEATING.
NONE INSIDE THESE WALLS HAS ANY INTEREST IN ANYTHING ELSE.
MERCENARY COMPANY. AMRA'S BASTARDS, OUT OF SHUMBALLA.
LOOKING FOR A FAIR PRICE FOR WAR IN THE MARKET OF SWORDS.
SEE HOW EASY THAT WAS?
TOLL.
LET 'EM THROUGH!
"EACH OUTER GATE AND INNER GATE ARE CONNECTED BY A TUNNEL AT LEAST FIVE HORSE GALLOPS LONG.

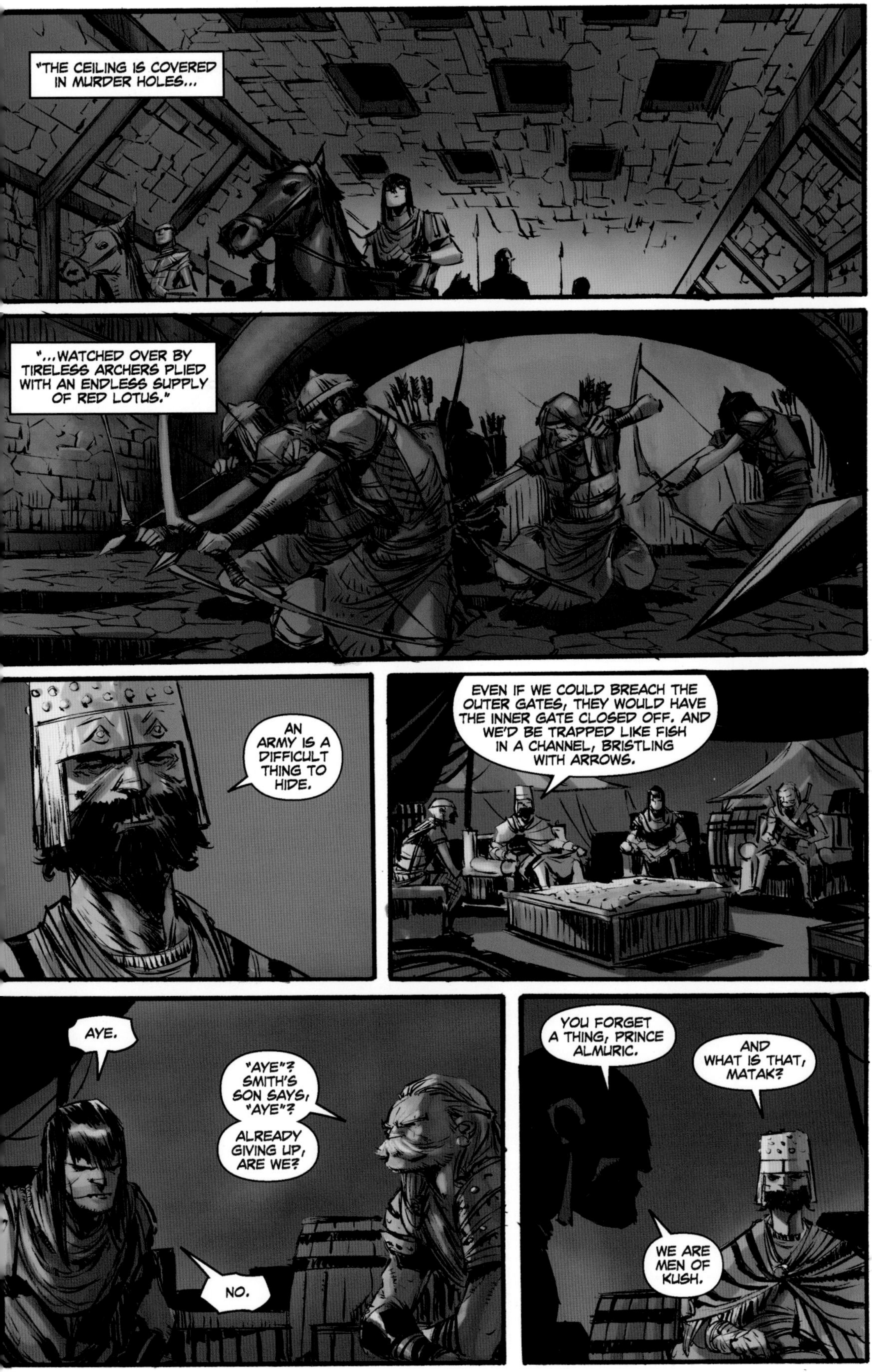
"THE CEILING IS COVERED IN MURDER HOLES...
"...WATCHED OVER BY TIRELESS ARCHERS PLIED WITH AN ENDLESS SUPPLY OF RED LOTUS."
AN ARMY IS A DIFFICULT THING TO HIDE.
EVEN IF WE COULD BREACH THE OUTER GATES, THEY WOULD HAVE THE INNER GATE CLOSED OFF. AND WE'D BE TRAPPED LIKE FISH IN A CHANNEL, BRISTLING WITH ARROWS.
AYE.
"AYE"? SMITH'S SON SAYS, "AYE"?
ALREADY GIVING UP, ARE WE?
NO.
YOU FORGET A THING, PRINCE ALMURIC.
AND WHAT IS THAT, MATAK?
WE ARE MEN OF KUSH.

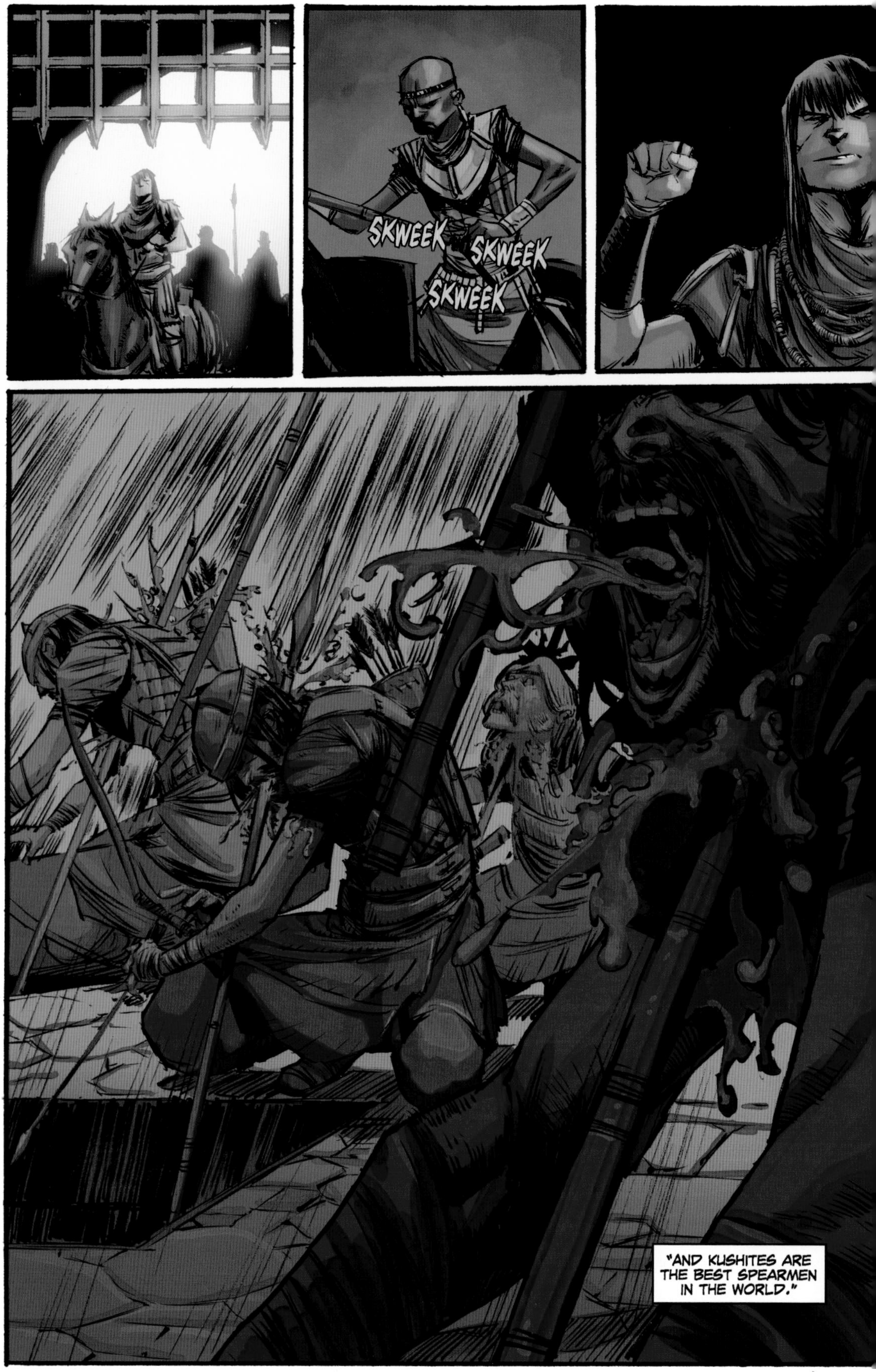
SKWEEK
SKWEEK
SKWEEK
"AND KUSHITES ARE THE BEST SPEARMEN IN THE WORLD."

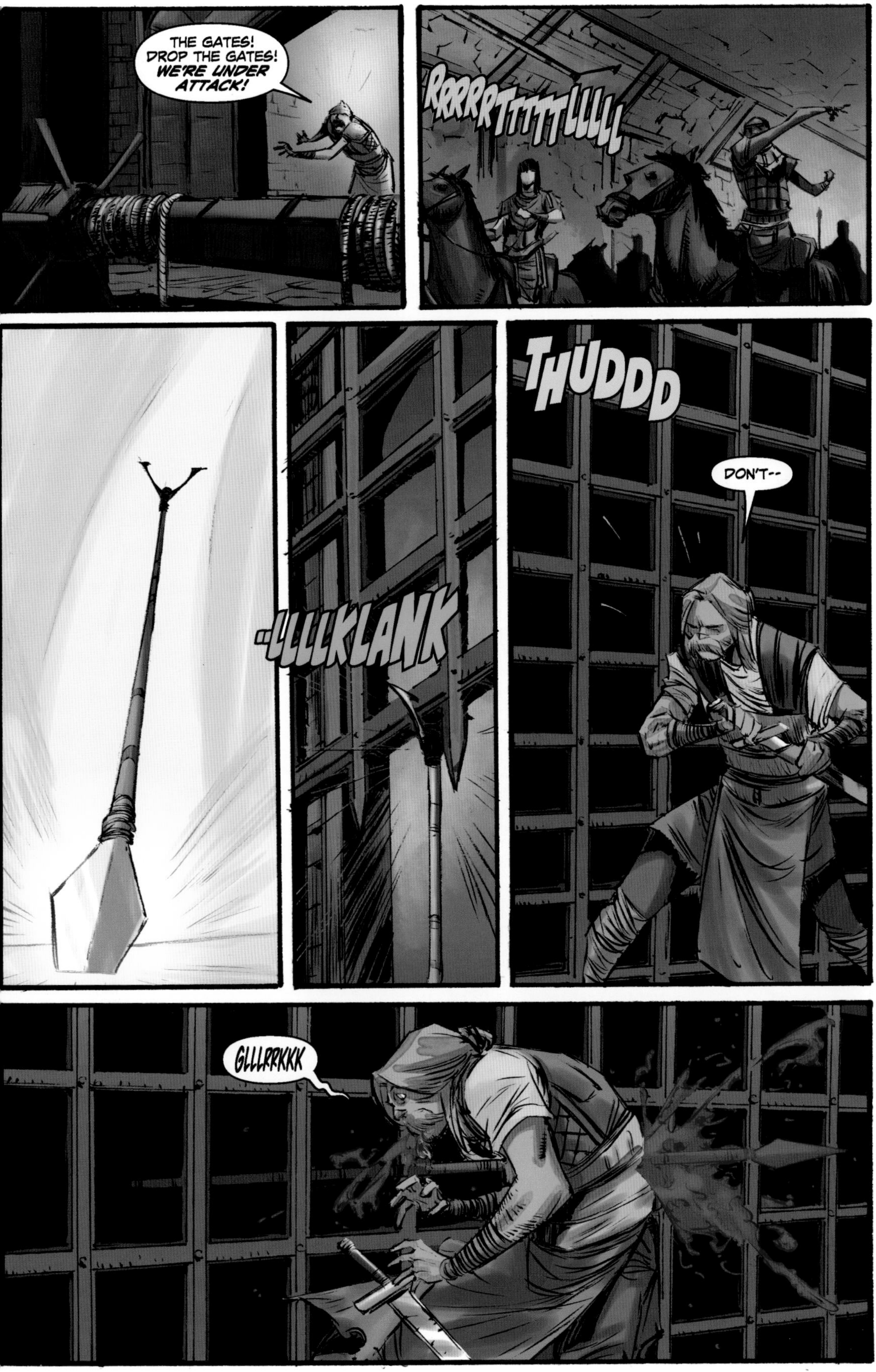
THE GATES! DROP THE GATES! WE'RE UNDER ATTACK!
RRRRRTTTTTLLLLL
THUDDD
-LLLLKLANK
DON'T--
GLLLRRKKK

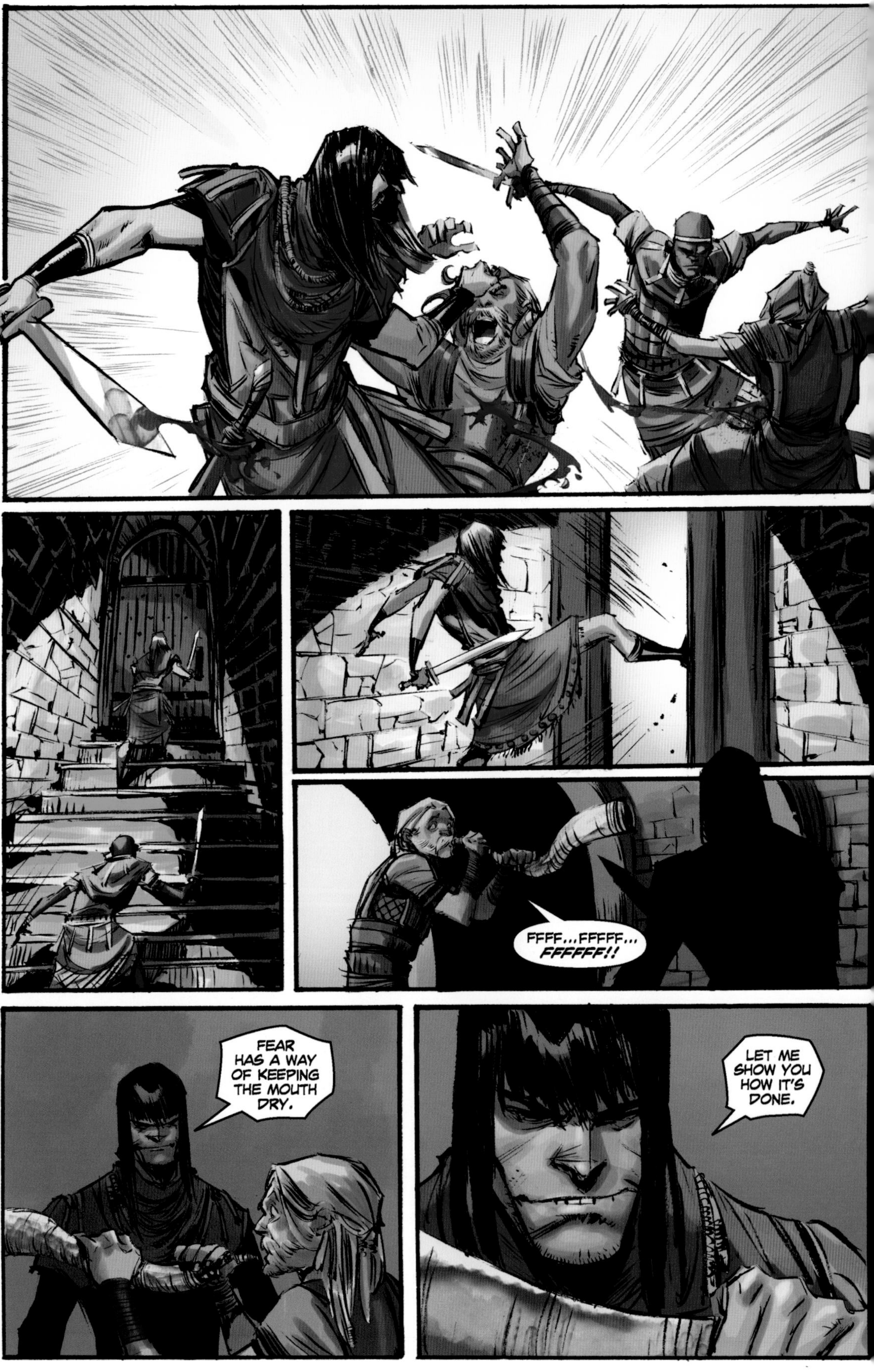
FFFF...FFFFF...
FFFFFF!!
FEAR HAS A WAY OF KEEPING THE MOUTH DRY.
LET ME SHOW YOU HOW IT'S DONE.

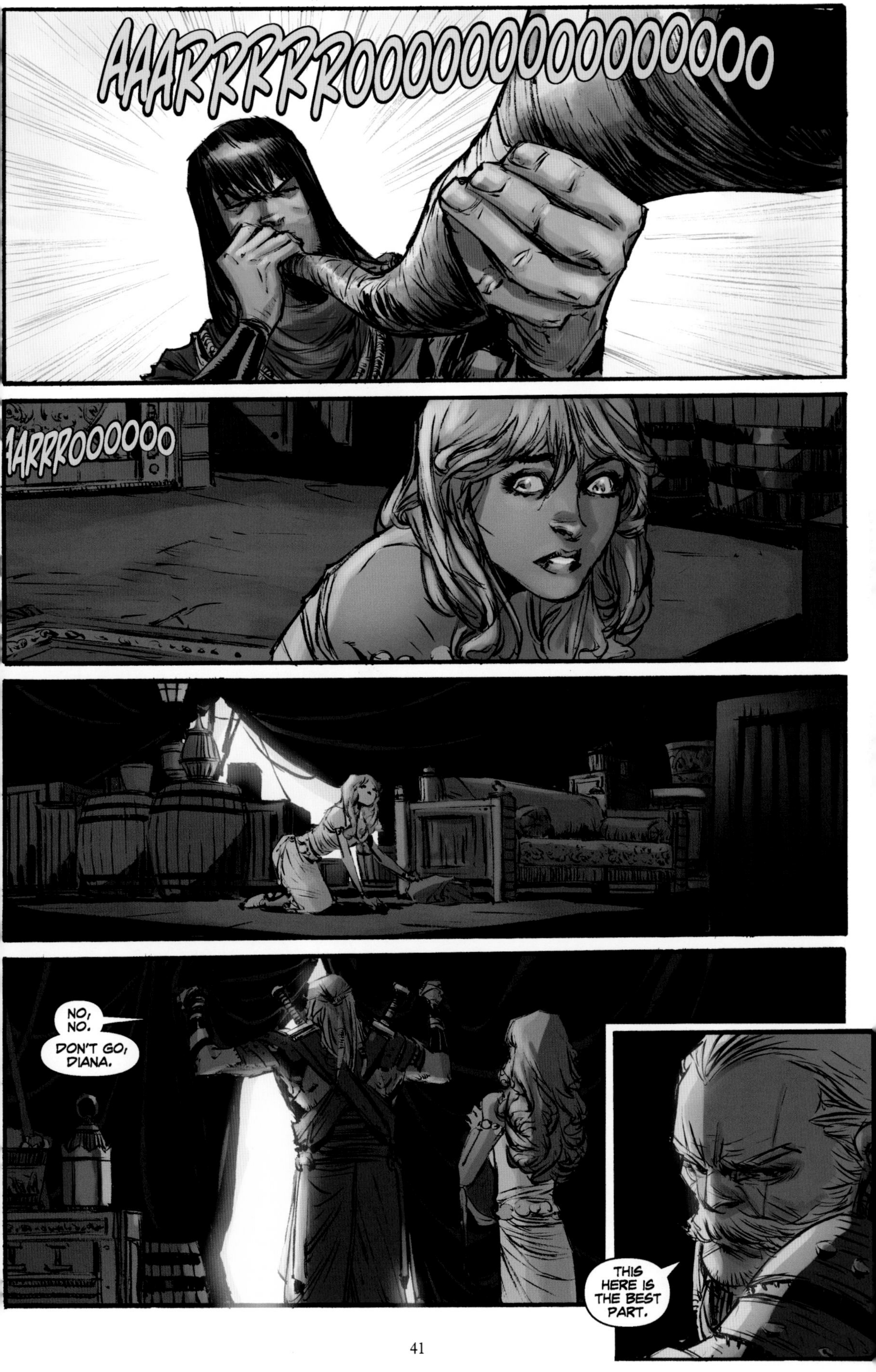
AAARRRRROOOOOOOOOOOOOOO
AARRROOOOOO
NO, NO.
DON'T GO, DIANA.
THIS HERE IS THE BEST PART.

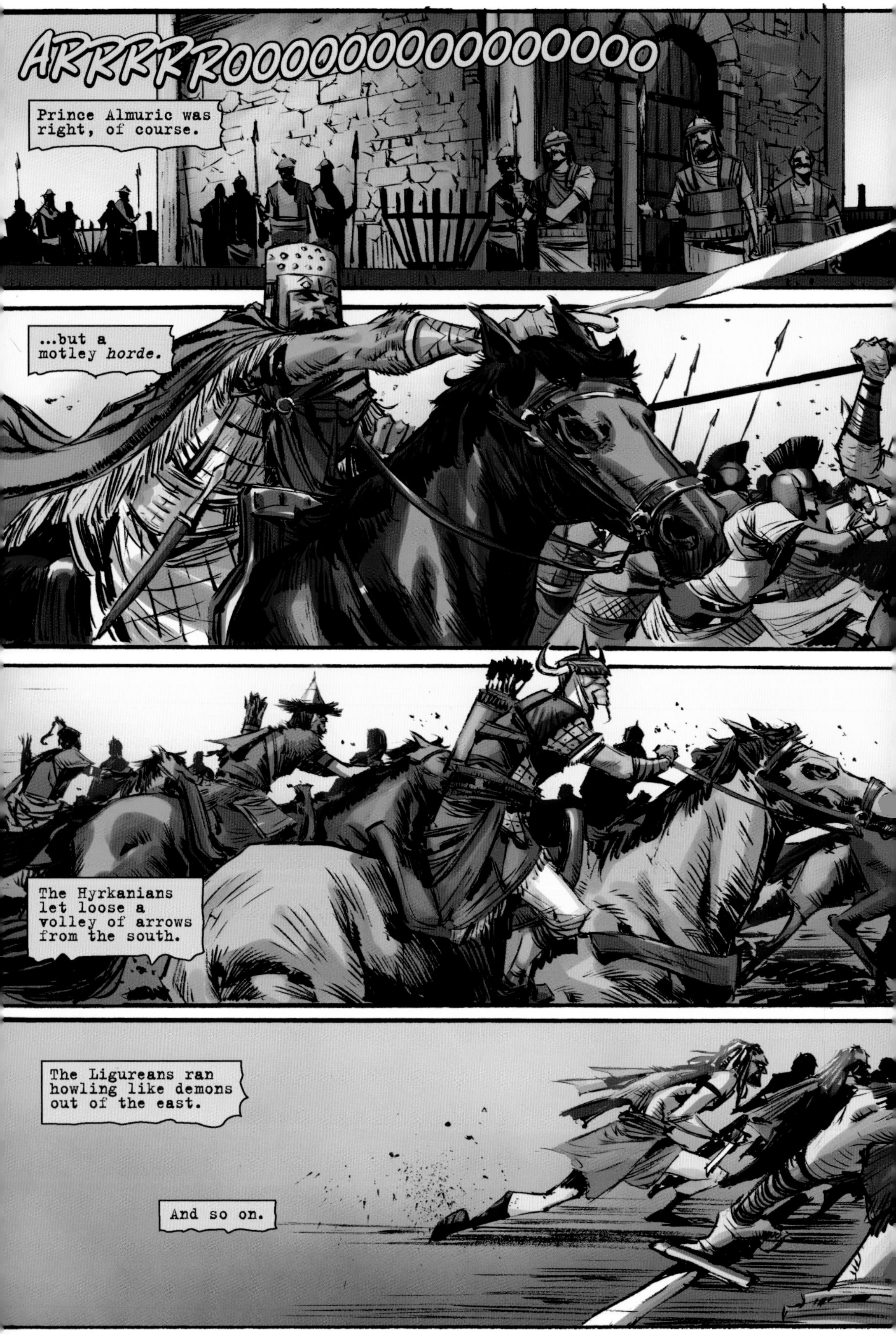
ARRRRROOOOOOOOOOOOOOO
Prince Almuric was right, of course.
...but a motley *horde*.
The Hyrkanians let loose a volley of arrows from the south.
The Ligureans ran howling like demons out of the east.
And so on.

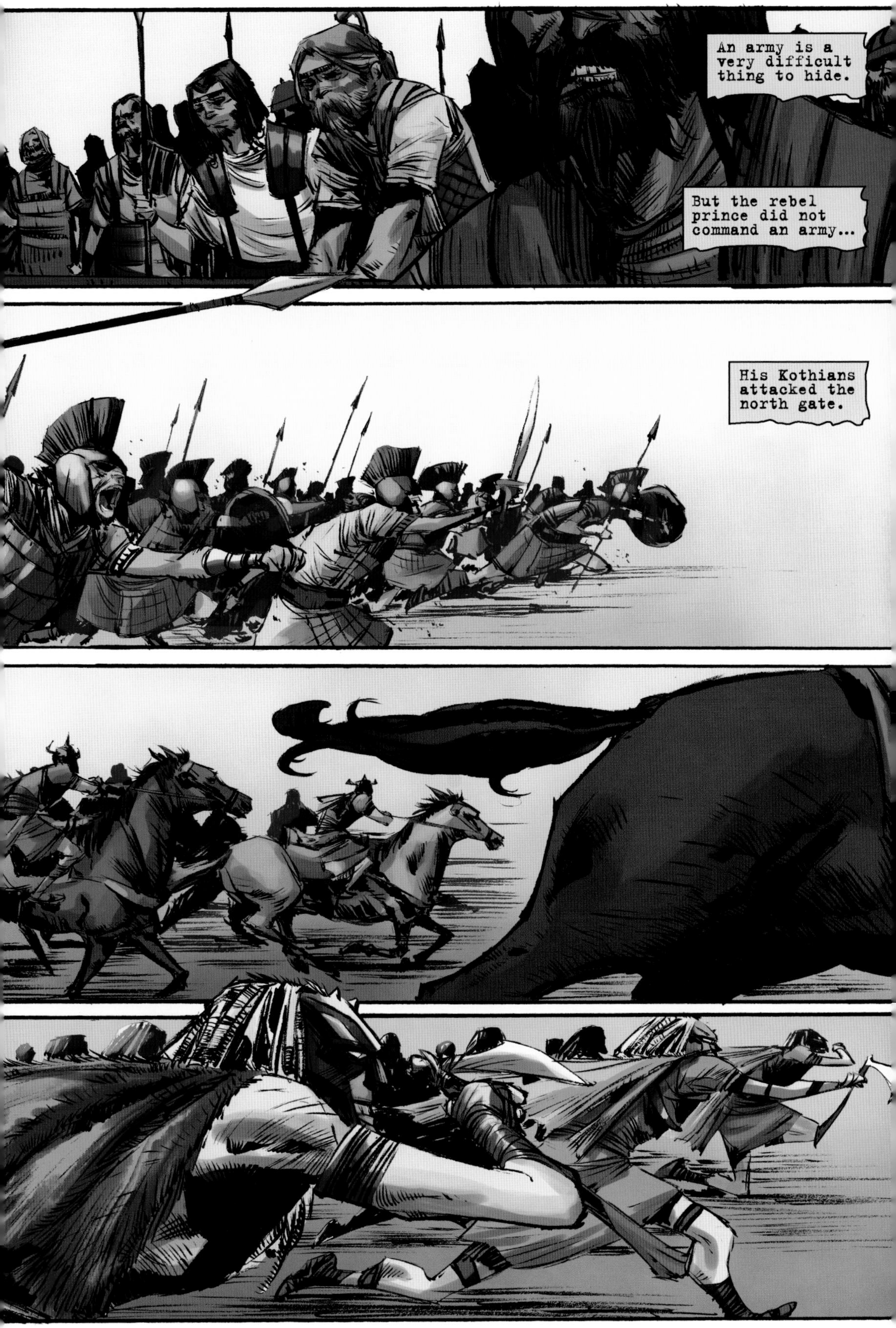
An army is a very difficult thing to hide.
But the rebel prince did not command an army...
His Kothians attacked the north gate.

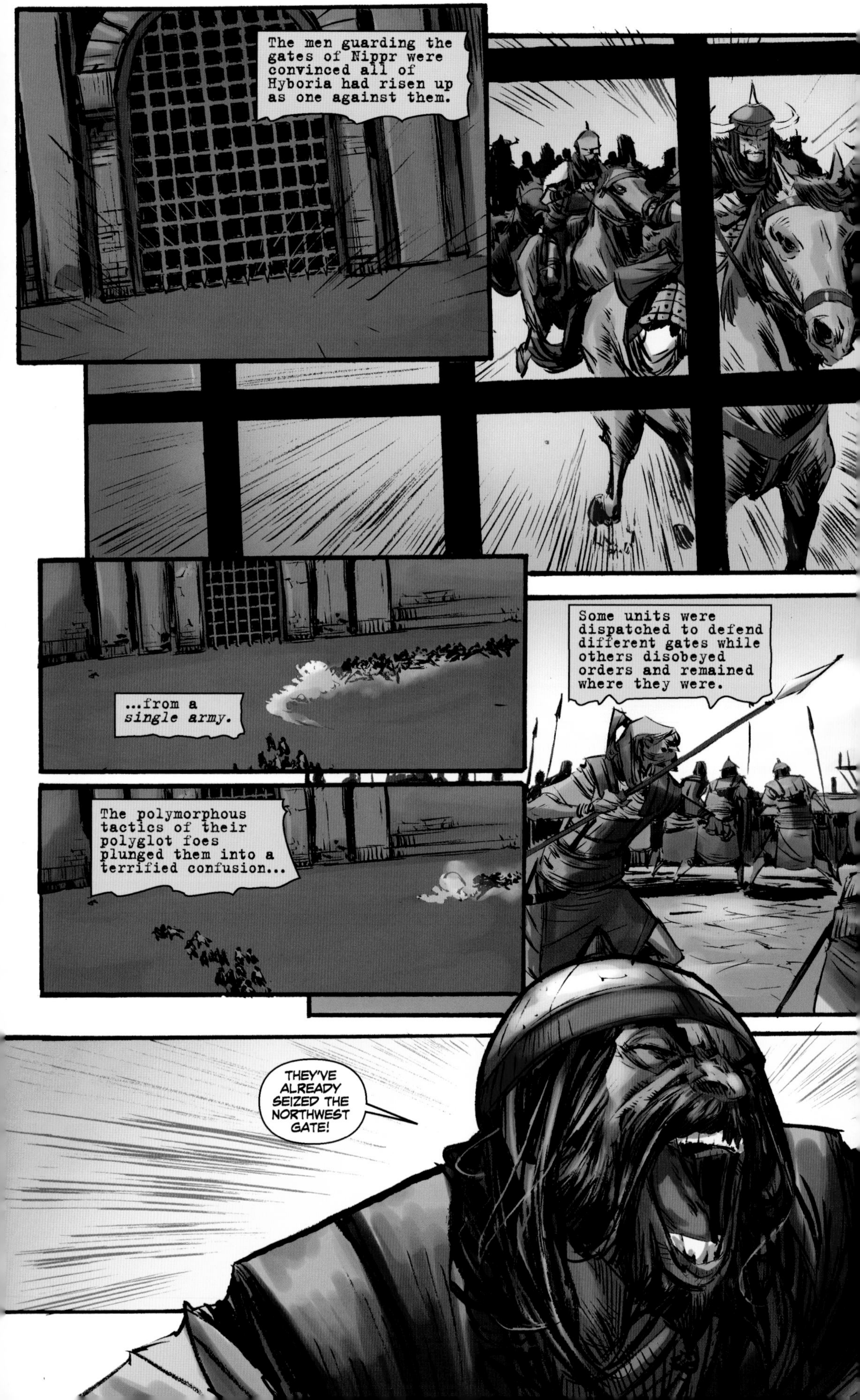
The men guarding the gates of Nippr were convinced all of Hyboria had risen up as one against them.
...from a *single army.*
The polymorphous tactics of their polyglot foes plunged them into a terrified confusion...
Some units were dispatched to defend different gates while others disobeyed orders and remained where they were.
THEY'VE ALREADY SEIZED THE NORTHWEST GATE!

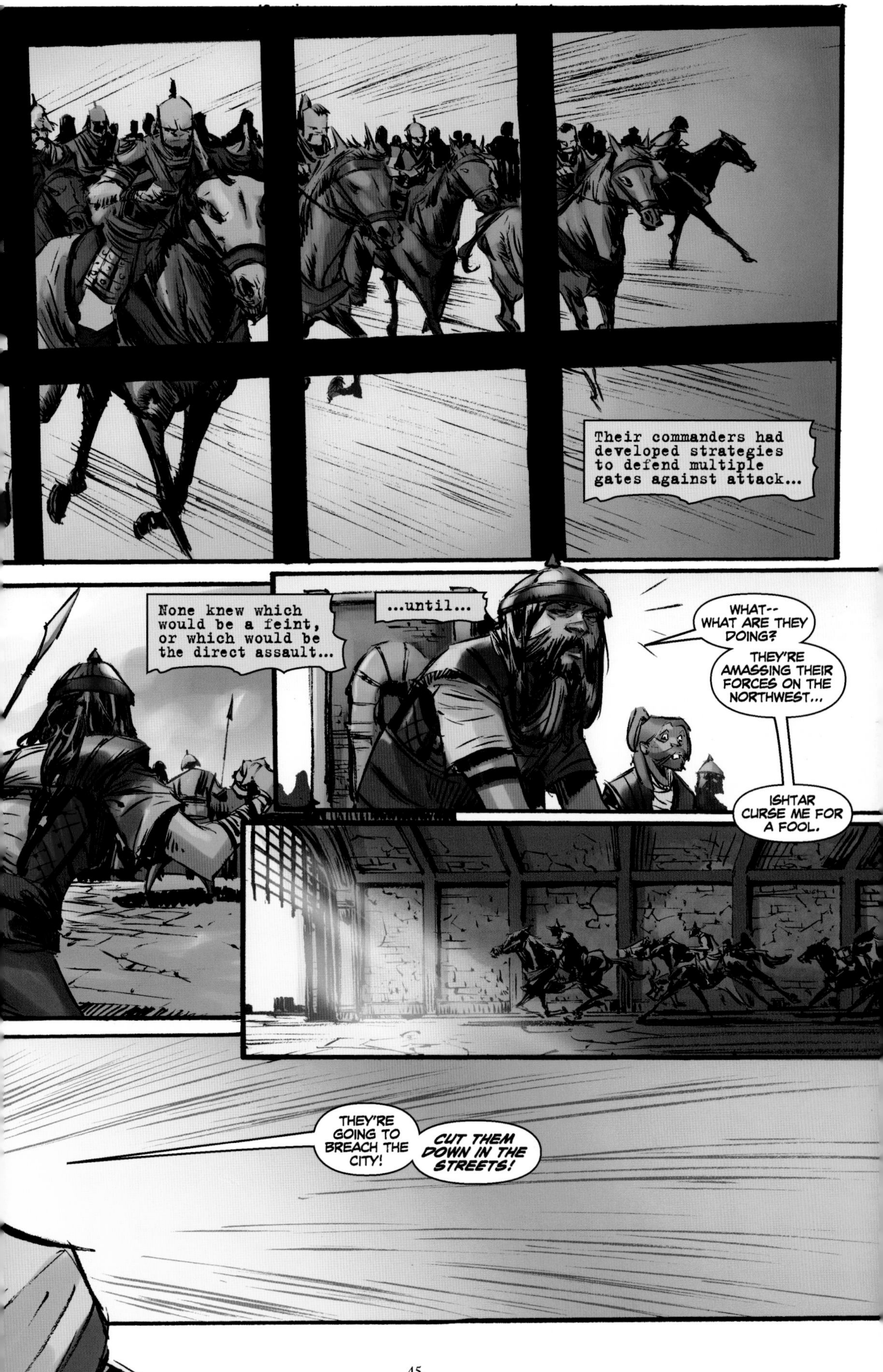
Their commanders had developed strategies to defend multiple gates against attack...
None knew which would be a feint, or which would be the direct assault...
...until...
WHAT-- WHAT ARE THEY DOING?
THEY'RE AMASSING THEIR FORCES ON THE NORTHWEST...
ISHTAR CURSE ME FOR A FOOL.
THEY'RE GOING TO BREACH THE CITY!
CUT THEM DOWN IN THE STREETS!

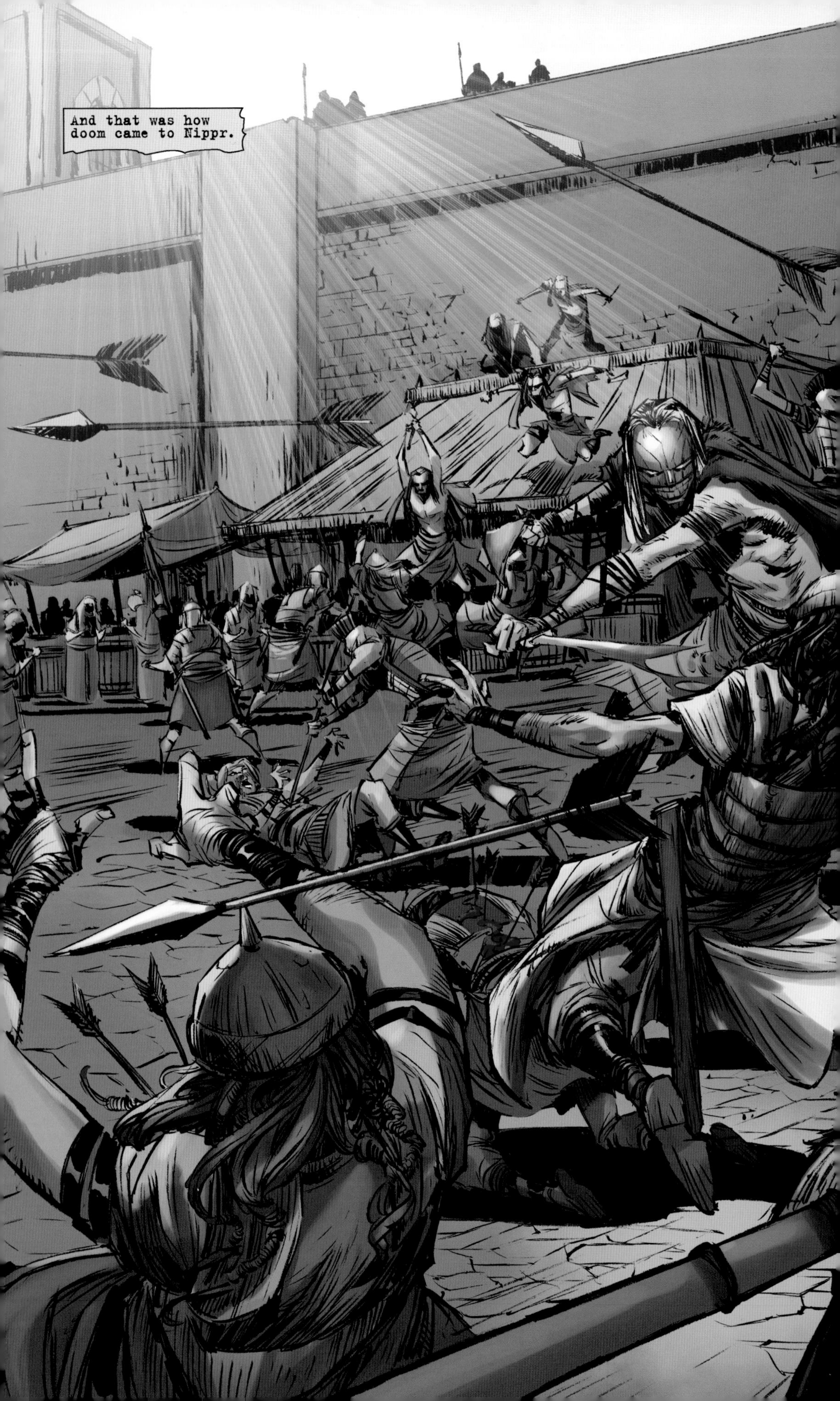
And that was how doom came to Nippr.

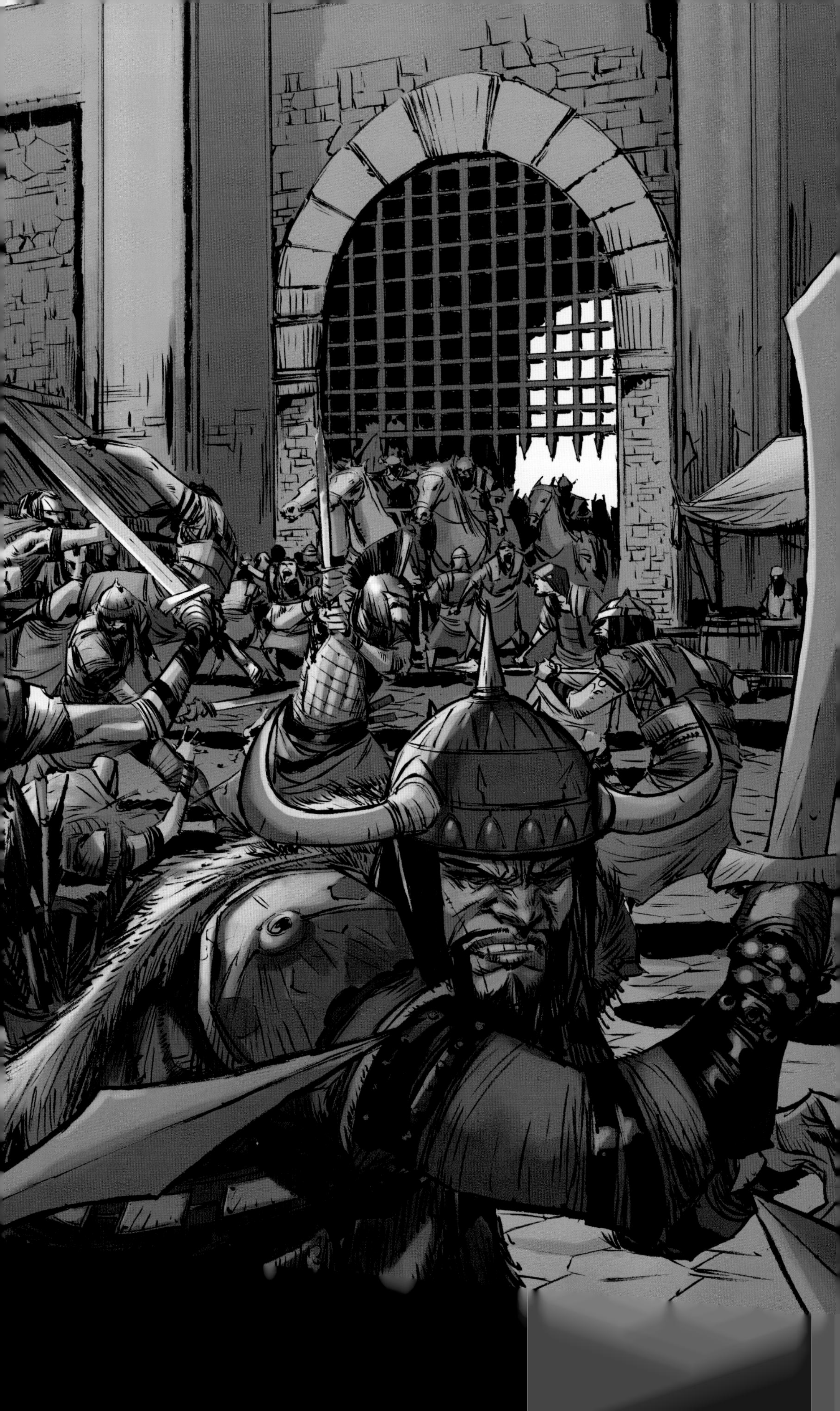

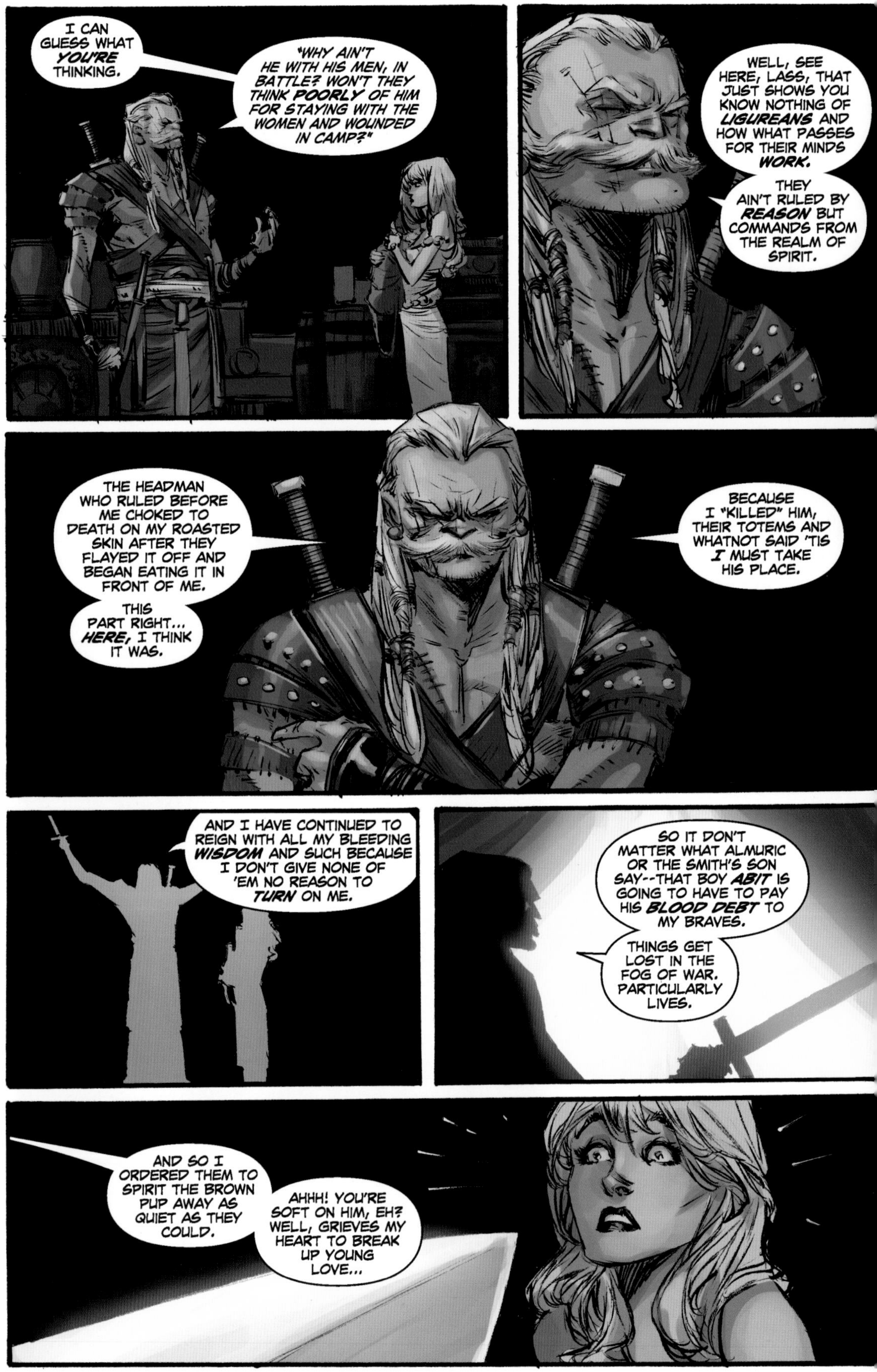
I CAN GUESS WHAT YOU'RE THINKING.
"WHY AIN'T HE WITH HIS MEN, IN BATTLE? WON'T THEY THINK POORLY OF HIM FOR STAYING WITH THE WOMEN AND WOUNDED IN CAMP?"
WELL, SEE HERE, LASS, THAT JUST SHOWS YOU KNOW NOTHING OF LIGUREANS AND HOW WHAT PASSES FOR THEIR MINDS WORK.
THEY AIN'T RULED BY REASON BUT COMMANDS FROM THE REALM OF SPIRIT.
THE HEADMAN WHO RULED BEFORE ME CHOKED TO DEATH ON MY ROASTED SKIN AFTER THEY FLAYED IT OFF AND BEGAN EATING IT IN FRONT OF ME.
THIS PART RIGHT... HERE, I THINK IT WAS.
BECAUSE I "KILLED" HIM, THEIR TOTEMS AND WHATNOT SAID 'TIS I MUST TAKE HIS PLACE.
AND I HAVE CONTINUED TO REIGN WITH ALL MY BLEEDING WISDOM AND SUCH BECAUSE I DON'T GIVE NONE OF 'EM NO REASON TO TURN ON ME.
SO IT DON'T MATTER WHAT ALMURIC OR THE SMITH'S SON SAY--THAT BOY ABIT IS GOING TO HAVE TO PAY HIS BLOOD DEBT TO MY BRAVES.
THINGS GET LOST IN THE FOG OF WAR. PARTICULARLY LIVES.
AND SO I ORDERED THEM TO SPIRIT THE BROWN PUP AWAY AS QUIET AS THEY COULD.
AHHH! YOU'RE SOFT ON HIM, EH? WELL, GRIEVES MY HEART TO BREAK UP YOUNG LOVE...

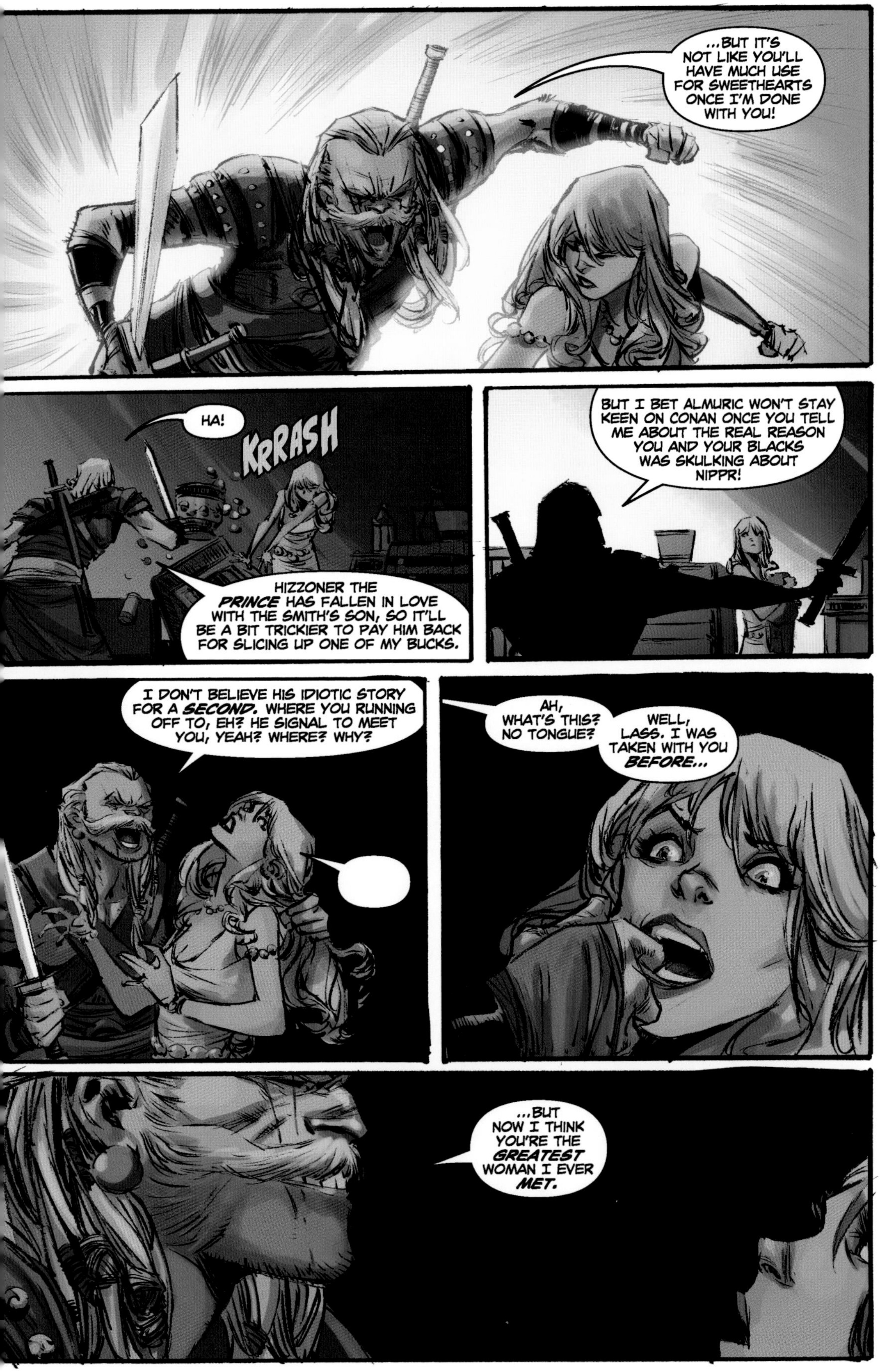

...BUT IT'S NOT LIKE YOU'LL HAVE MUCH USE FOR SWEETHEARTS ONCE I'M DONE WITH YOU!
HA!
KRRASH
HIZZONER THE PRINCE HAS FALLEN IN LOVE WITH THE SMITH'S SON, SO IT'LL BE A BIT TRICKIER TO PAY HIM BACK FOR SLICING UP ONE OF MY BUCKS.
BUT I BET ALMURIC WON'T STAY KEEN ON CONAN ONCE YOU TELL ME ABOUT THE REAL REASON YOU AND YOUR BLACKS WAS SKULKING ABOUT NIPPR!
I DON'T BELIEVE HIS IDIOTIC STORY FOR A SECOND. WHERE YOU RUNNING OFF TO, EH? HE SIGNAL TO MEET YOU, YEAH? WHERE? WHY?
AH, WHAT'S THIS? NO TONGUE?
WELL, LASS, I WAS TAKEN WITH YOU BEFORE...
...BUT NOW I THINK YOU'RE THE GREATEST WOMAN I EVER MET.

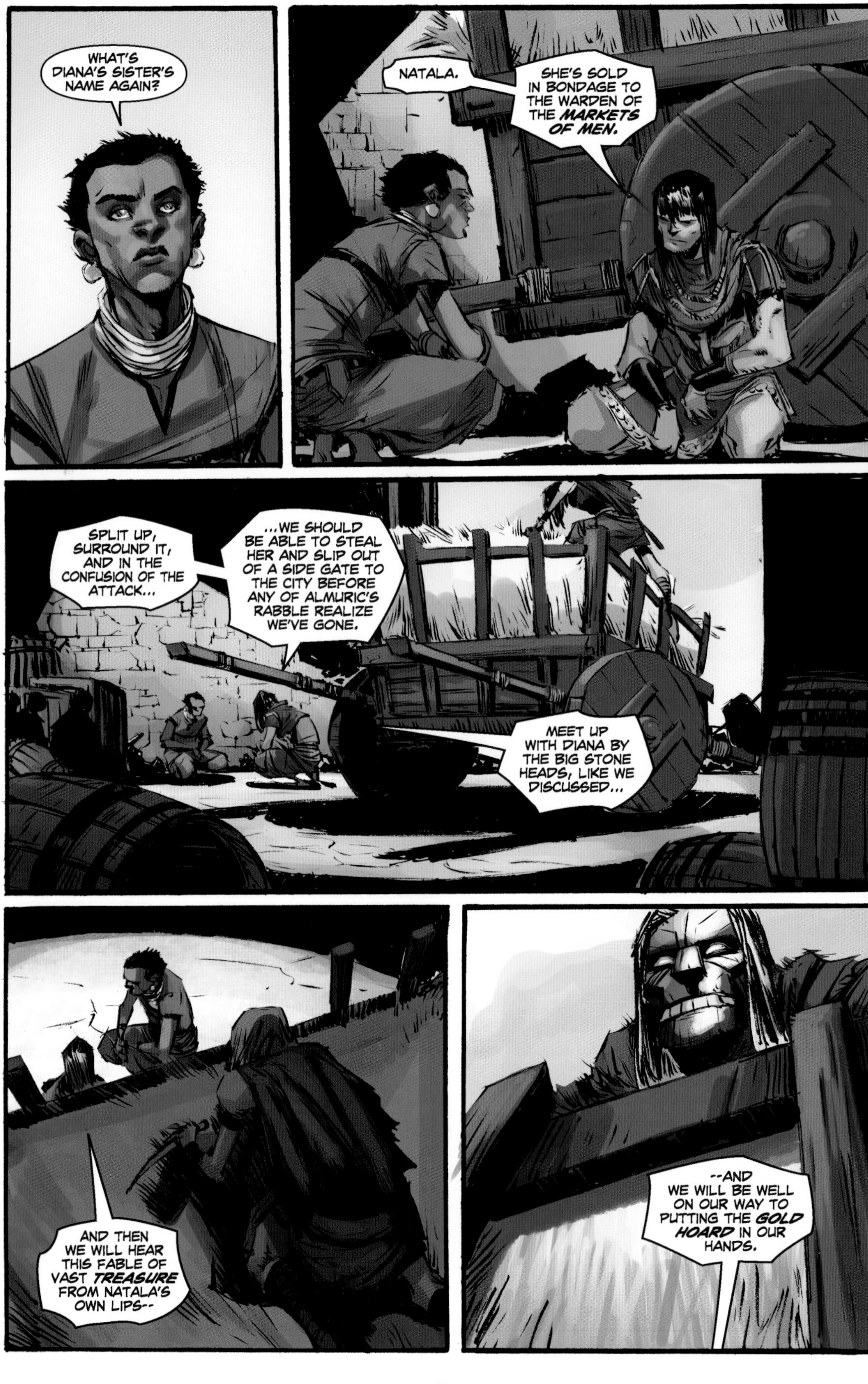
WHAT'S DIANA'S SISTER'S NAME AGAIN?
NATALA.
SHE'S SOLD IN BONDAGE TO THE WARDEN OF THE MARKETS OF MEN.
SPLIT UP, SURROUND IT, AND IN THE CONFUSION OF THE ATTACK...
...WE SHOULD BE ABLE TO STEAL HER AND SLIP OUT OF A SIDE GATE TO THE CITY BEFORE ANY OF ALMURIC'S RABBLE REALIZE WE'VE GONE.
MEET UP WITH DIANA BY THE BIG STONE HEADS, LIKE WE DISCUSSED...
AND THEN WE WILL HEAR THIS FABLE OF VAST TREASURE FROM NATALA'S OWN LIPS--
--AND WE WILL BE WELL ON OUR WAY TO PUTTING THE GOLD HOARD IN OUR HANDS.

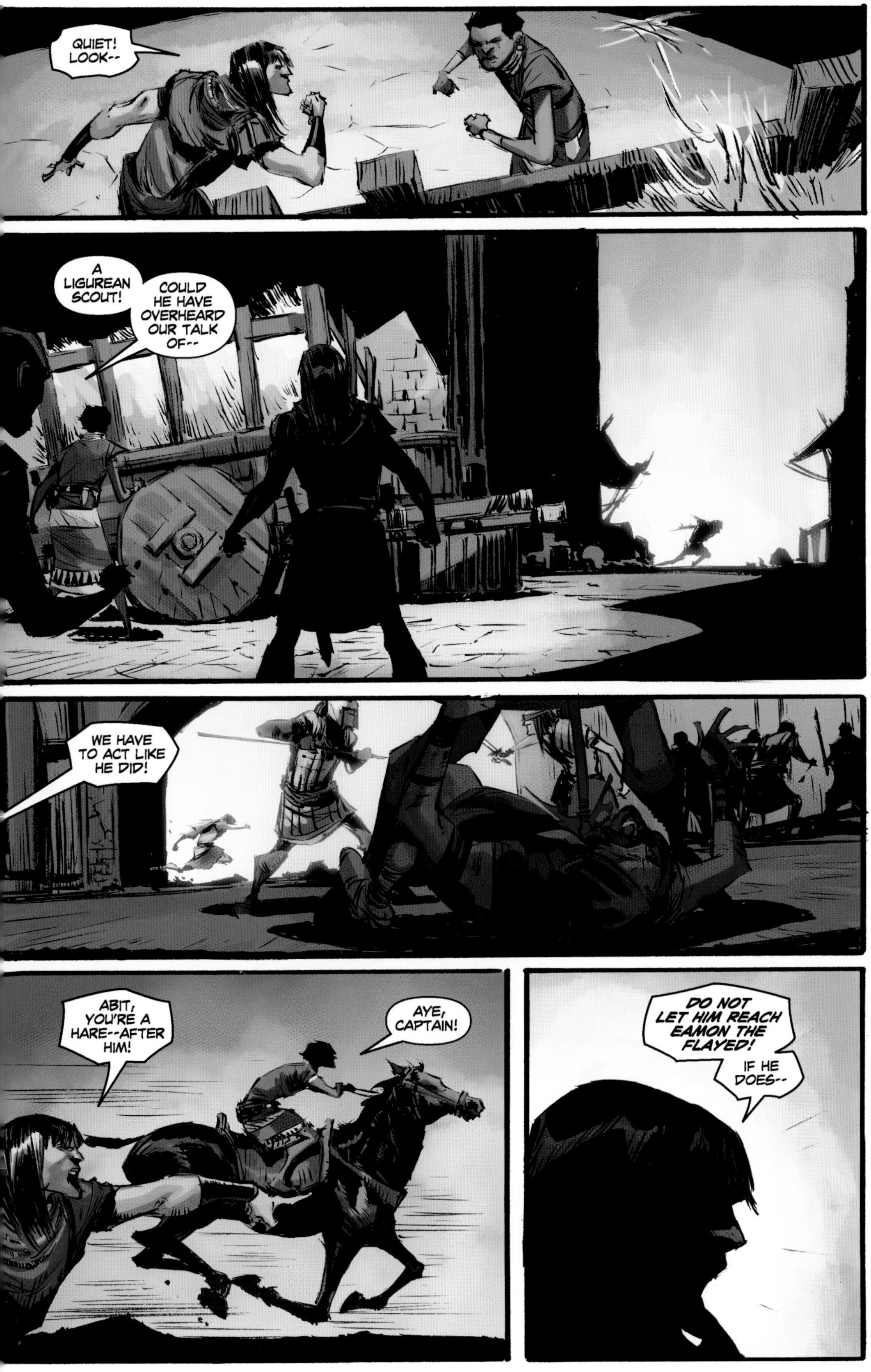
QUIET! LOOK--
A LIGUREAN SCOUT!
COULD HE HAVE OVERHEARD OUR TALK OF--
WE HAVE TO ACT LIKE HE DID!
ABIT, YOU'RE A HARE--AFTER HIM!
AYE, CAPTAIN!
DO NOT LET HIM REACH EAMON THE FLAYED!
IF HE DOES--

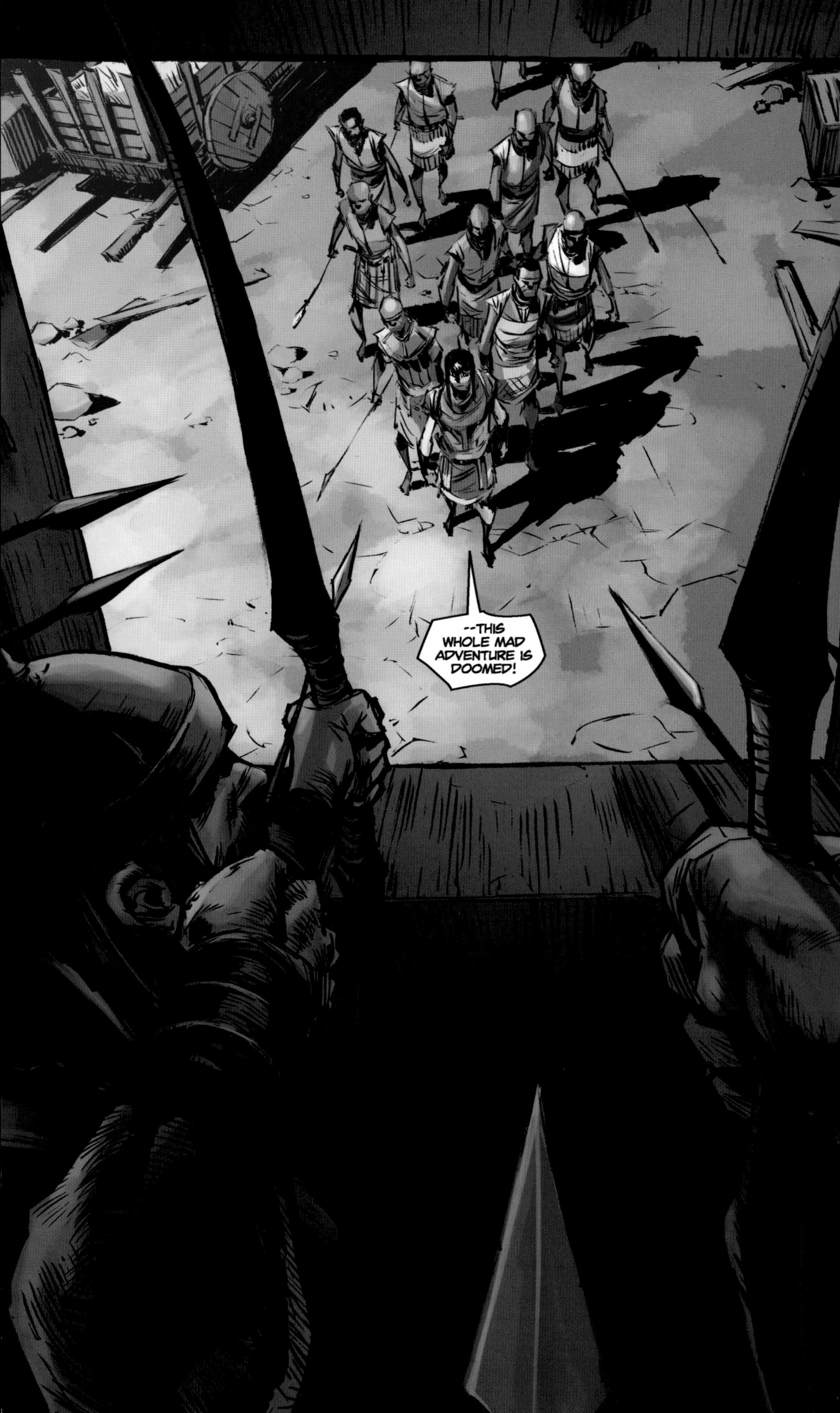
--THIS WHOLE MAD ADVENTURE IS DOOMED!

CHAPTER THREE

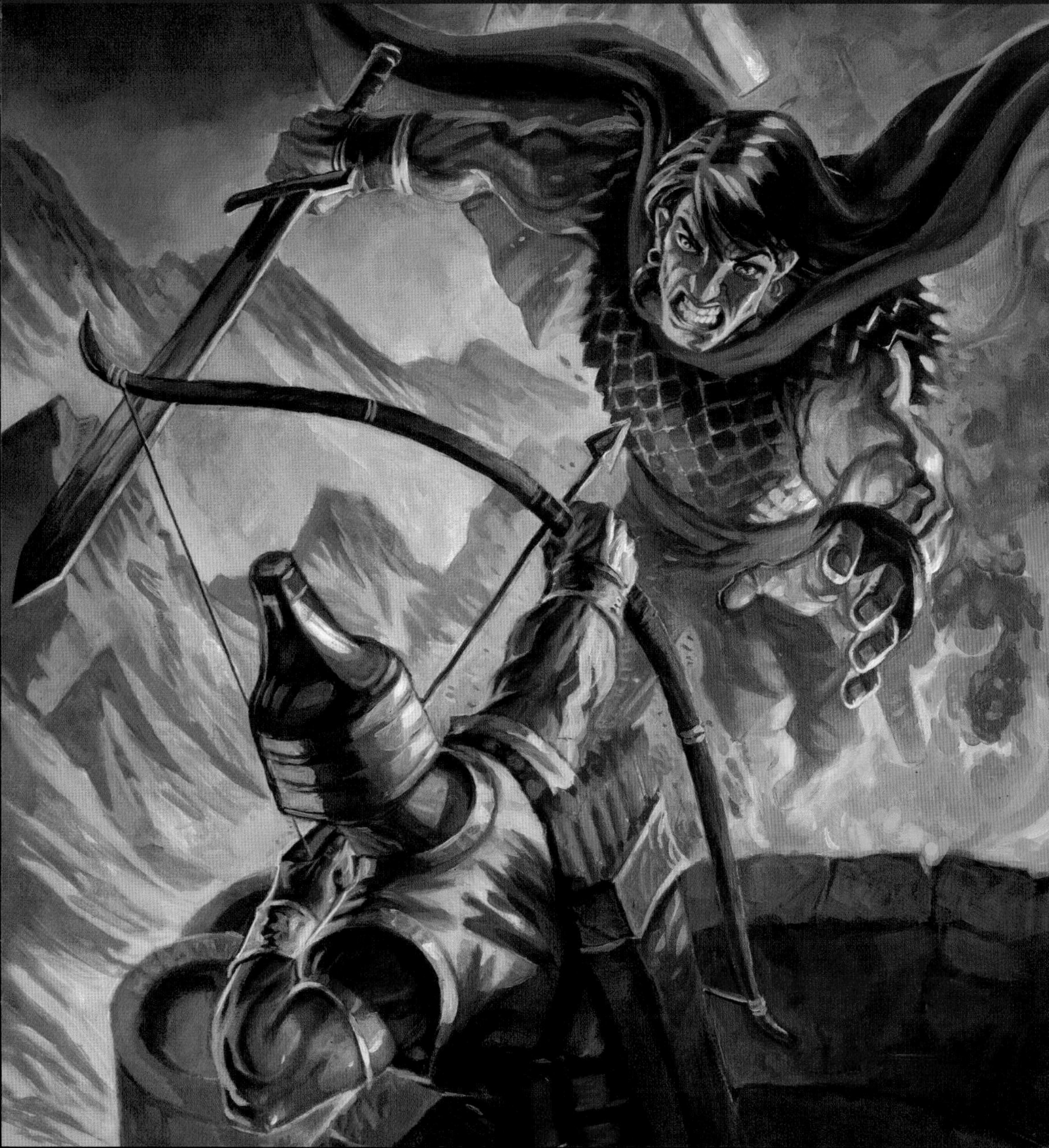

"Go. When they ask, tell them *Amra's Bastards* freed you."

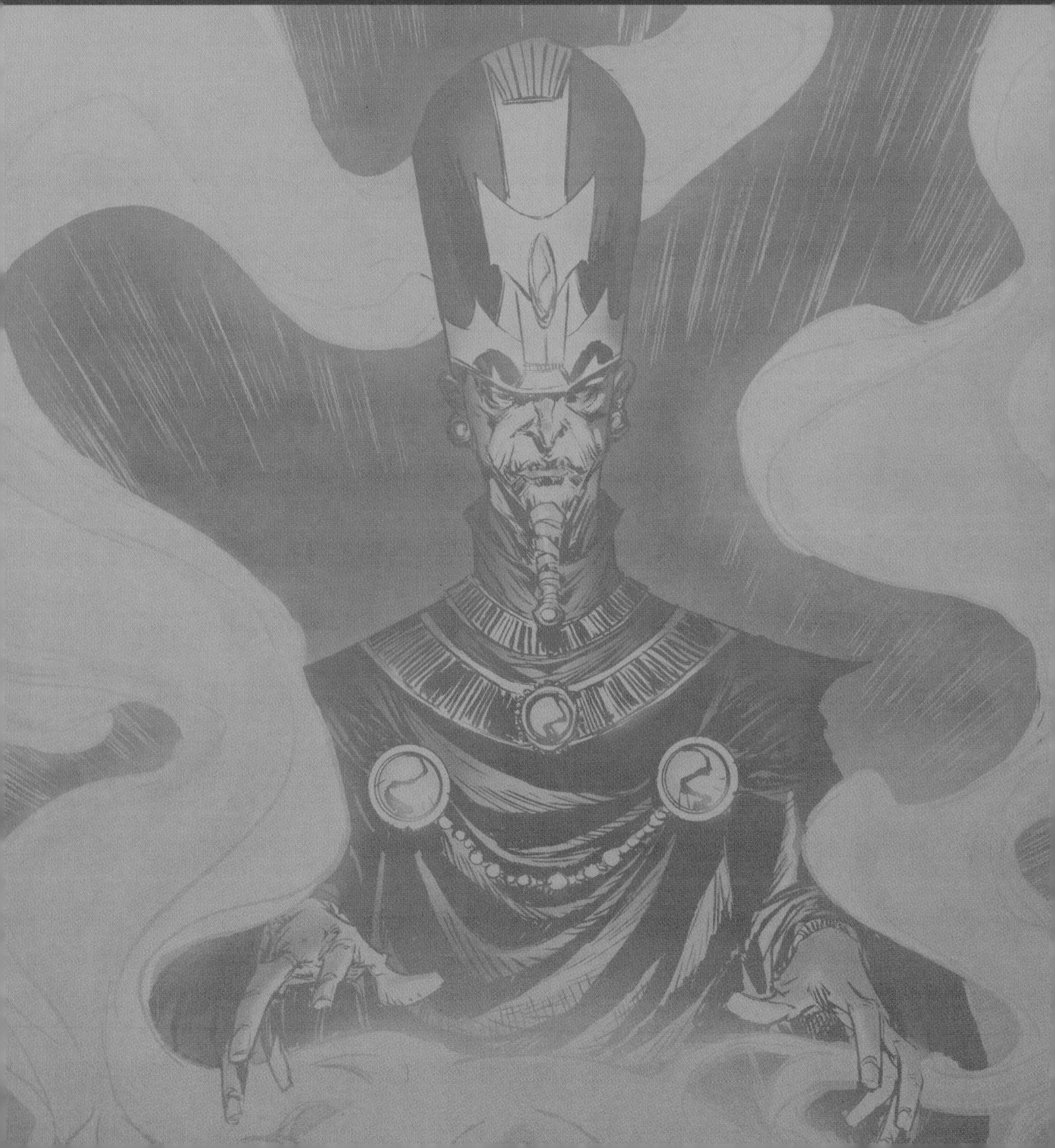

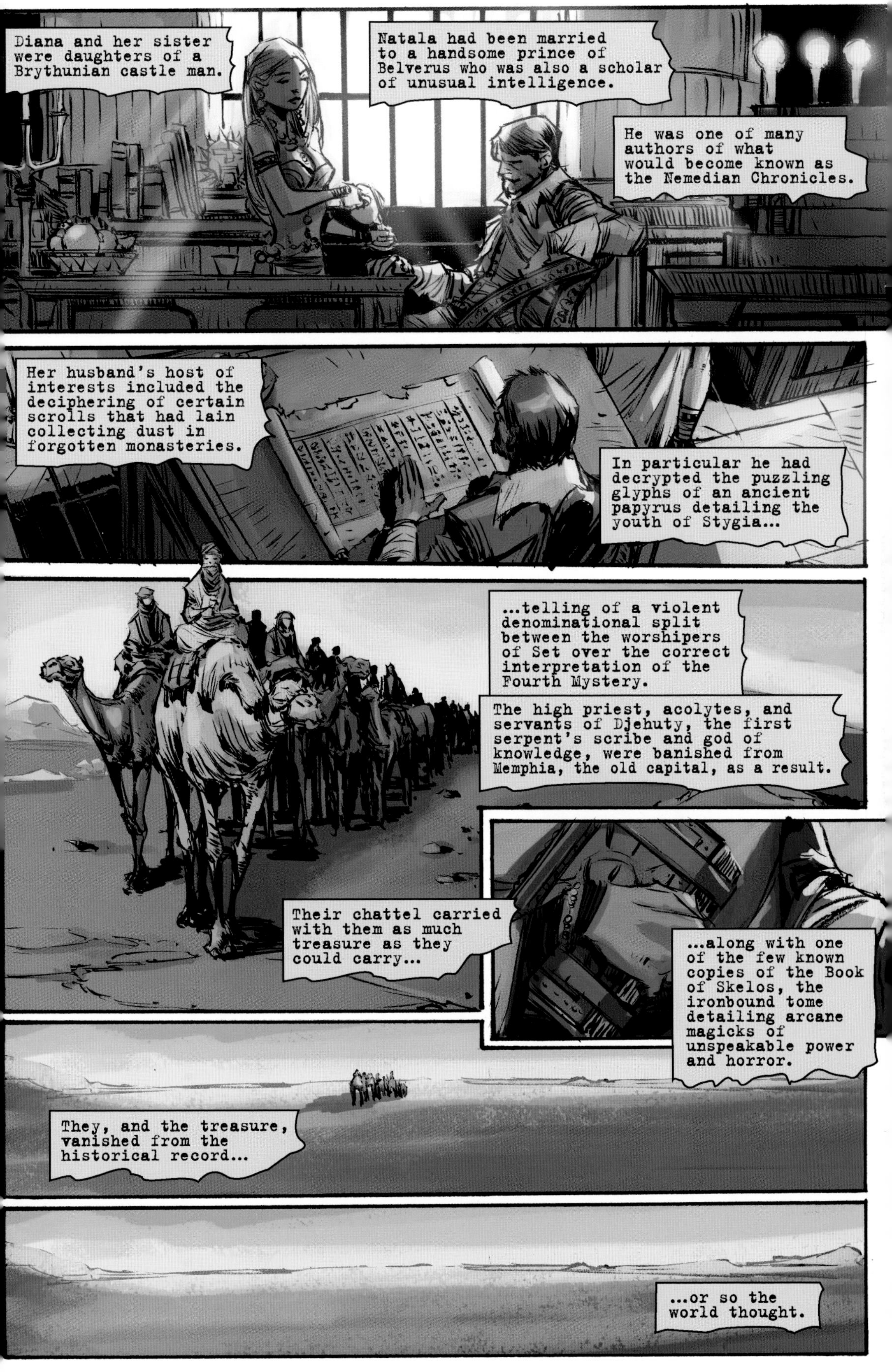

Diana and her sister were daughters of a Brythunian castle man.
Natala had been married to a handsome prince of Belverus who was also a scholar of unusual intelligence.
He was one of many authors of what would become known as the Nemedian Chronicles.
Her husband's host of interests included the deciphering of certain scrolls that had lain collecting dust in forgotten monasteries.
In particular he had decrypted the puzzling glyphs of an ancient papyrus detailing the youth of Stygia...
...telling of a violent denominational split between the worshipers of Set over the correct interpretation of the Fourth Mystery.
The high priest, acolytes, and servants of Djehuty, the first serpent's scribe and god of knowledge, were banished from Memphia, the old capital, as a result.
Their chattel carried with them as much treasure as they could carry...
...along with one of the few known copies of the Book of Skelos, the ironbound tome detailing arcane magicks of unspeakable power and horror.
They, and the treasure, vanished from the historical record...
...or so the world thought.

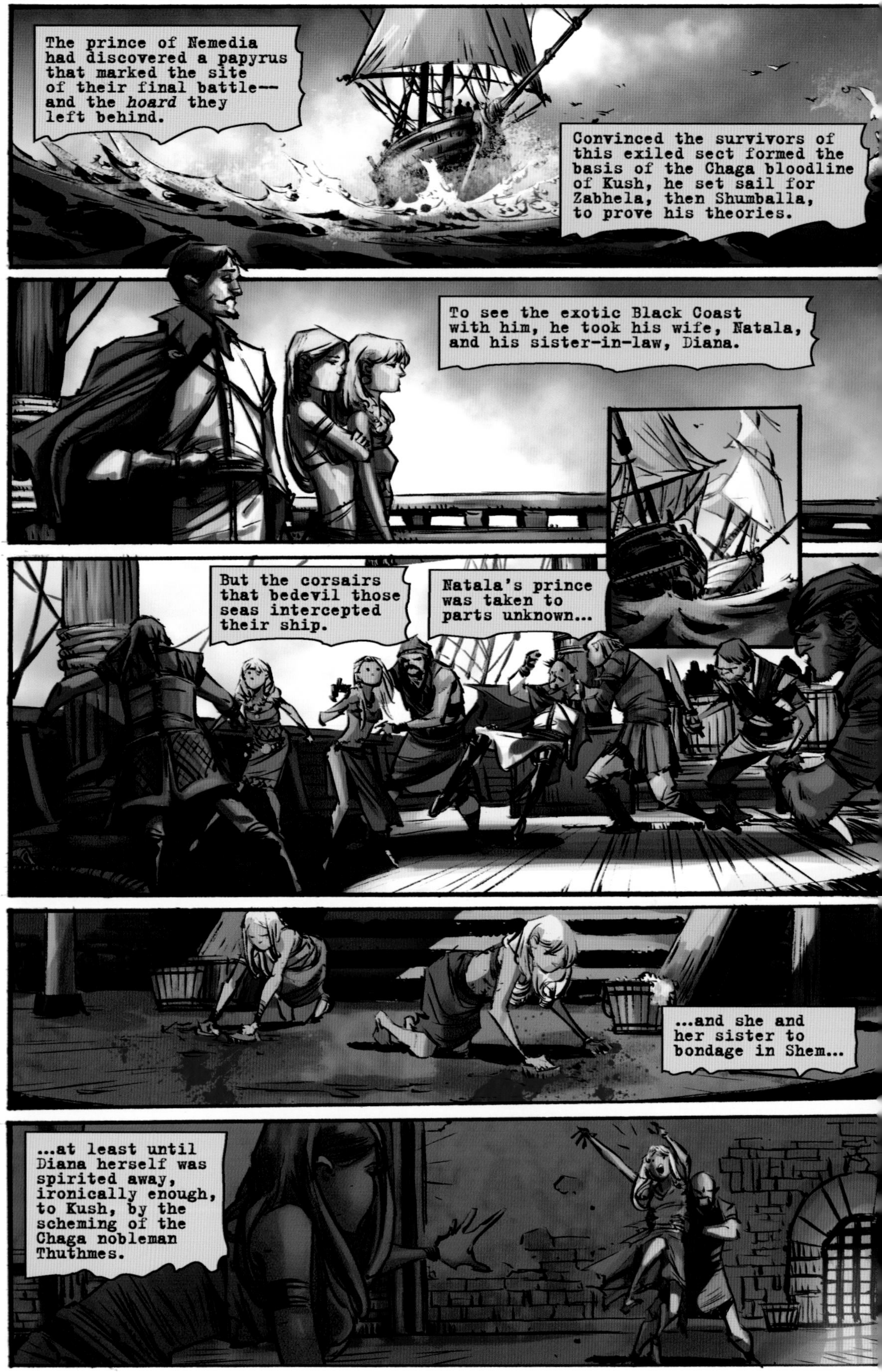
The prince of Nemedia had discovered a papyrus that marked the site of their final battle-- and the *hoard* they left behind.
Convinced the survivors of this exiled sect formed the basis of the Chaga bloodline of Kush, he set sail for Zabhela, then Shumballa, to prove his theories.
To see the exotic Black Coast with him, he took his wife, Natala, and his sister-in-law, Diana.
But the corsairs that bedevil those seas intercepted their ship.
Natala's prince was taken to parts unknown...
...and she and her sister to bondage in Shem...
...at least until Diana herself was spirited away, ironically enough, to Kush, by the scheming of the Chaga nobleman Thuthmes.

There had been the sound of *rushing wind* where Diana's heart had been ever since she had been ripped from her sister's embrace.

A SHAME YE CAN'T TALK, AN' TELL ME WHAT THE SMITH'S SON'S *REALLY* UP TO, LASS.

Now she was but a few short leagues from where Natala was held captive.

BUT DON'T THINK I THINK THE LESS O' YE FOR IT, OH NO!

The hole inside her was on the verge of closing.

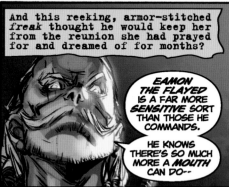

And this reeking, armor-stitched *freak* thought he would keep her from the reunion she had prayed for and dreamed of for months?

EAMON THE FLAYED IS A FAR MORE *SENSITIVE* SORT THAN THOSE HE COMMANDS.

HE KNOWS THERE'S SO MUCH MORE A *MOUTH* CAN DO--

FSSSSSSS

She'd make sure it would be the last mistake he'd ever make.

EEEYYAAAAAAAA!!

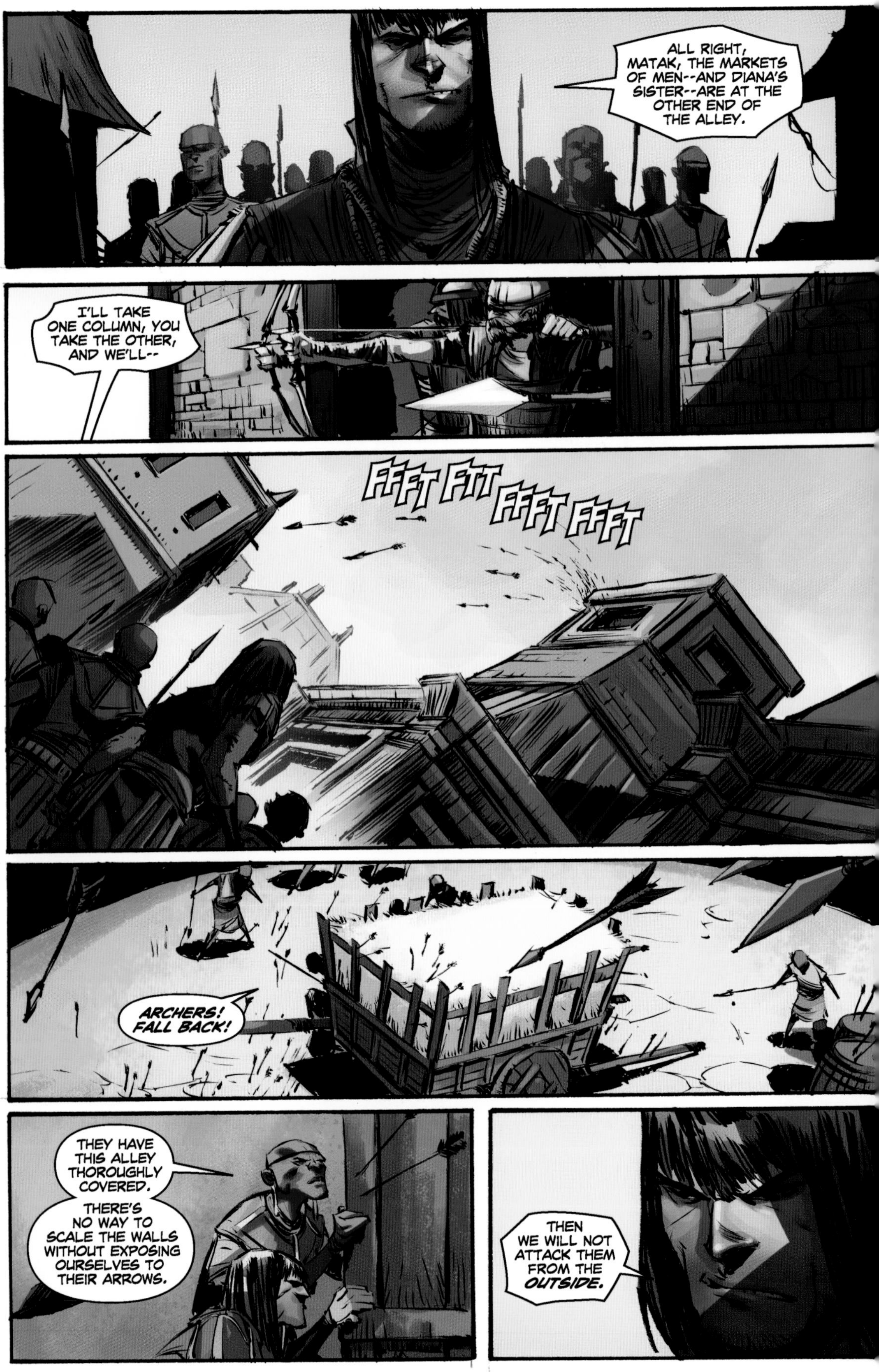
ALL RIGHT, MATAK, THE MARKETS OF MEN--AND DIANA'S SISTER--ARE AT THE OTHER END OF THE ALLEY.
I'LL TAKE ONE COLUMN, YOU TAKE THE OTHER, AND WE'LL--
FFFT FTT FFFT FFFT
ARCHERS! FALL BACK!
THEY HAVE THIS ALLEY THOROUGHLY COVERED.
THERE'S NO WAY TO SCALE THE WALLS WITHOUT EXPOSING OURSELVES TO THEIR ARROWS.
THEN WE WILL NOT ATTACK THEM FROM THE OUTSIDE.

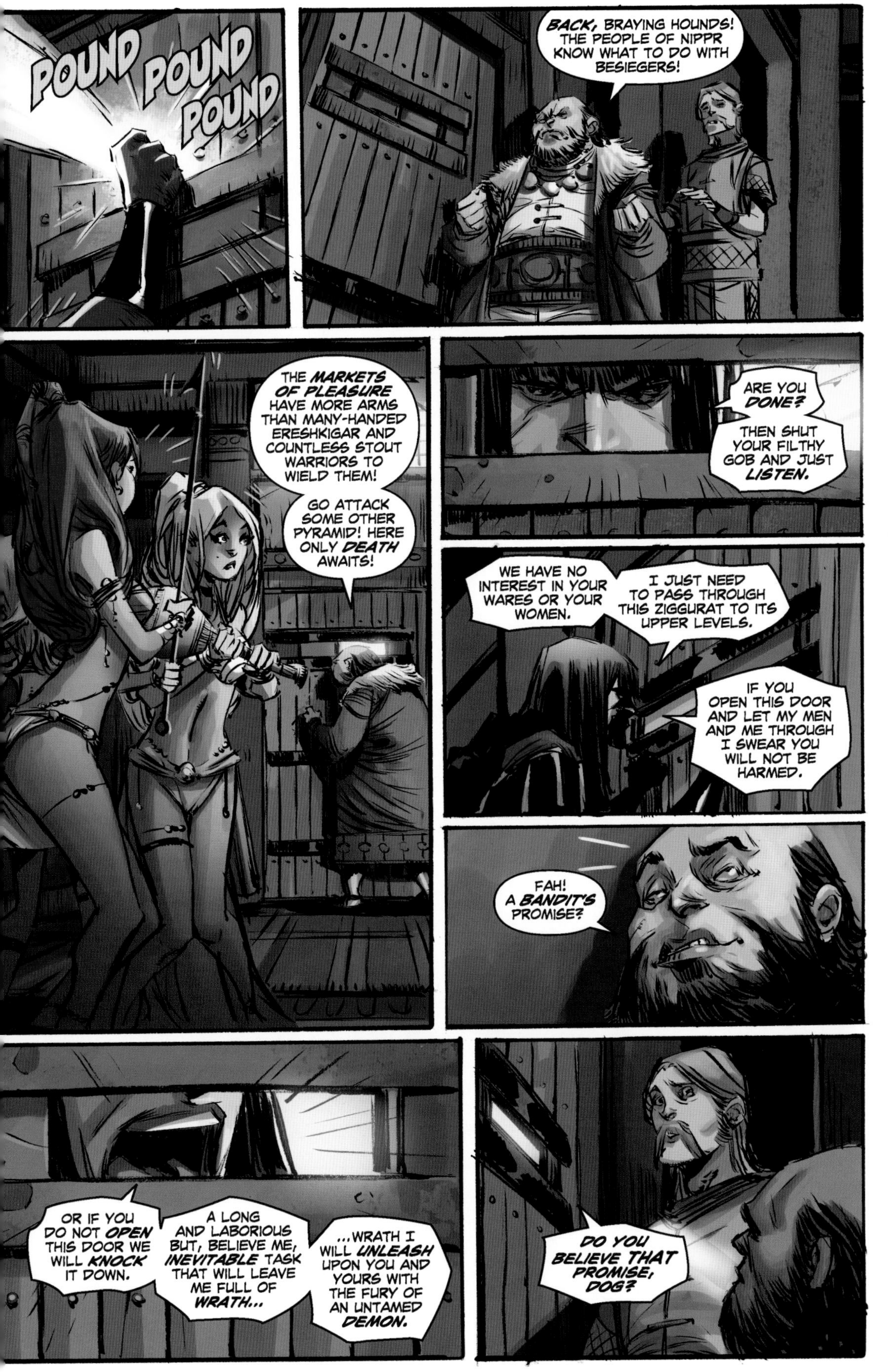
POUND POUND POUND
BACK, BRAYING HOUNDS! THE PEOPLE OF NIPPR KNOW WHAT TO DO WITH BESIEGERS!
THE MARKETS OF PLEASURE HAVE MORE ARMS THAN MANY-HANDED ERESHKIGAR AND COUNTLESS STOUT WARRIORS TO WIELD THEM!
GO ATTACK SOME OTHER PYRAMID! HERE ONLY DEATH AWAITS!
ARE YOU DONE?
THEN SHUT YOUR FILTHY GOB AND JUST LISTEN.
WE HAVE NO INTEREST IN YOUR WARES OR YOUR WOMEN.
I JUST NEED TO PASS THROUGH THIS ZIGGURAT TO ITS UPPER LEVELS.
IF YOU OPEN THIS DOOR AND LET MY MEN AND ME THROUGH I SWEAR YOU WILL NOT BE HARMED.
FAH! A BANDIT'S PROMISE?
OR IF YOU DO NOT OPEN THIS DOOR WE WILL KNOCK IT DOWN.
A LONG AND LABORIOUS BUT, BELIEVE ME, INEVITABLE TASK THAT WILL LEAVE ME FULL OF WRATH...
...WRATH I WILL UNLEASH UPON YOU AND YOURS WITH THE FURY OF AN UNTAMED DEMON.
DO YOU BELIEVE THAT PROMISE, DOG?

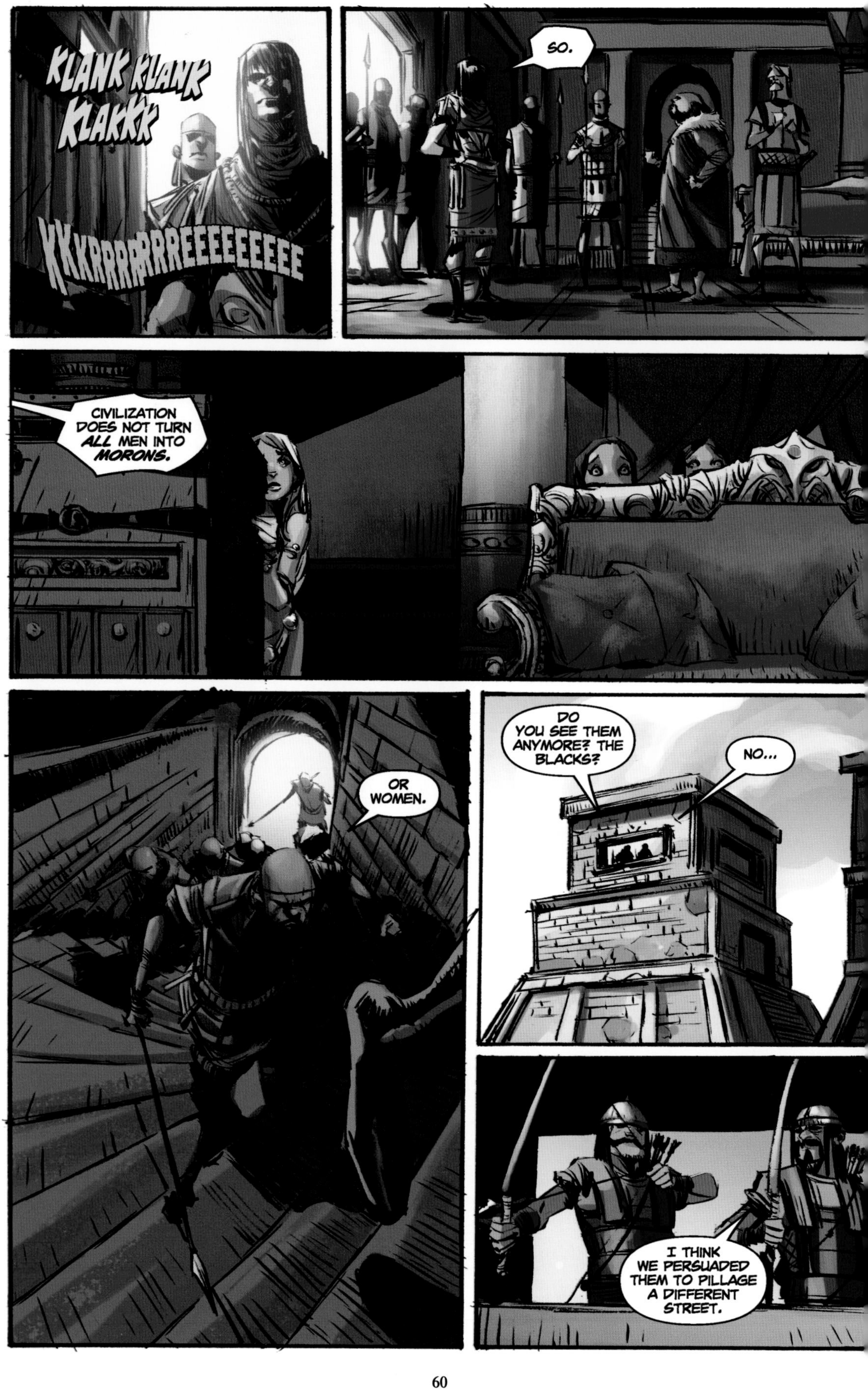
KLANK KLANK KLAKKK
KKKRRRRRRREEEEEEEEE
SO.
CIVILIZATION DOES NOT TURN ALL MEN INTO MORONS.
OR WOMEN.
DO YOU SEE THEM ANYMORE? THE BLACKS?
NO...
I THINK WE PERSUADED THEM TO PILLAGE A DIFFERENT STREET.

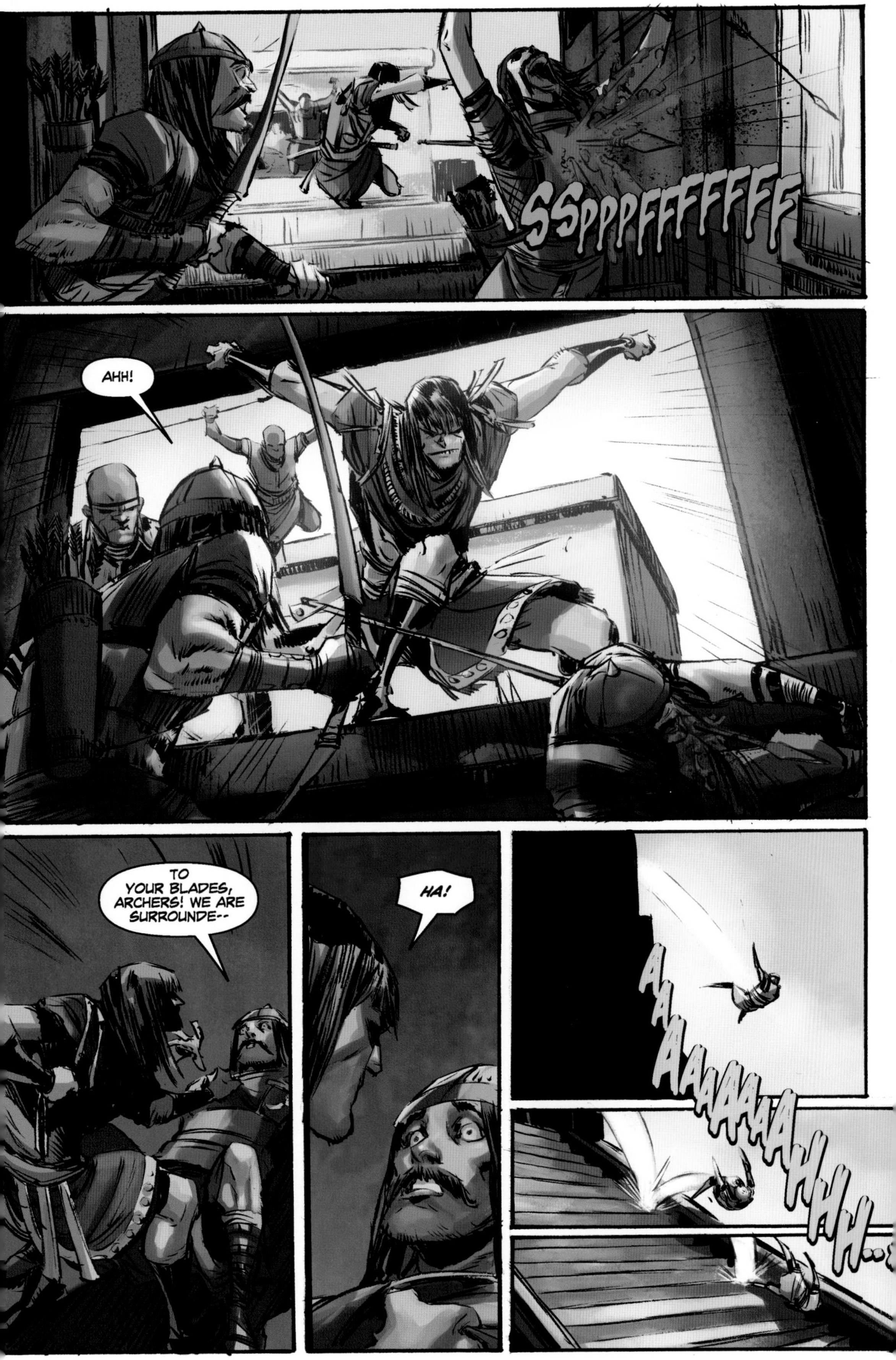
SSPPPFFFFFFF
AHH!
TO YOUR BLADES, ARCHERS! WE ARE SURROUNDE--
HA!
AAAAAAAAAAAHHHH...

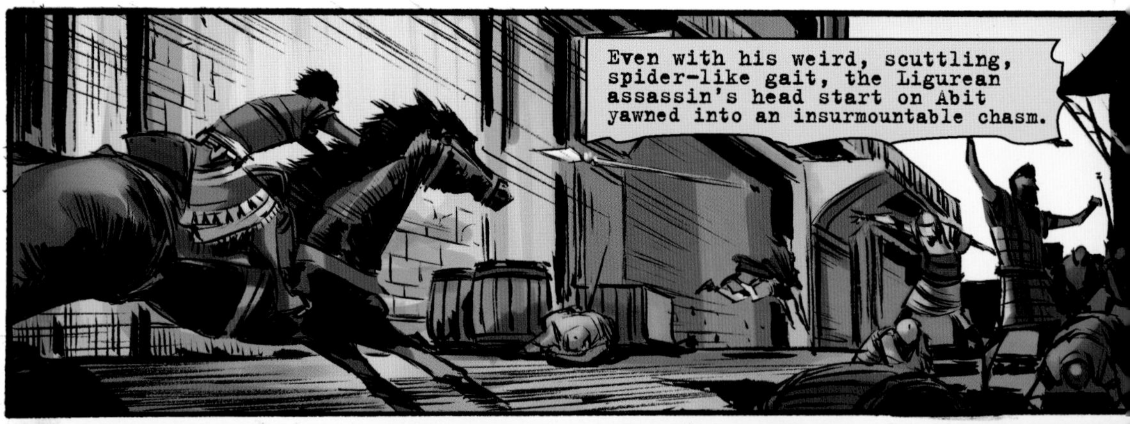
Even with his weird, scuttling, spider-like gait, the Ligurean assassin's head start on Abit yawned into an insurmountable chasm.

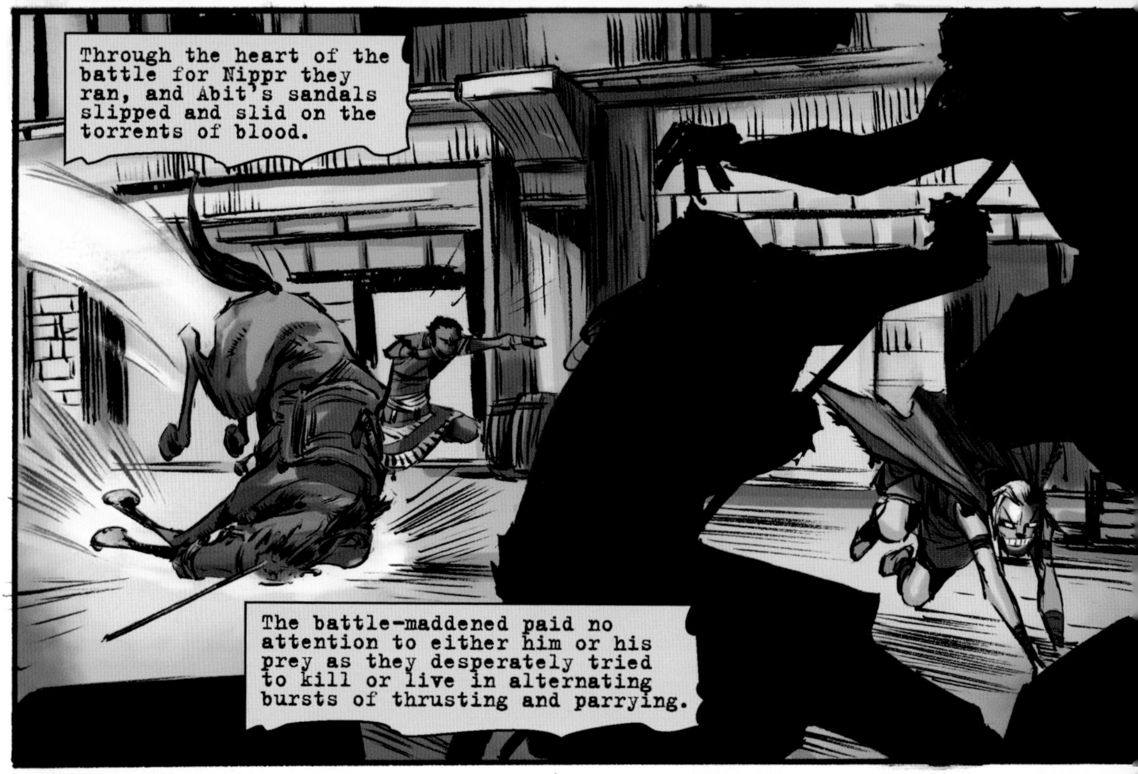
Through the heart of the battle for Nippr they ran, and Abit's sandals slipped and slid on the torrents of blood.
The battle-maddened paid no attention to either him or his prey as they desperately tried to kill or live in alternating bursts of thrusting and parrying.

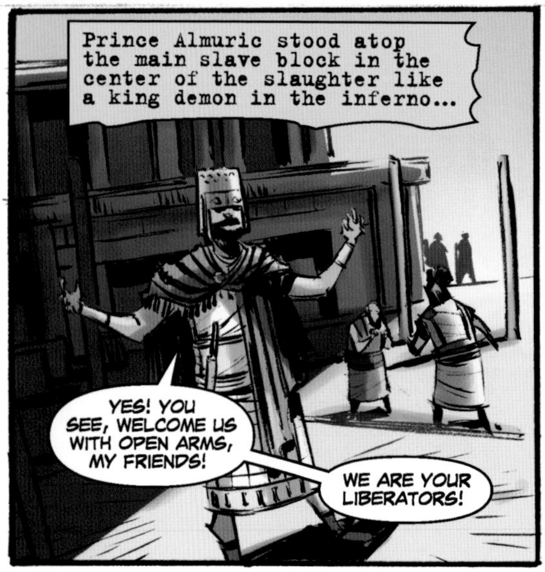
Prince Almuric stood atop the main slave block in the center of the slaughter like a king demon in the inferno...
YES! YOU SEE, WELCOME US WITH OPEN ARMS, MY FRIENDS!
WE ARE YOUR LIBERATORS!

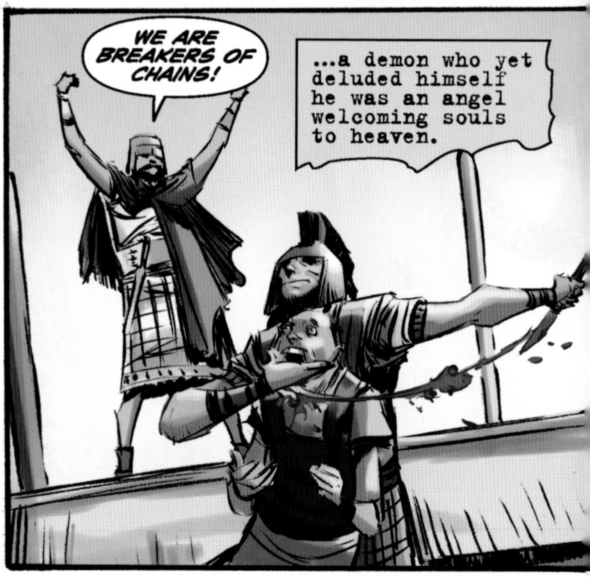
WE ARE BREAKERS OF CHAINS!
...a demon who yet deluded himself he was an angel welcoming souls to heaven.

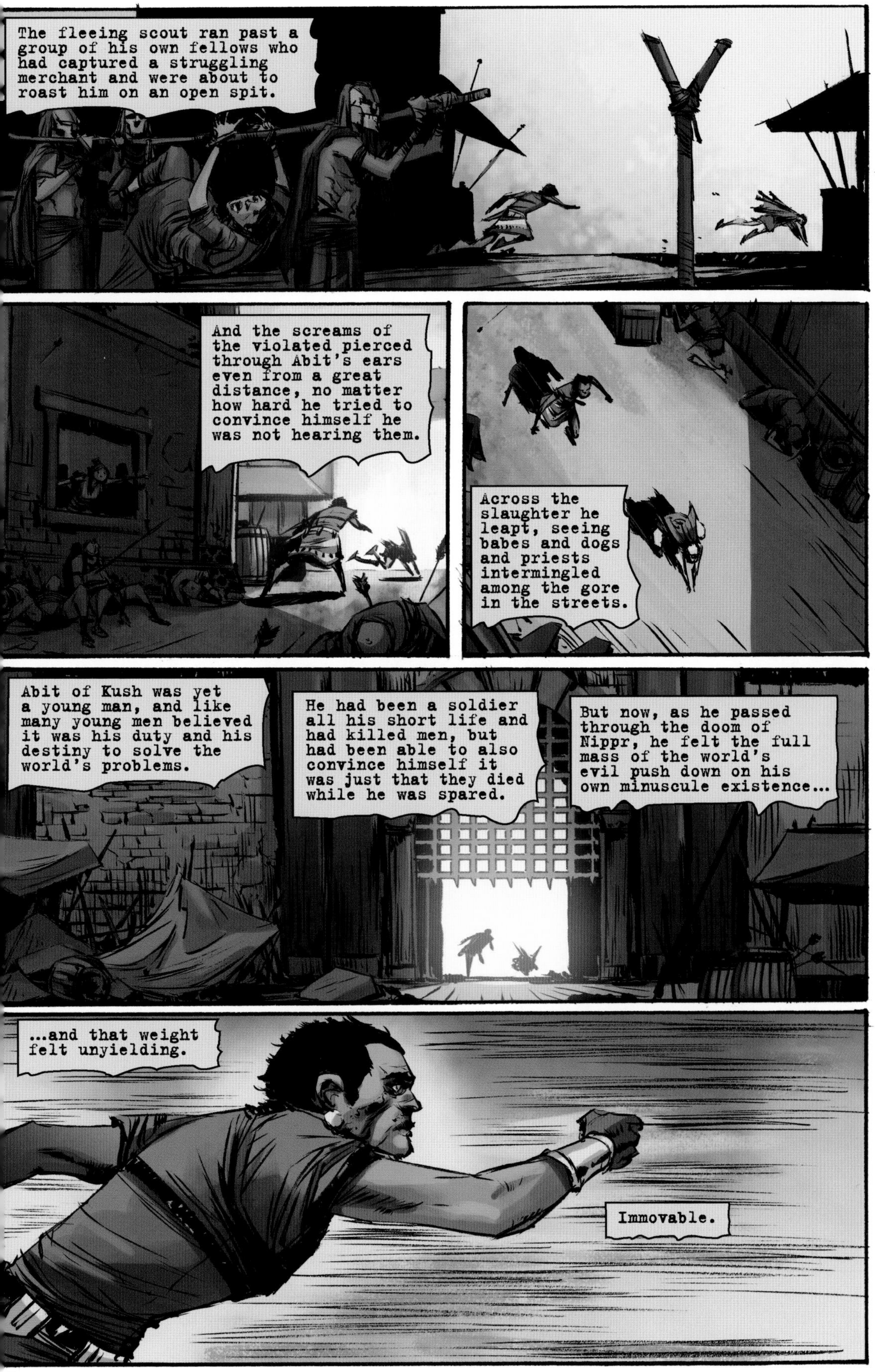

The fleeing scout ran past a group of his own fellows who had captured a struggling merchant and were about to roast him on an open spit.
And the screams of the violated pierced through Abit's ears even from a great distance, no matter how hard he tried to convince himself he was not hearing them.
Across the slaughter he leapt, seeing babes and dogs and priests intermingled among the gore in the streets.
Abit of Kush was yet a young man, and like many young men believed it was his duty and his destiny to solve the world's problems.
He had been a soldier all his short life and had killed men, but had been able to also convince himself it was just that they died while he was spared.
But now, as he passed through the doom of Nippr, he felt the full mass of the world's evil push down on his own minuscule existence...
...and that weight felt unyielding.
Immovable.

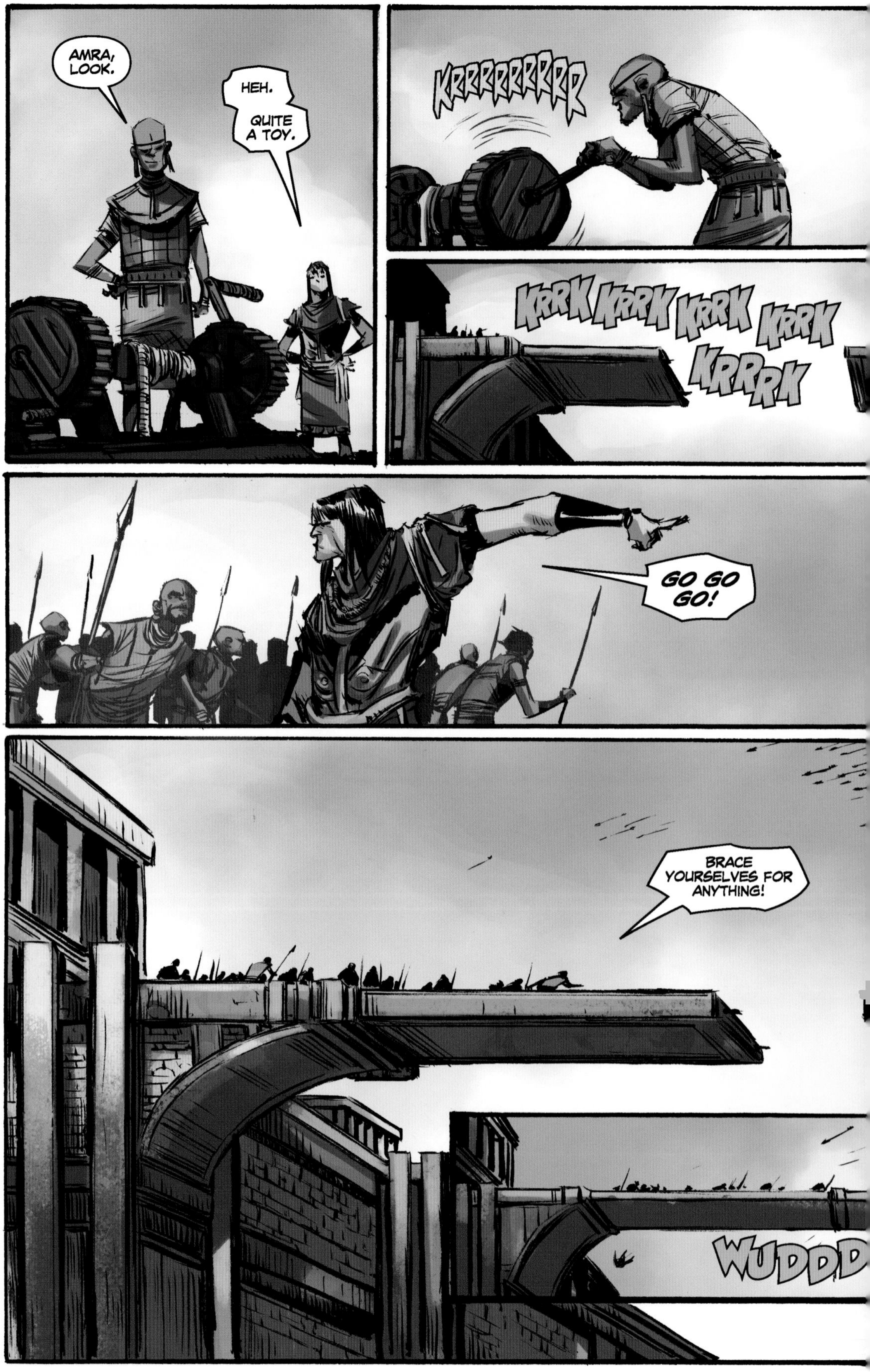
AMRA, LOOK.
HEH.
QUITE A TOY.
KRRRRRRRRR
KRRK KRRK KRRK KRRK
KRRRK
GO GO GO!
BRACE YOURSELVES FOR ANYTHING!
WUDDD

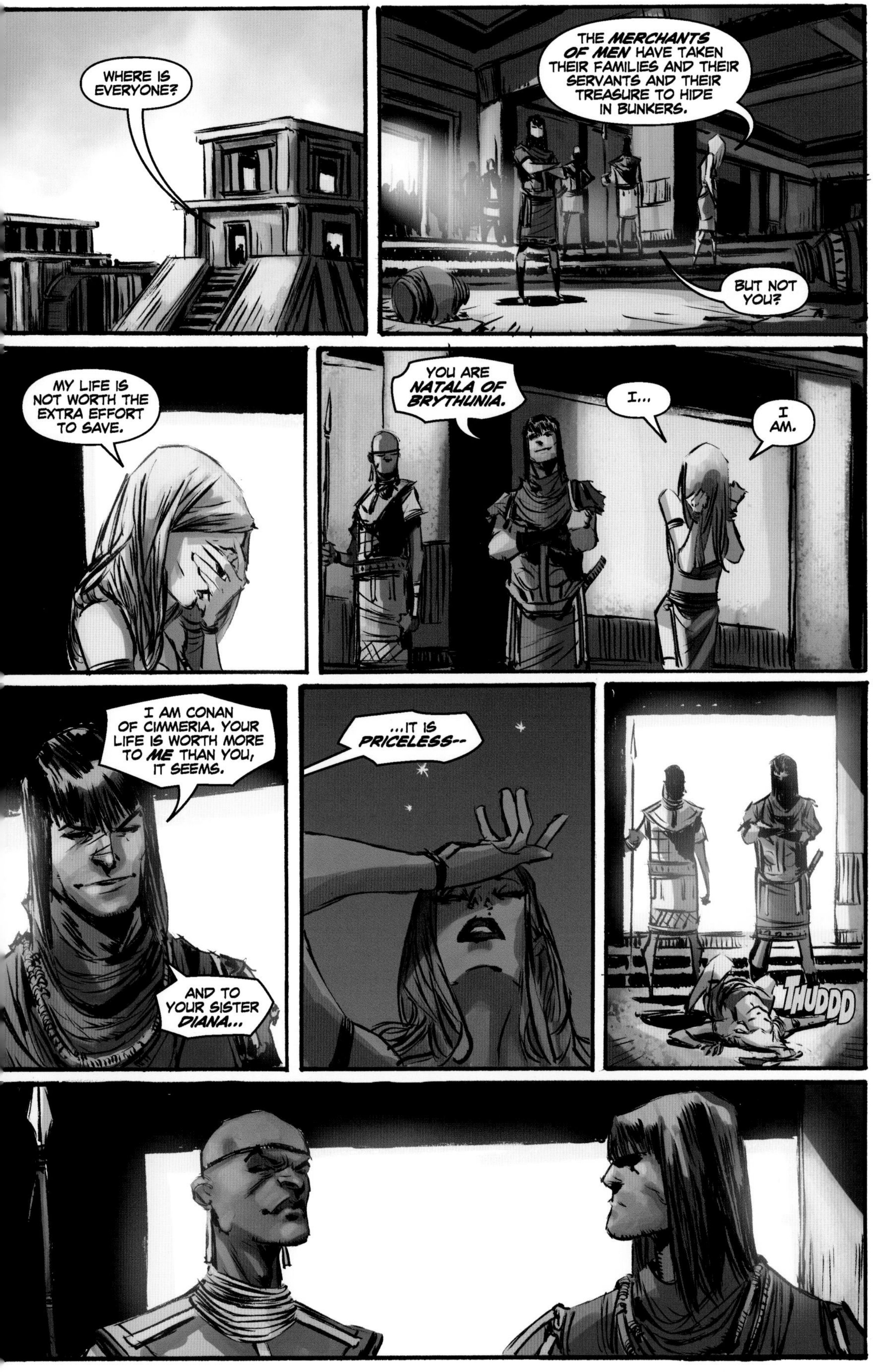
WHERE IS EVERYONE?
THE MERCHANTS OF MEN HAVE TAKEN THEIR FAMILIES AND THEIR SERVANTS AND THEIR TREASURE TO HIDE IN BUNKERS.
BUT NOT YOU?
MY LIFE IS NOT WORTH THE EXTRA EFFORT TO SAVE.
YOU ARE NATALA OF BRYTHUNIA.
I...
I AM.
I AM CONAN OF CIMMERIA. YOUR LIFE IS WORTH MORE TO ME THAN YOU, IT SEEMS.
AND TO YOUR SISTER DIANA...
...IT IS PRICELESS--
THUDDD

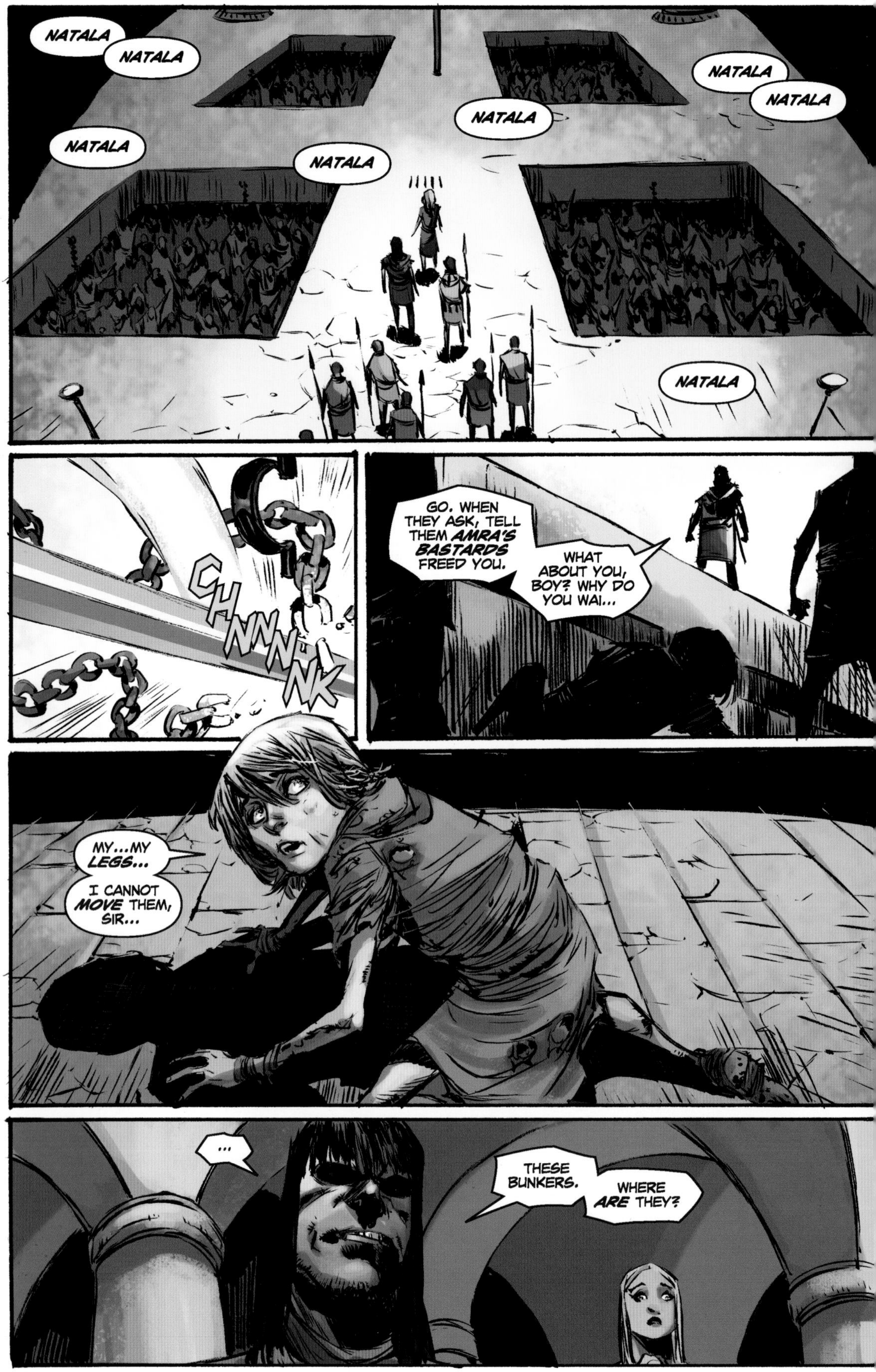
NATALA
NATALA
NATALA
NATALA
NATALA
NATALA
NATALA
NATALA
CHNNNNK
GO. WHEN THEY ASK, TELL THEM AMRA'S BASTARDS FREED YOU.
WHAT ABOUT YOU, BOY? WHY DO YOU WAI...
MY...MY LEGS...
I CANNOT MOVE THEM, SIR...
...
THESE BUNKERS.
WHERE ARE THEY?

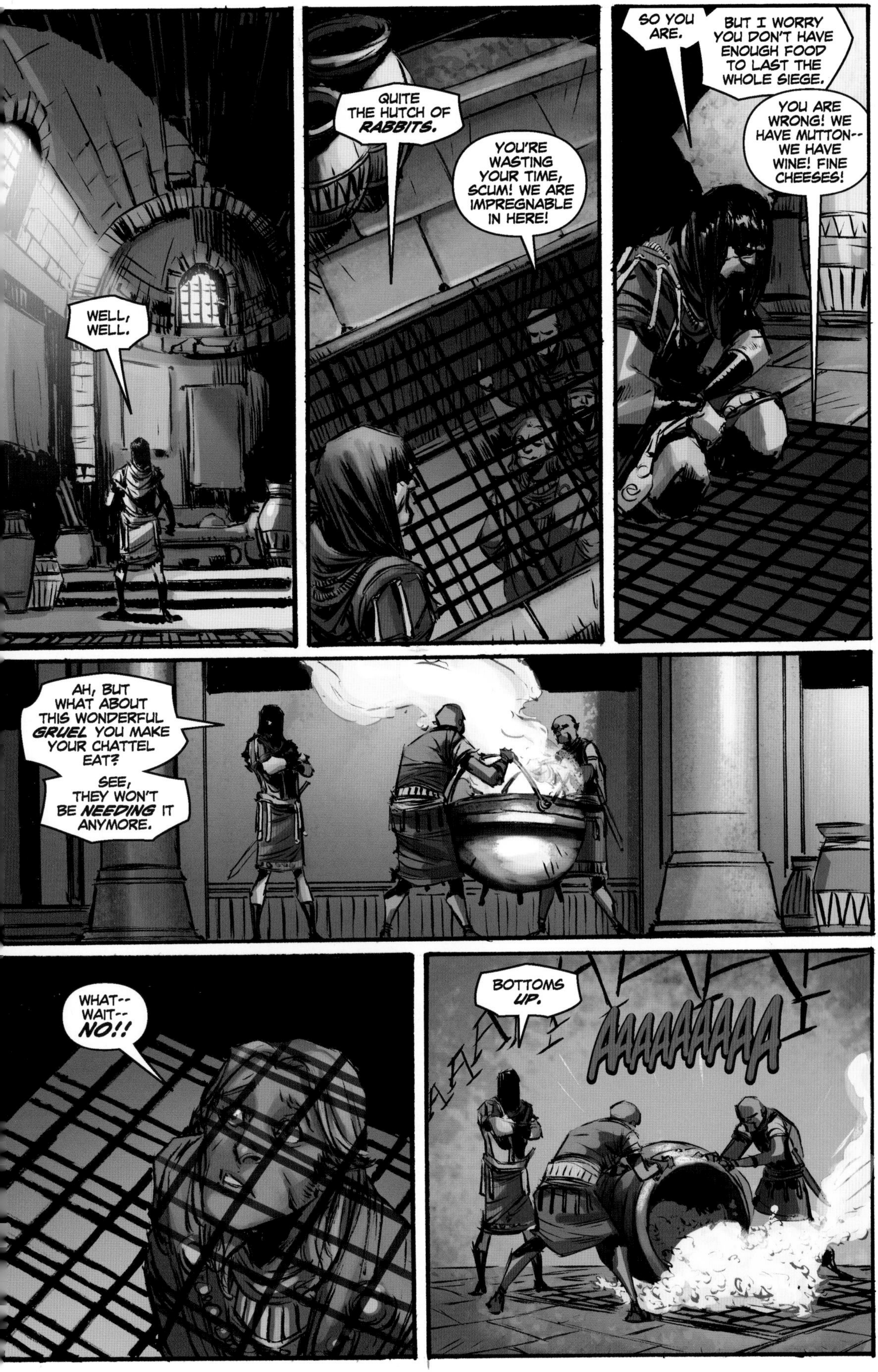
WELL, WELL.
QUITE THE HUTCH OF RABBITS.
YOU'RE WASTING YOUR TIME, SCUM! WE ARE IMPREGNABLE IN HERE!
SO YOU ARE.
BUT I WORRY YOU DON'T HAVE ENOUGH FOOD TO LAST THE WHOLE SIEGE.
YOU ARE WRONG! WE HAVE MUTTON-- WE HAVE WINE! FINE CHEESES!
AH, BUT WHAT ABOUT THIS WONDERFUL GRUEL YOU MAKE YOUR CHATTEL EAT?
SEE, THEY WON'T BE NEEDING IT ANYMORE.
WHAT-- WAIT-- NO!!
BOTTOMS UP.
AAAAAAAAA

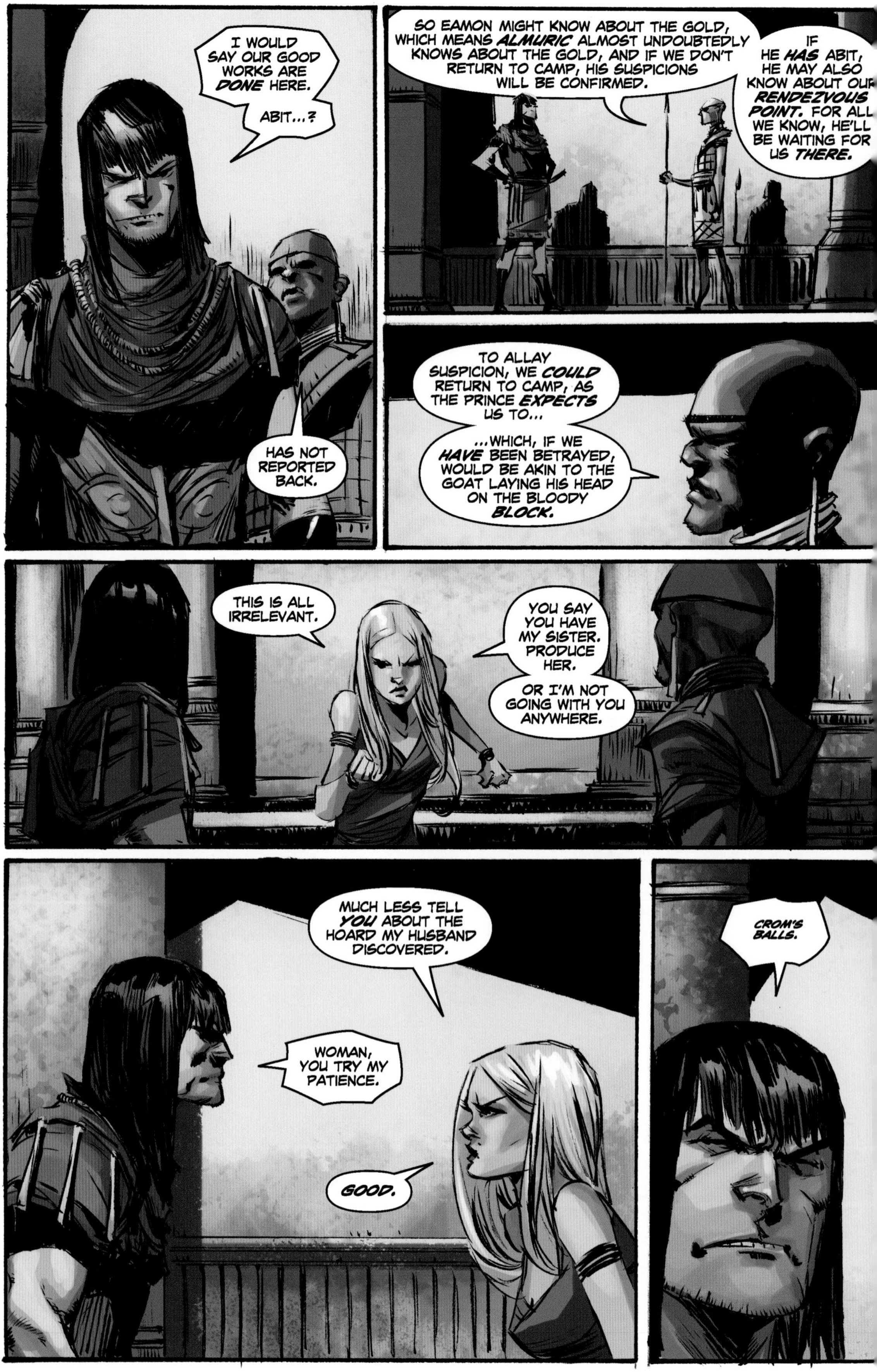

I WOULD SAY OUR GOOD WORKS ARE DONE HERE.
ABIT...?
HAS NOT REPORTED BACK.
SO EAMON MIGHT KNOW ABOUT THE GOLD, WHICH MEANS ALMURIC ALMOST UNDOUBTEDLY KNOWS ABOUT THE GOLD, AND IF WE DON'T RETURN TO CAMP, HIS SUSPICIONS WILL BE CONFIRMED.
IF HE HAS ABIT, HE MAY ALSO KNOW ABOUT OUR RENDEZVOUS POINT. FOR ALL WE KNOW, HE'LL BE WAITING FOR US THERE.
TO ALLAY SUSPICION, WE COULD RETURN TO CAMP, AS THE PRINCE EXPECTS US TO...
...WHICH, IF WE HAVE BEEN BETRAYED, WOULD BE AKIN TO THE GOAT LAYING HIS HEAD ON THE BLOODY BLOCK.
THIS IS ALL IRRELEVANT.
YOU SAY YOU HAVE MY SISTER. PRODUCE HER.
OR I'M NOT GOING WITH YOU ANYWHERE.
MUCH LESS TELL YOU ABOUT THE HOARD MY HUSBAND DISCOVERED.
WOMAN, YOU TRY MY PATIENCE.
GOOD.
CROM'S BALLS.

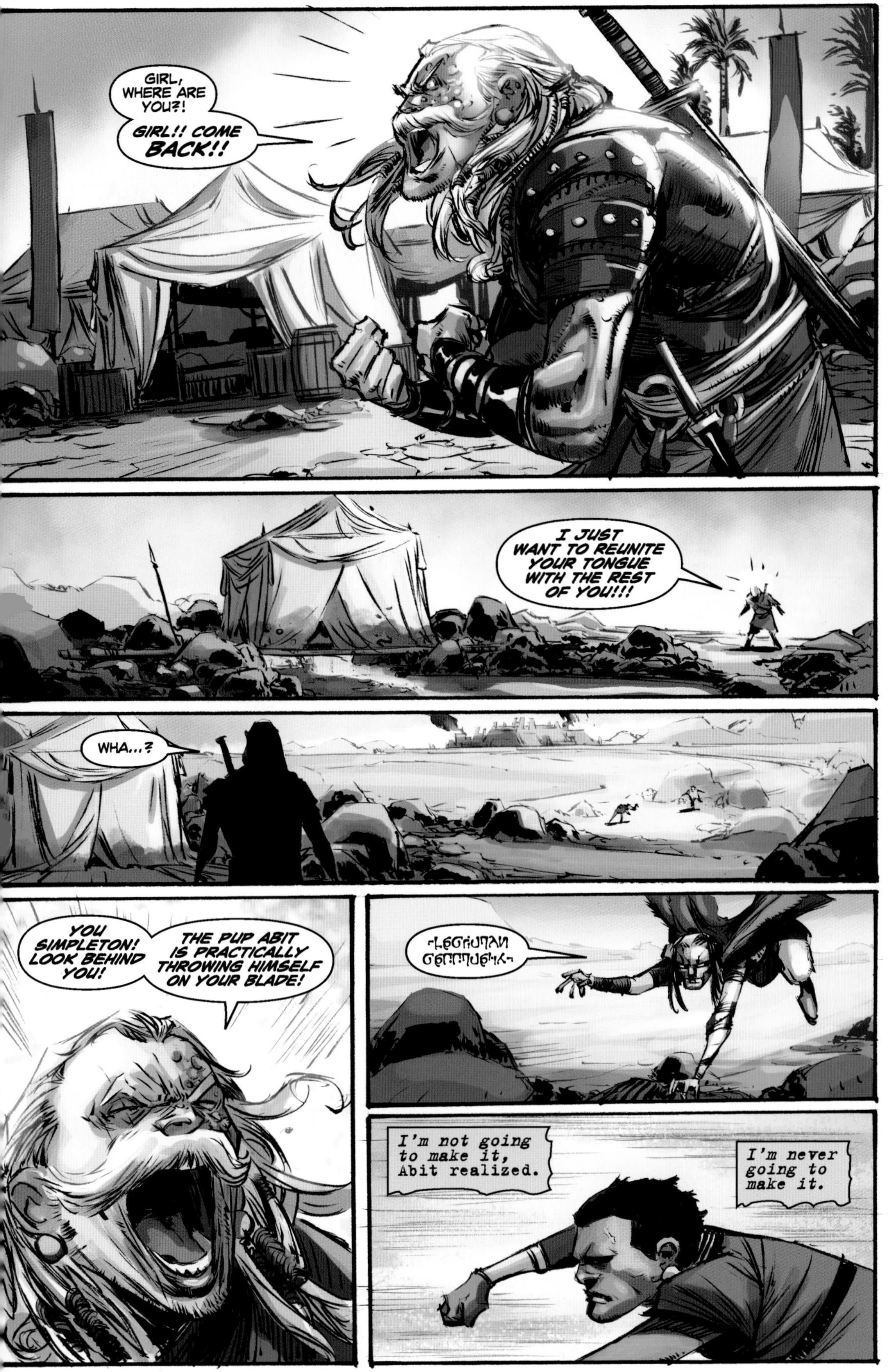
GIRL, WHERE ARE YOU?!
GIRL!! COME BACK!!
I JUST WANT TO REUNITE YOUR TONGUE WITH THE REST OF YOU!!!
WHA...?
YOU SIMPLETON! LOOK BEHIND YOU!
THE PUP ABIT IS PRACTICALLY THROWING HIMSELF ON YOUR BLADE!
I'm not going to make it, Abit realized.
I'm never going to make it.

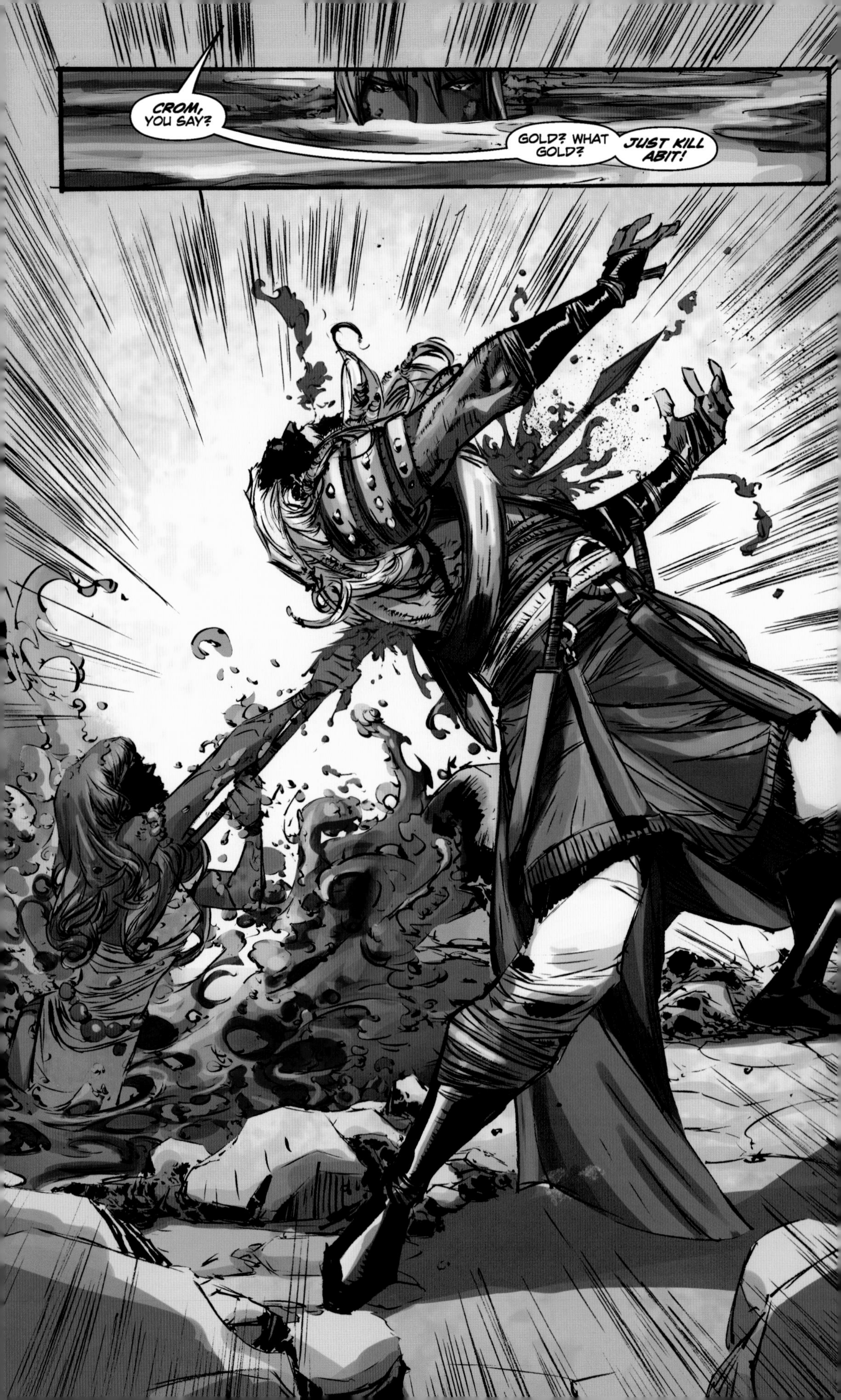
CROM, YOU SAY?
GOLD? WHAT GOLD?
JUST KILL ABIT!

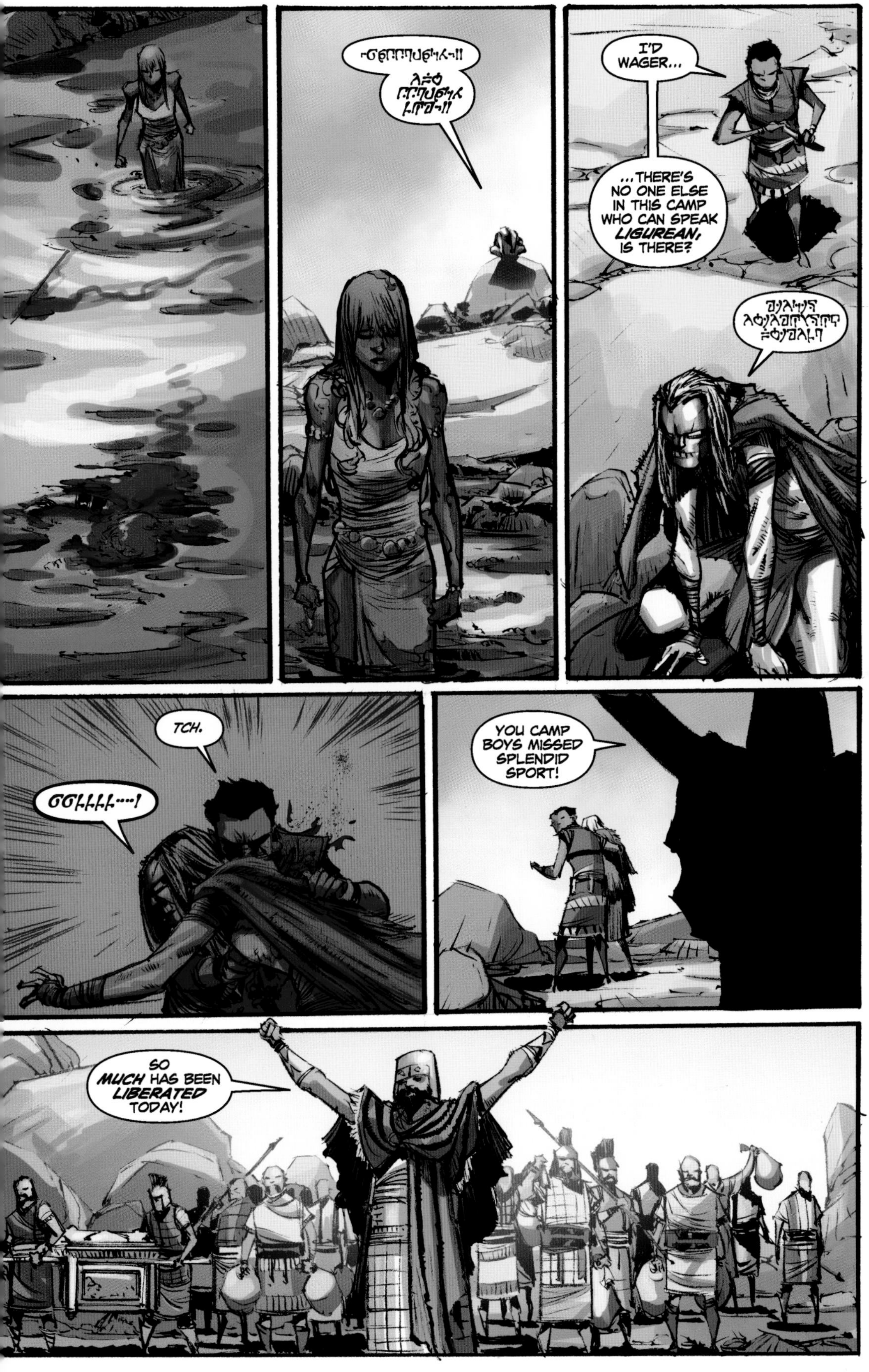
I'D WAGER...
...THERE'S NO ONE ELSE IN THIS CAMP WHO CAN SPEAK LIGUREAN, IS THERE?
TCH.
YOU CAMP BOYS MISSED SPLENDID SPORT!
SO MUCH HAS BEEN LIBERATED TODAY!

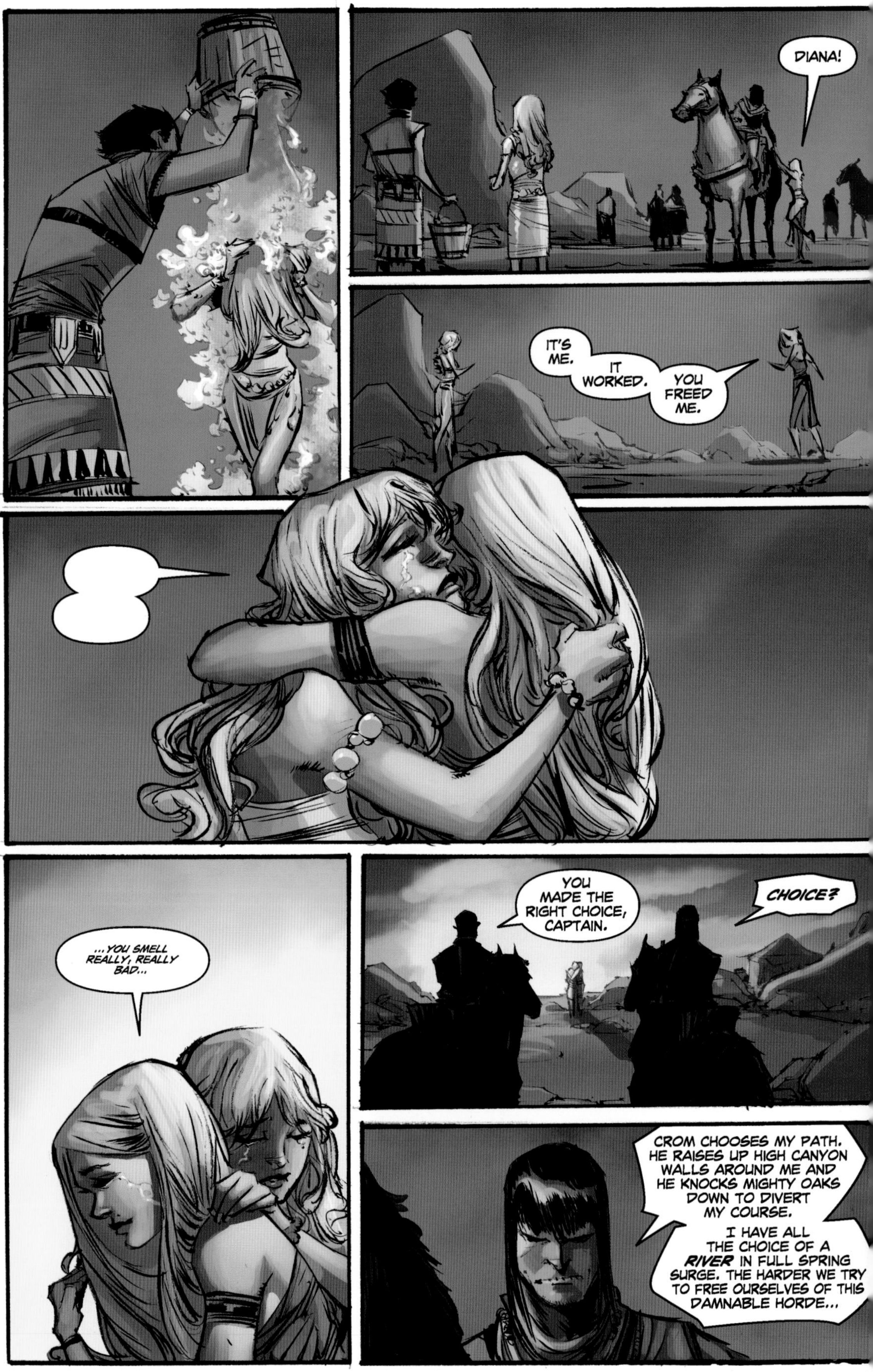
DIANA!
IT'S ME.
IT WORKED.
YOU FREED ME.
...YOU SMELL REALLY, REALLY BAD...
YOU MADE THE RIGHT CHOICE, CAPTAIN.
CHOICE?
CROM CHOOSES MY PATH. HE RAISES UP HIGH CANYON WALLS AROUND ME AND HE KNOCKS MIGHTY OAKS DOWN TO DIVERT MY COURSE.
I HAVE ALL THE CHOICE OF A *RIVER* IN FULL SPRING SURGE. THE HARDER WE TRY TO FREE OURSELVES OF THIS DAMNABLE HORDE...

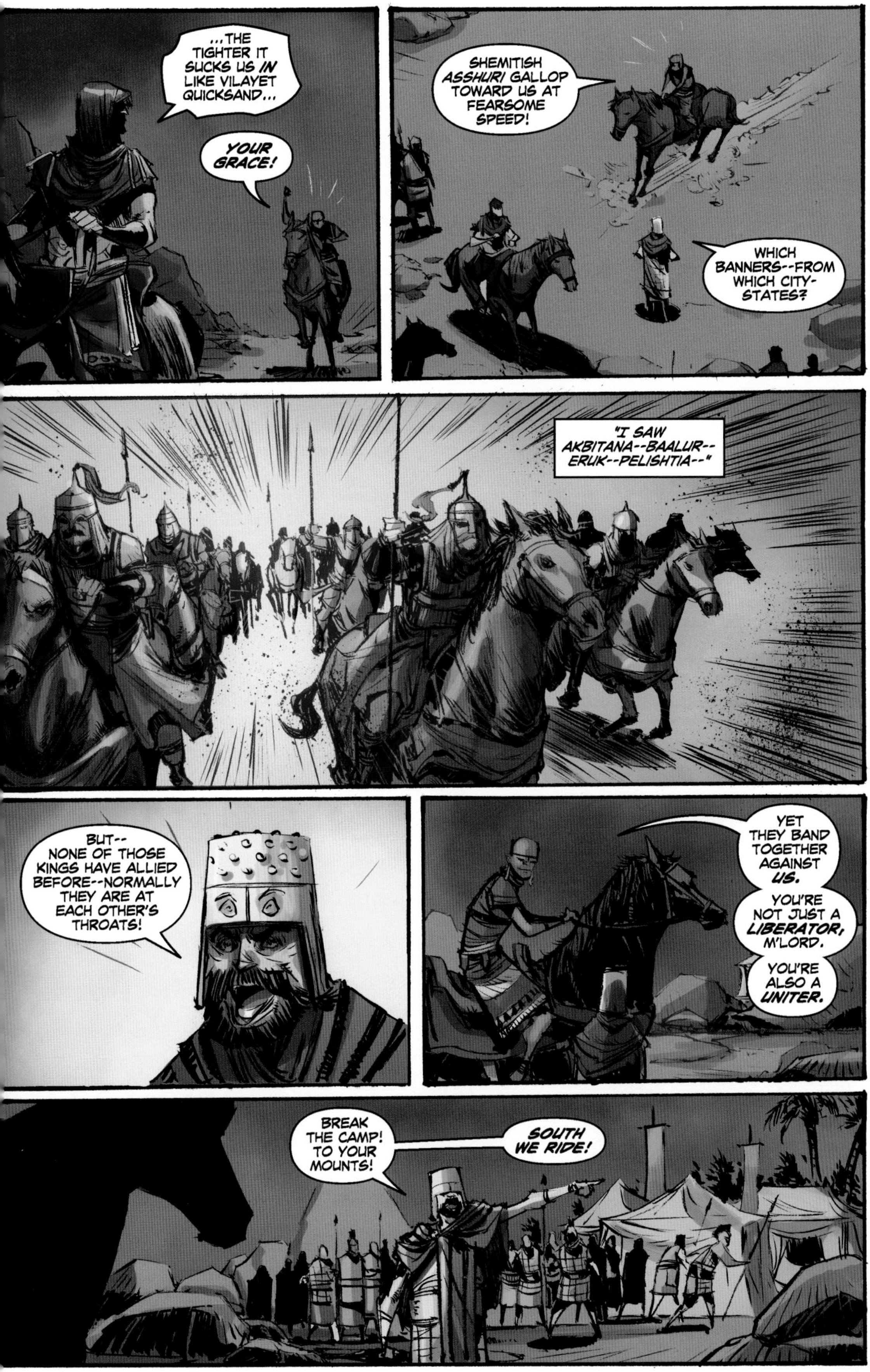

...THE TIGHTER IT SUCKS US IN LIKE VILAYET QUICKSAND...
YOUR GRACE!
SHEMITISH ASSHURI GALLOP TOWARD US AT FEARSOME SPEED!
WHICH BANNERS--FROM WHICH CITY-STATES?
"I SAW AKBITANA--BAALUR--ERUK--PELISHTIA--"
BUT--NONE OF THOSE KINGS HAVE ALLIED BEFORE--NORMALLY THEY ARE AT EACH OTHER'S THROATS!
YET THEY BAND TOGETHER AGAINST US.
YOU'RE NOT JUST A LIBERATOR, M'LORD.
YOU'RE ALSO A UNITER.
BREAK THE CAMP! TO YOUR MOUNTS!
SOUTH WE RIDE!

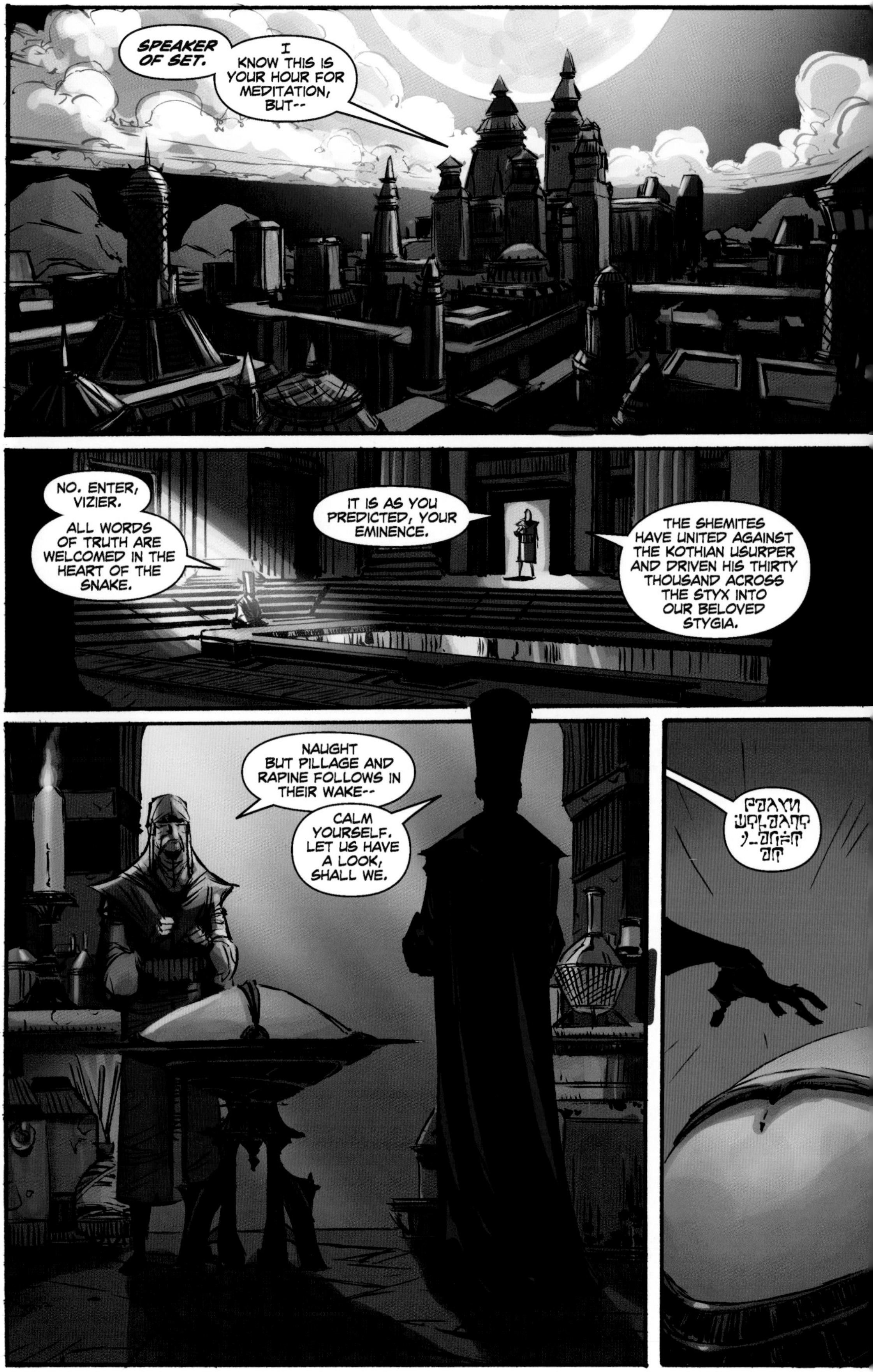
SPEAKER OF SET.
I KNOW THIS IS YOUR HOUR FOR MEDITATION, BUT--
NO. ENTER, VIZIER.
ALL WORDS OF TRUTH ARE WELCOMED IN THE HEART OF THE SNAKE.
IT IS AS YOU PREDICTED, YOUR EMINENCE.
THE SHEMITES HAVE UNITED AGAINST THE KOTHIAN USURPER AND DRIVEN HIS THIRTY THOUSAND ACROSS THE STYX INTO OUR BELOVED STYGIA.
NAUGHT BUT PILLAGE AND RAPINE FOLLOWS IN THEIR WAKE--
CALM YOURSELF. LET US HAVE A LOOK, SHALL WE.

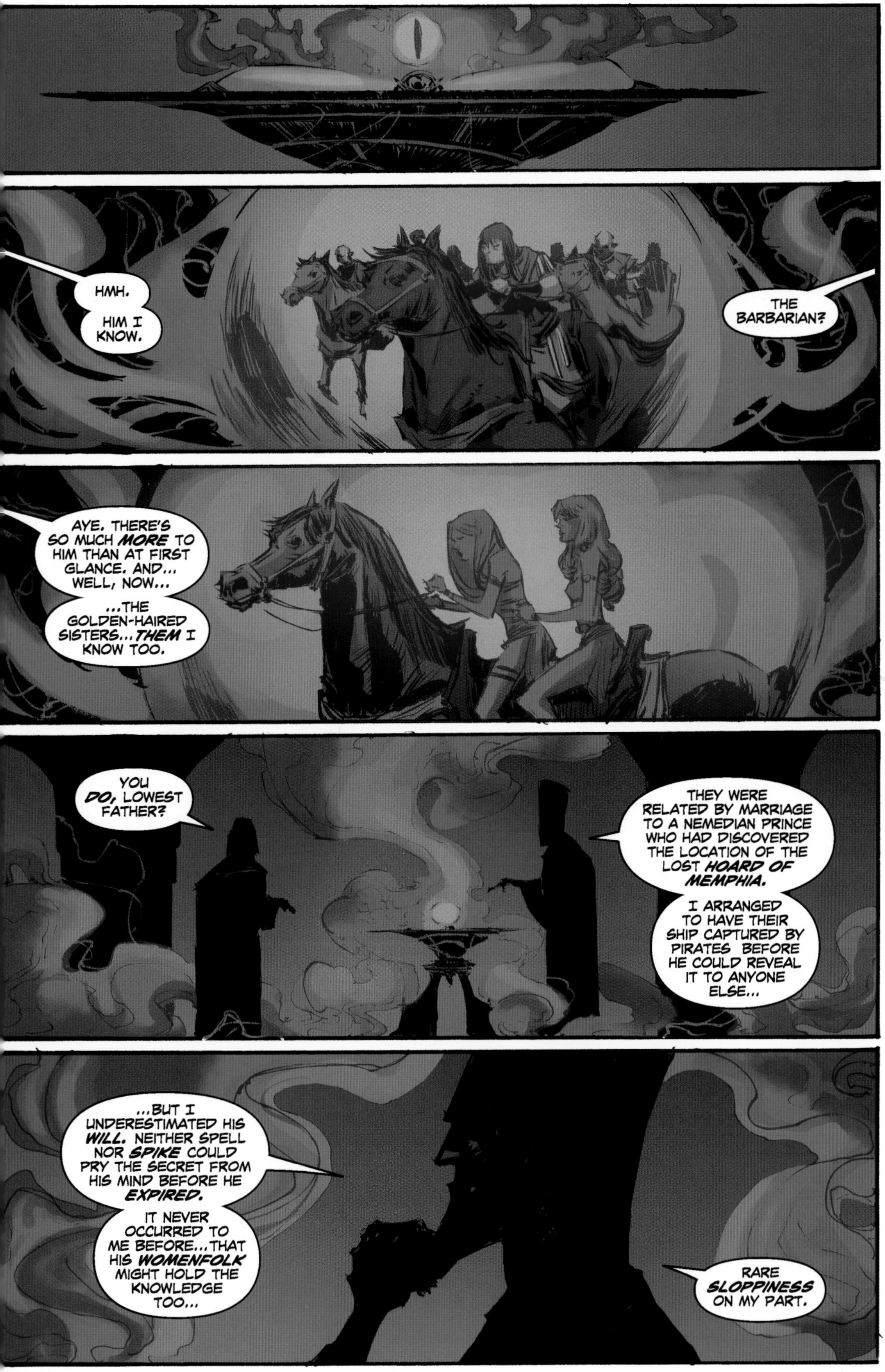
HMH.
HIM I KNOW.
THE BARBARIAN?
AYE. THERE'S SO MUCH MORE TO HIM THAN AT FIRST GLANCE. AND... WELL, NOW...
...THE GOLDEN-HAIRED SISTERS...THEM I KNOW TOO.
YOU DO, LOWEST FATHER?
THEY WERE RELATED BY MARRIAGE TO A NEMEDIAN PRINCE WHO HAD DISCOVERED THE LOCATION OF THE LOST HOARD OF MEMPHIA.
I ARRANGED TO HAVE THEIR SHIP CAPTURED BY PIRATES BEFORE HE COULD REVEAL IT TO ANYONE ELSE...
...BUT I UNDERESTIMATED HIS WILL. NEITHER SPELL NOR SPIKE COULD PRY THE SECRET FROM HIS MIND BEFORE HE EXPIRED.
IT NEVER OCCURRED TO ME BEFORE...THAT HIS WOMENFOLK MIGHT HOLD THE KNOWLEDGE TOO...
RARE SLOPPINESS ON MY PART.

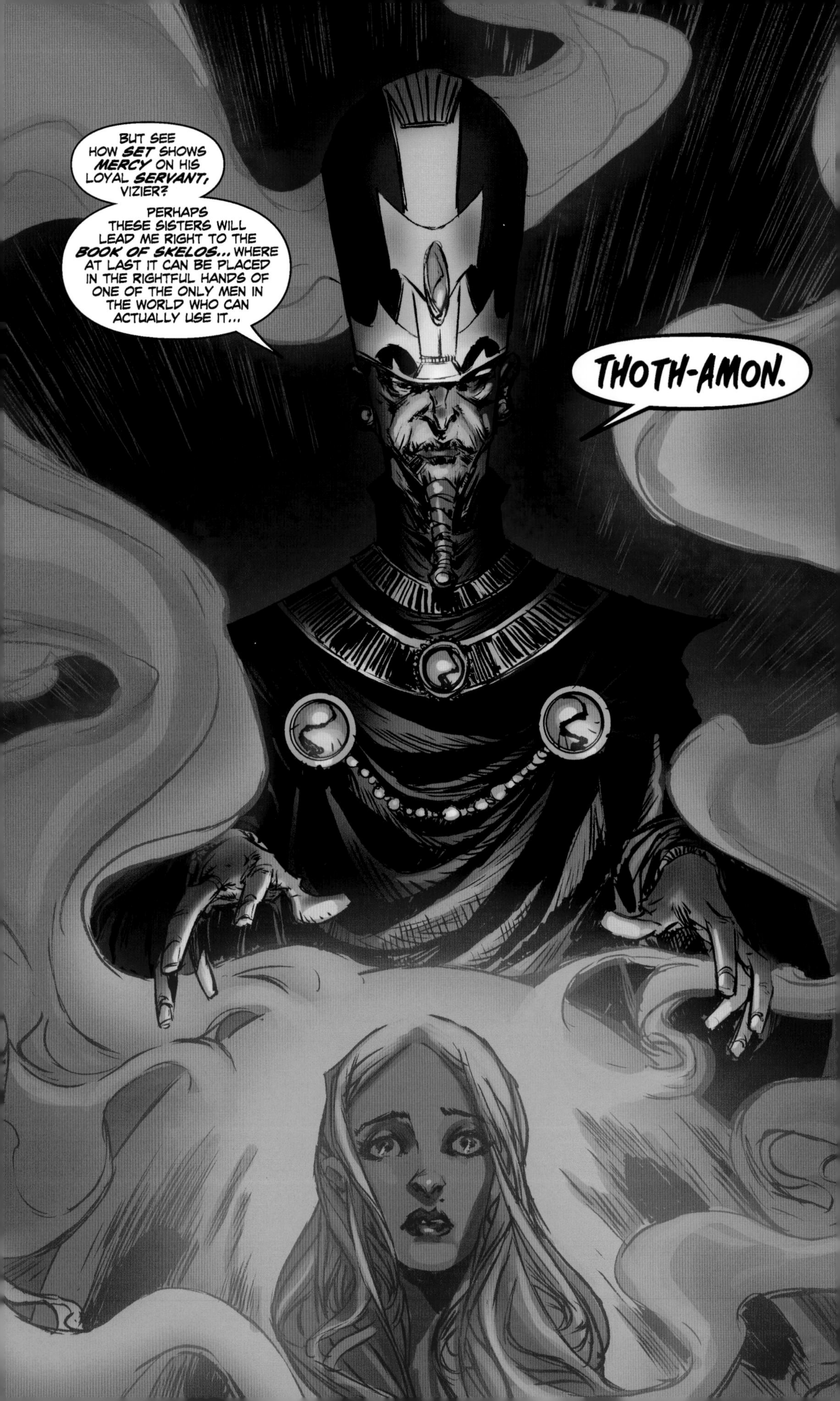

BUT SEE HOW SET SHOWS MERCY ON HIS LOYAL SERVANT, VIZIER?
PERHAPS THESE SISTERS WILL LEAD ME RIGHT TO THE BOOK OF SKELOS... WHERE AT LAST IT CAN BE PLACED IN THE RIGHTFUL HANDS OF ONE OF THE ONLY MEN IN THE WORLD WHO CAN ACTUALLY USE IT...
THOTH-AMON.

CHAPTER FOUR

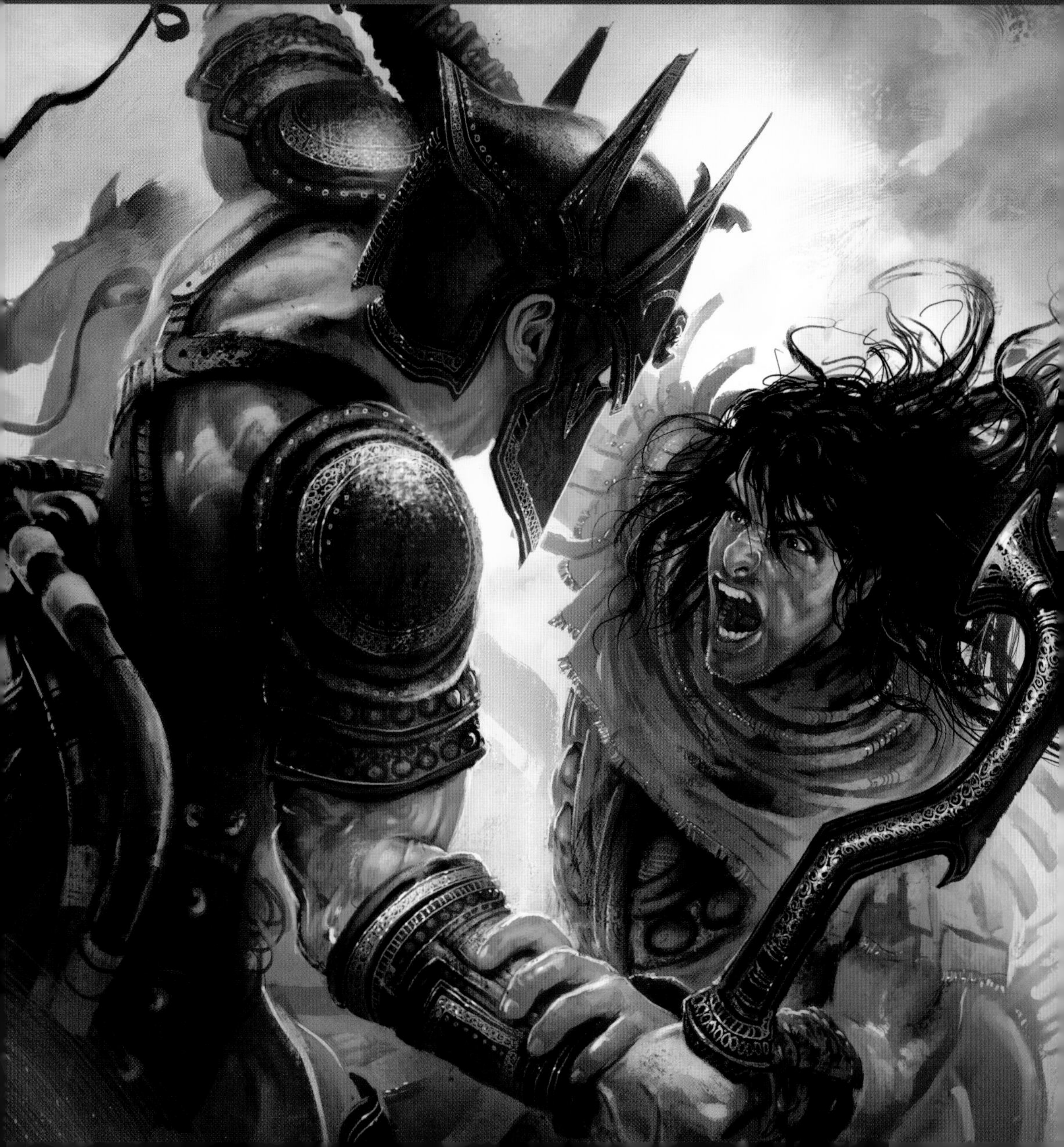

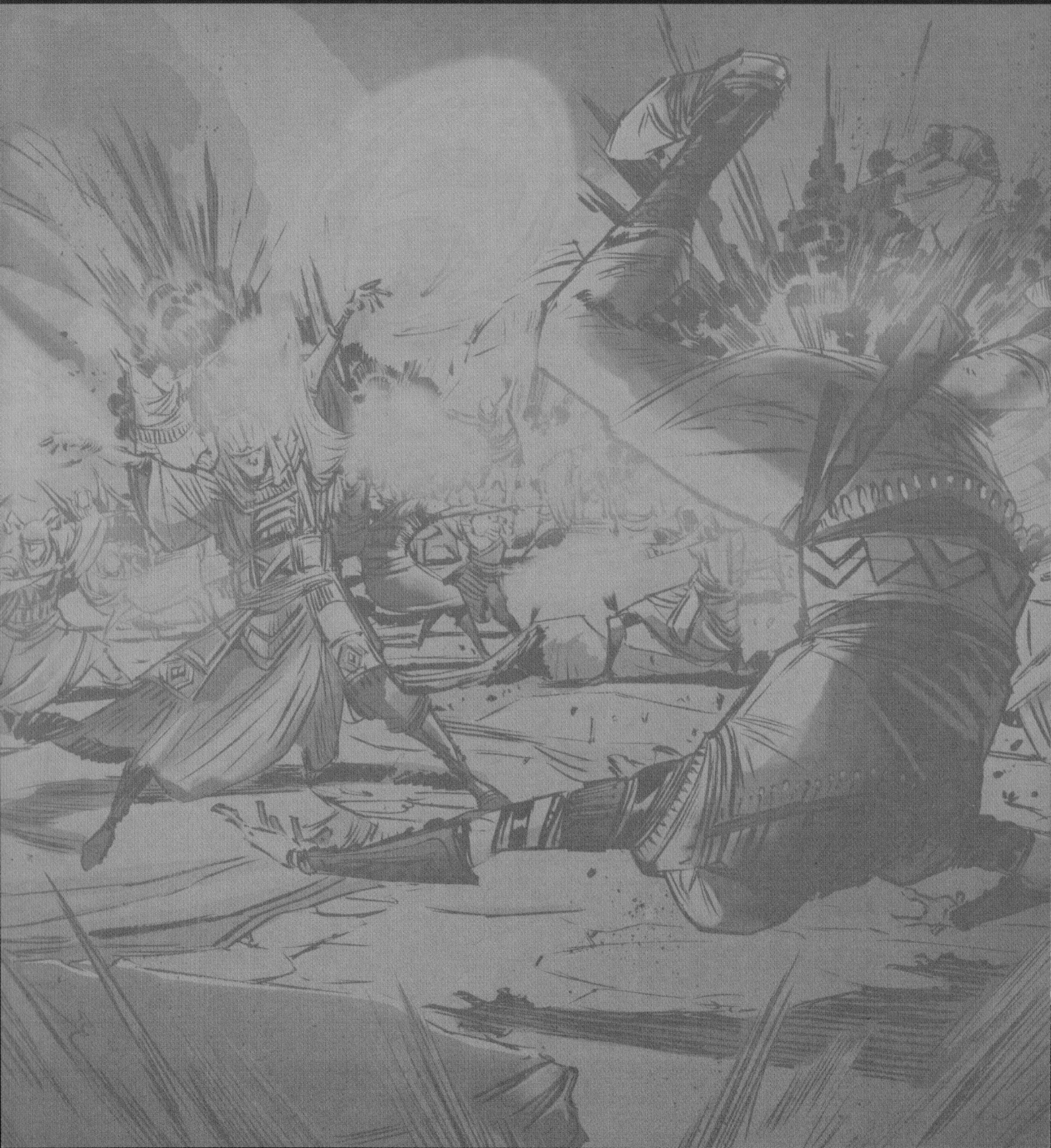

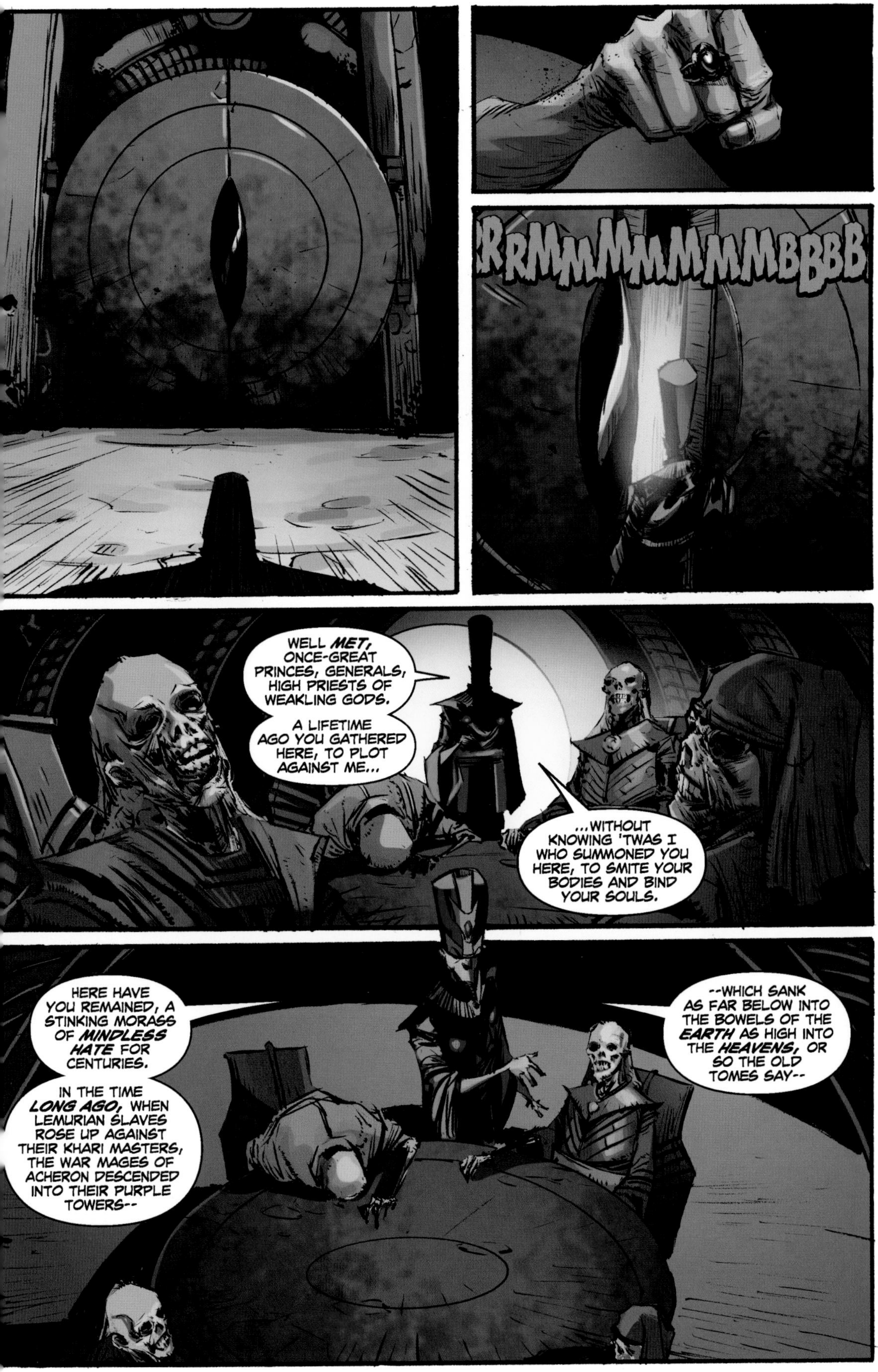
RRRMMMMMMMMMBBBB
WELL MET, ONCE-GREAT PRINCES, GENERALS, HIGH PRIESTS OF WEAKLING GODS.
A LIFETIME AGO YOU GATHERED HERE, TO PLOT AGAINST ME...
...WITHOUT KNOWING 'TWAS I WHO SUMMONED YOU HERE, TO SMITE YOUR BODIES AND BIND YOUR SOULS.
HERE HAVE YOU REMAINED, A STINKING MORASS OF MINDLESS HATE FOR CENTURIES.
IN THE TIME LONG AGO, WHEN LEMURIAN SLAVES ROSE UP AGAINST THEIR KHARI MASTERS, THE WAR MAGES OF ACHERON DESCENDED INTO THEIR PURPLE TOWERS--
--WHICH SANK AS FAR BELOW INTO THE BOWELS OF THE EARTH AS HIGH INTO THE HEAVENS, OR SO THE OLD TOMES SAY--

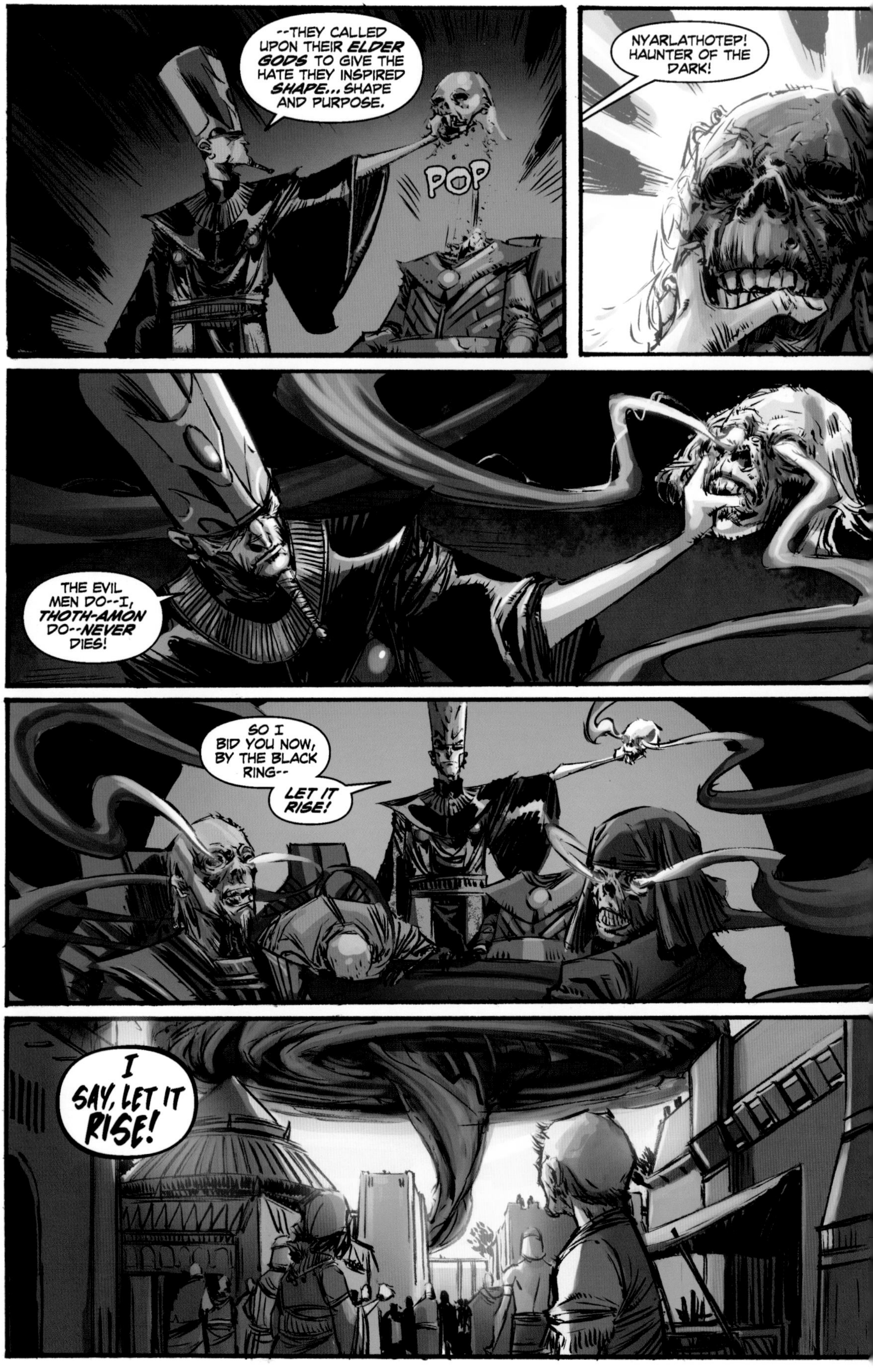
--THEY CALLED UPON THEIR ELDER GODS TO GIVE THE HATE THEY INSPIRED SHAPE... SHAPE AND PURPOSE.
POP
NYARLATHOTEP! HAUNTER OF THE DARK!
THE EVIL MEN DO--I, THOTH-AMON DO--NEVER DIES!
SO I BID YOU NOW, BY THE BLACK RING--
LET IT RISE!
I SAY, LET IT RISE!

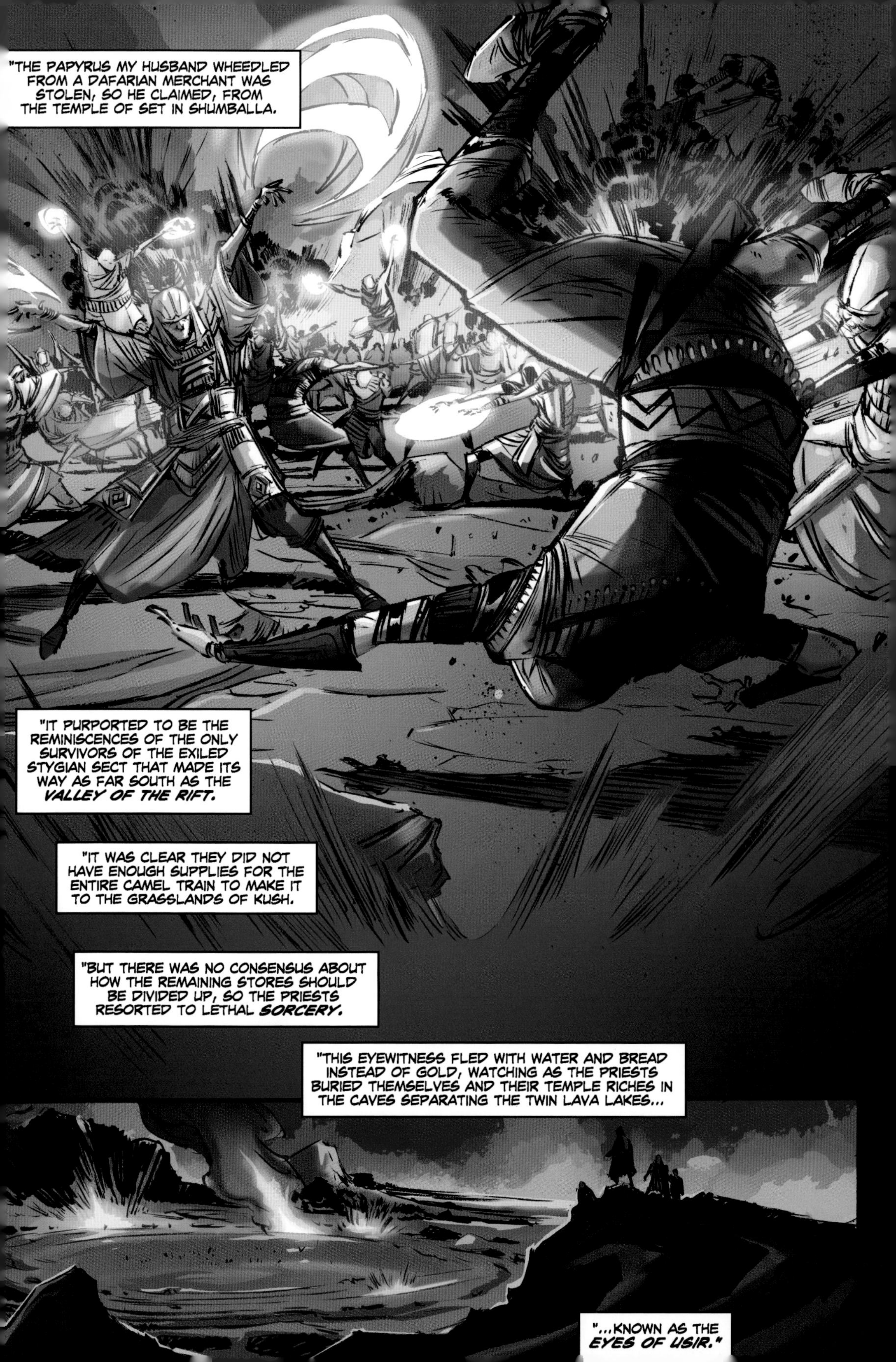
"THE PAPYRUS MY HUSBAND WHEEDLED FROM A DAFARIAN MERCHANT WAS STOLEN, SO HE CLAIMED, FROM THE TEMPLE OF SET IN SHUMBALLA.
"IT PURPORTED TO BE THE REMINISCENCES OF THE ONLY SURVIVORS OF THE EXILED STYGIAN SECT THAT MADE ITS WAY AS FAR SOUTH AS THE *VALLEY OF THE RIFT.*
"IT WAS CLEAR THEY DID NOT HAVE ENOUGH SUPPLIES FOR THE ENTIRE CAMEL TRAIN TO MAKE IT TO THE GRASSLANDS OF KUSH.
"BUT THERE WAS NO CONSENSUS ABOUT HOW THE REMAINING STORES SHOULD BE DIVIDED UP, SO THE PRIESTS RESORTED TO LETHAL *SORCERY.*
"THIS EYEWITNESS FLED WITH WATER AND BREAD INSTEAD OF GOLD, WATCHING AS THE PRIESTS BURIED THEMSELVES AND THEIR TEMPLE RICHES IN THE CAVES SEPARATING THE TWIN LAVA LAKES...
"...KNOWN AS THE *EYES OF USIR.*"

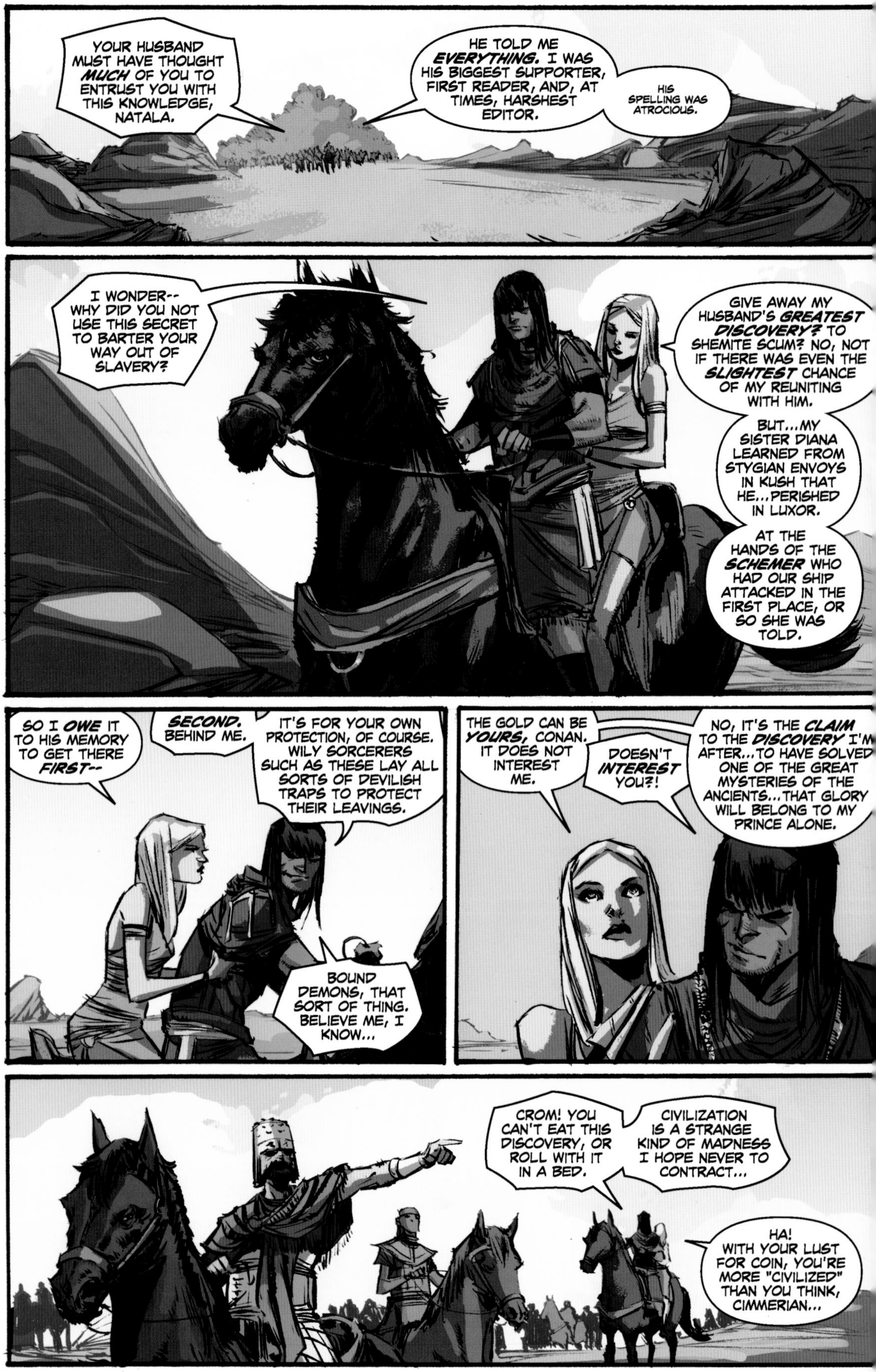
YOUR HUSBAND MUST HAVE THOUGHT MUCH OF YOU TO ENTRUST YOU WITH THIS KNOWLEDGE, NATALA.
HE TOLD ME EVERYTHING. I WAS HIS BIGGEST SUPPORTER, FIRST READER, AND, AT TIMES, HARSHEST EDITOR.
HIS SPELLING WAS ATROCIOUS.
I WONDER-- WHY DID YOU NOT USE THIS SECRET TO BARTER YOUR WAY OUT OF SLAVERY?
GIVE AWAY MY HUSBAND'S GREATEST DISCOVERY? TO SHEMITE SCUM? NO, NOT IF THERE WAS EVEN THE SLIGHTEST CHANCE OF MY REUNITING WITH HIM.
BUT...MY SISTER DIANA LEARNED FROM STYGIAN ENVOYS IN KUSH THAT HE...PERISHED IN LUXOR.
AT THE HANDS OF THE SCHEMER WHO HAD OUR SHIP ATTACKED IN THE FIRST PLACE, OR SO SHE WAS TOLD.
SO I OWE IT TO HIS MEMORY TO GET THERE FIRST--
SECOND. BEHIND ME.
IT'S FOR YOUR OWN PROTECTION, OF COURSE. WILY SORCERERS SUCH AS THESE LAY ALL SORTS OF DEVILISH TRAPS TO PROTECT THEIR LEAVINGS.
BOUND DEMONS, THAT SORT OF THING. BELIEVE ME, I KNOW...
THE GOLD CAN BE YOURS, CONAN. IT DOES NOT INTEREST ME.
DOESN'T INTEREST YOU?!
NO, IT'S THE CLAIM TO THE DISCOVERY I'M AFTER...TO HAVE SOLVED ONE OF THE GREAT MYSTERIES OF THE ANCIENTS...THAT GLORY WILL BELONG TO MY PRINCE ALONE.
CROM! YOU CAN'T EAT THIS DISCOVERY, OR ROLL WITH IT IN A BED.
CIVILIZATION IS A STRANGE KIND OF MADNESS I HOPE NEVER TO CONTRACT...
HA! WITH YOUR LUST FOR COIN, YOU'RE MORE "CIVILIZED" THAN YOU THINK, CIMMERIAN...

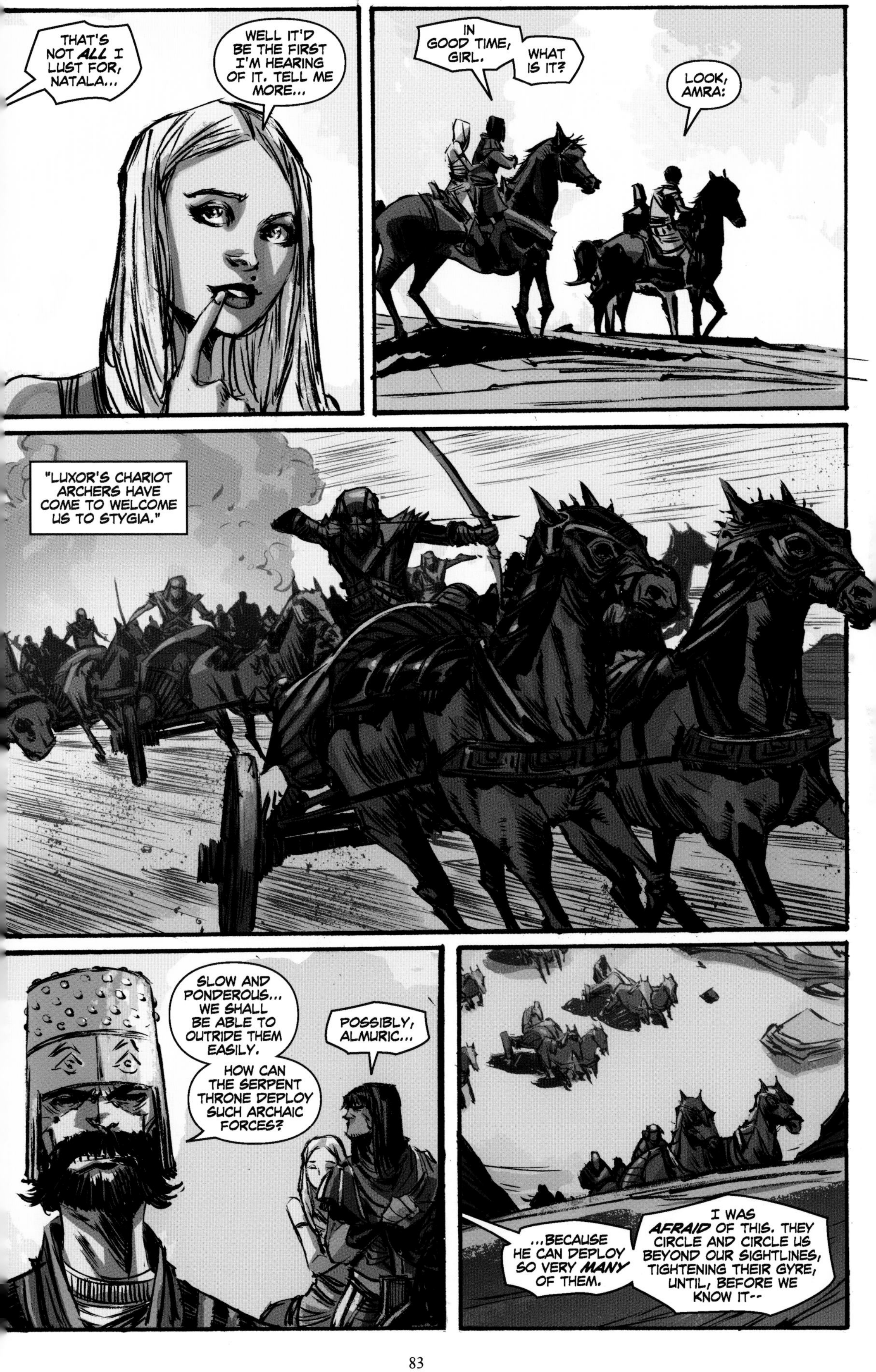

THAT'S NOT ALL I LUST FOR, NATALA...
WELL IT'D BE THE FIRST I'M HEARING OF IT. TELL ME MORE...
IN GOOD TIME, GIRL.
WHAT IS IT?
LOOK, AMRA:
"LUXOR'S CHARIOT ARCHERS HAVE COME TO WELCOME US TO STYGIA."
SLOW AND PONDEROUS... WE SHALL BE ABLE TO OUTRIDE THEM EASILY.
HOW CAN THE SERPENT THRONE DEPLOY SUCH ARCHAIC FORCES?
POSSIBLY, ALMURIC...
I WAS AFRAID OF THIS. THEY CIRCLE AND CIRCLE US BEYOND OUR SIGHTLINES, TIGHTENING THEIR GYRE, UNTIL, BEFORE WE KNOW IT--
...BECAUSE HE CAN DEPLOY SO VERY MANY OF THEM.

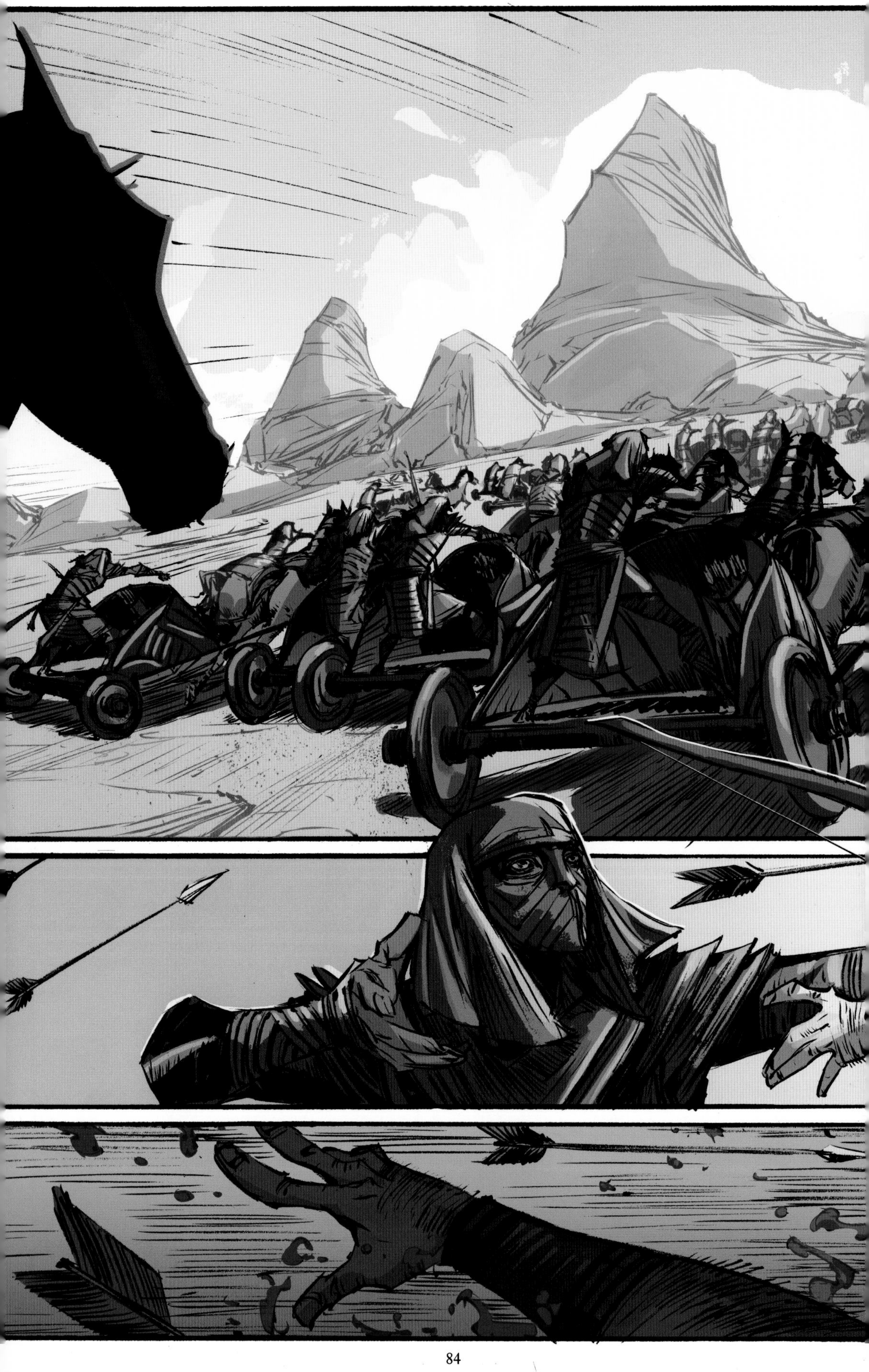

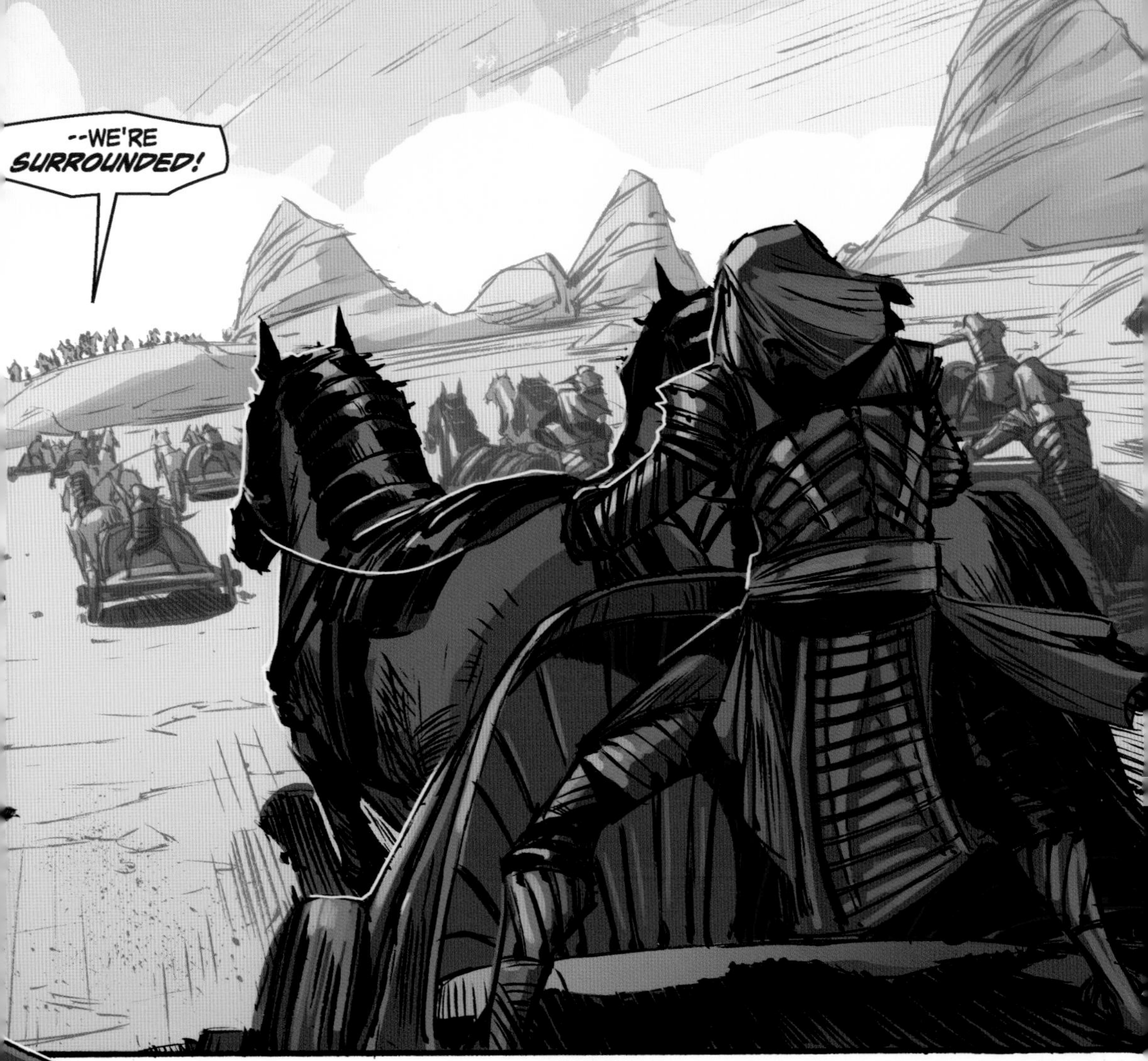
--WE'RE SURROUNDED!

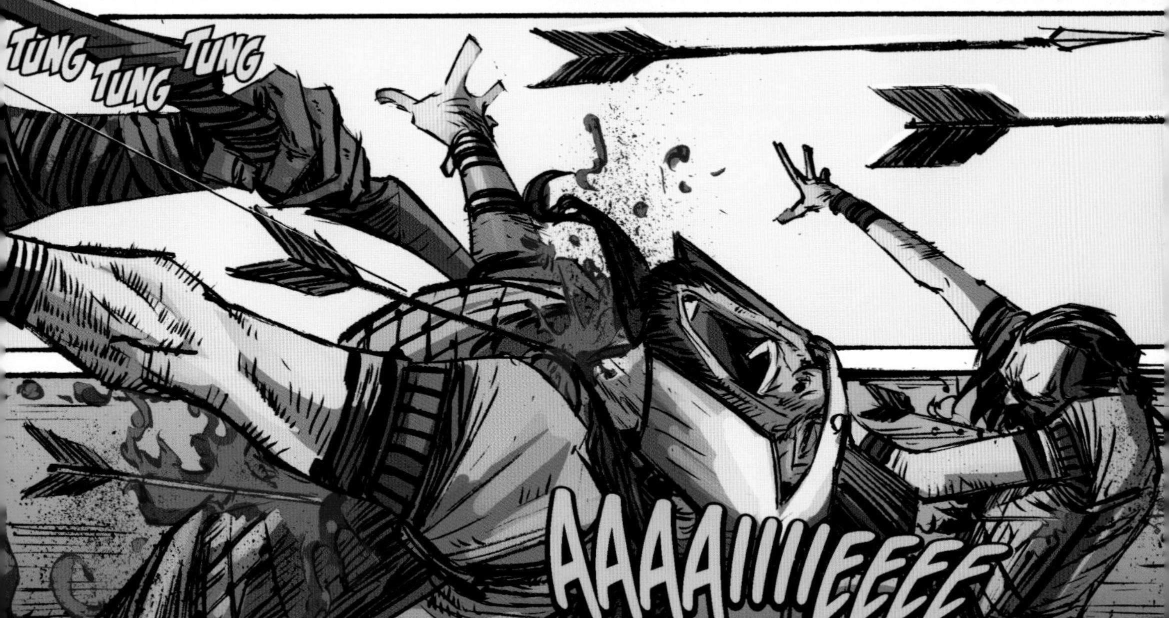
TUNG TUNG TUNG
AAAAIIIIEEEE

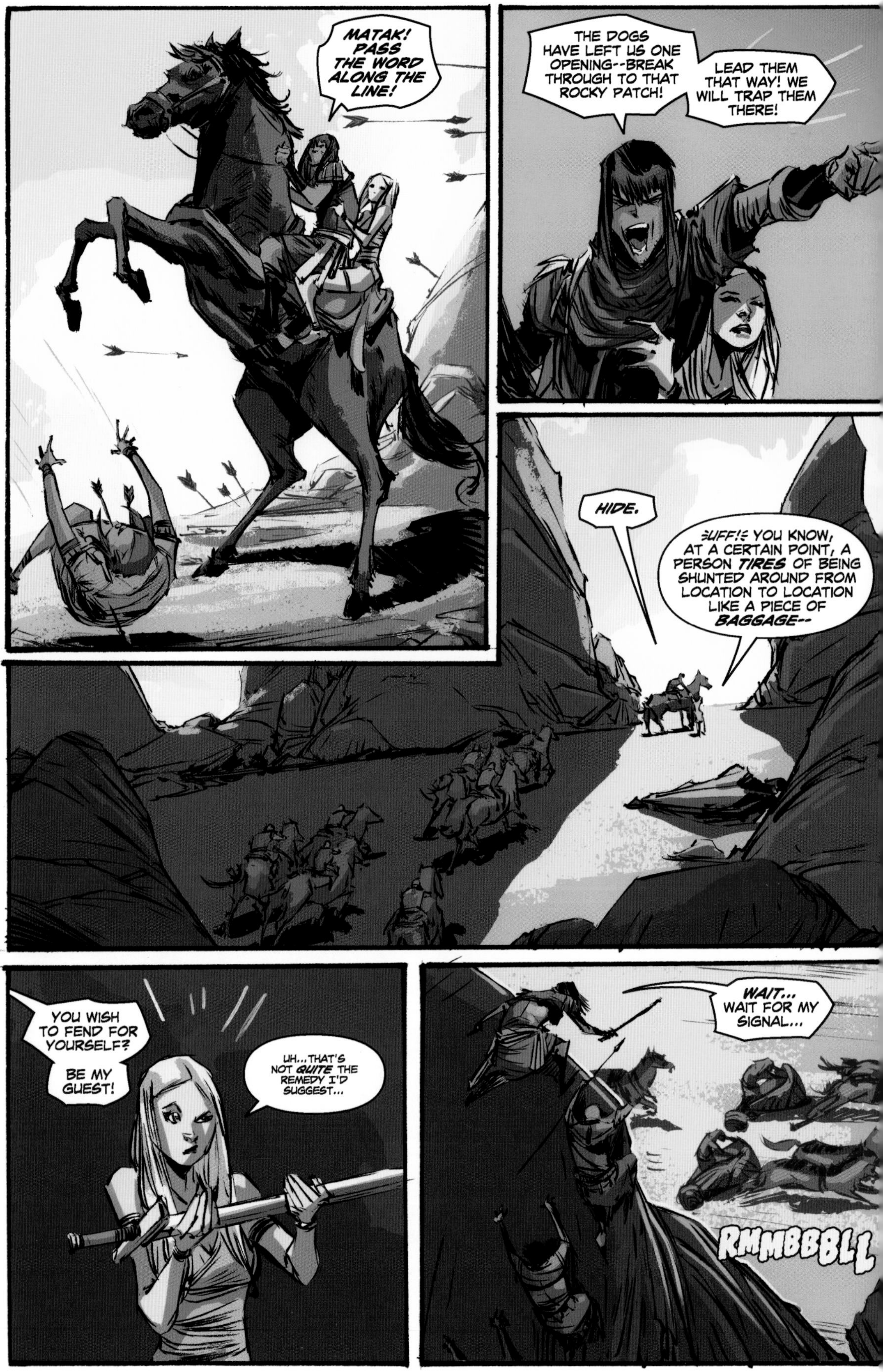
MATAK! PASS THE WORD ALONG THE LINE!
THE DOGS HAVE LEFT US ONE OPENING--BREAK THROUGH TO THAT ROCKY PATCH!
LEAD THEM THAT WAY! WE WILL TRAP THEM THERE!
HIDE.
SUFF!S YOU KNOW, AT A CERTAIN POINT, A PERSON TIRES OF BEING SHUNTED AROUND FROM LOCATION TO LOCATION LIKE A PIECE OF BAGGAGE--
YOU WISH TO FEND FOR YOURSELF?
BE MY GUEST!
UH...THAT'S NOT QUITE THE REMEDY I'D SUGGEST...
WAIT... WAIT FOR MY SIGNAL...
RMMBBBLL

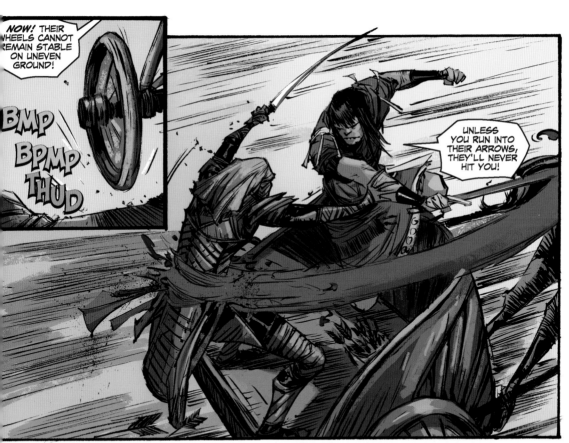

NOW! THEIR WHEELS CANNOT REMAIN STABLE ON UNEVEN GROUND!

BMP
BPMP
THUD

UNLESS YOU RUN INTO THEIR ARROWS, THEY'LL NEVER HIT YOU!

SSSKKKRRRSSSSHH

GGGYYAAHHH!

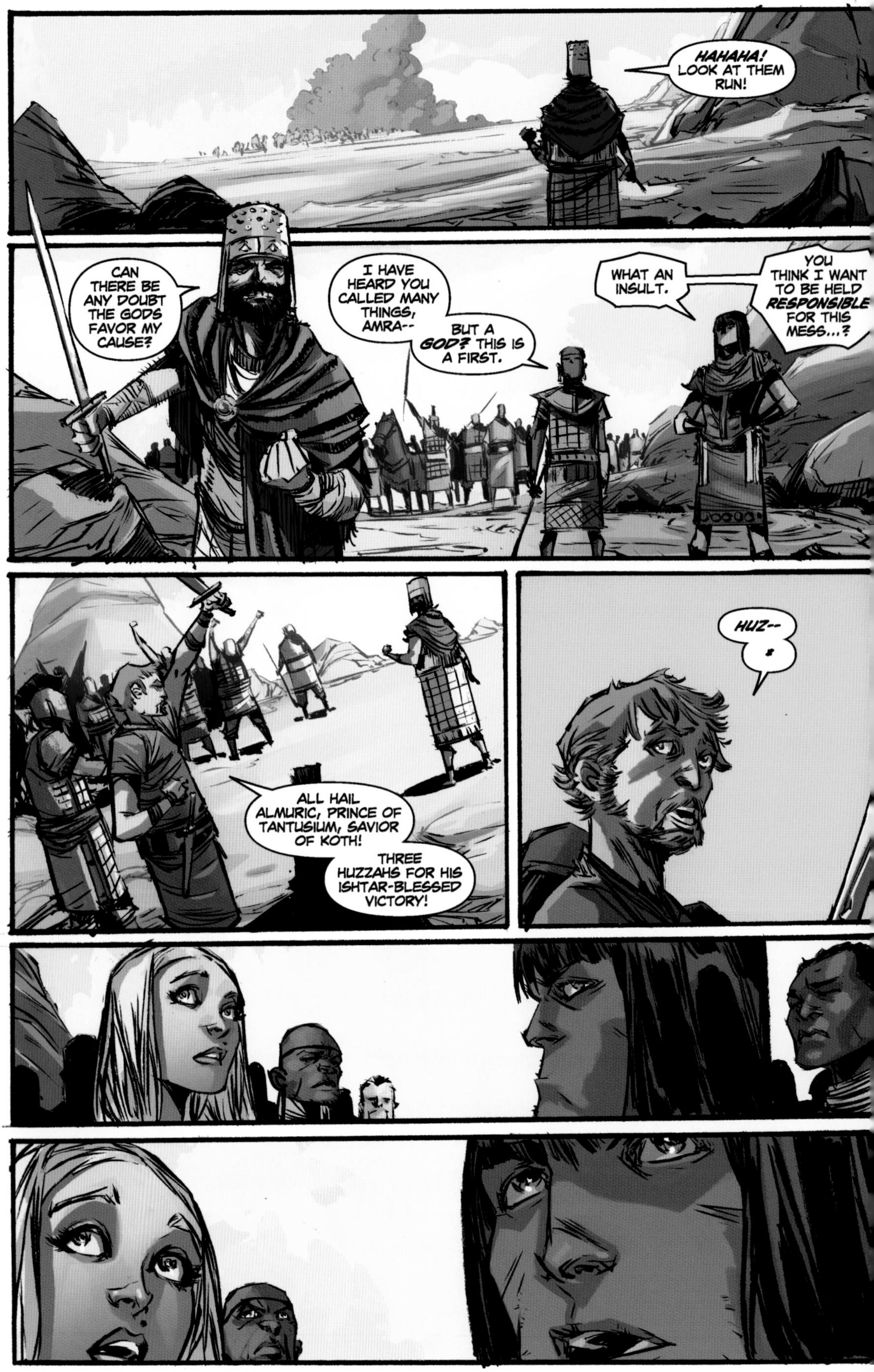

HAHAHA! LOOK AT THEM RUN!
CAN THERE BE ANY DOUBT THE GODS FAVOR MY CAUSE?
I HAVE HEARD YOU CALLED MANY THINGS, AMRA--
BUT A GOD? THIS IS A FIRST.
WHAT AN INSULT.
YOU THINK I WANT TO BE HELD RESPONSIBLE FOR THIS MESS...?
ALL HAIL ALMURIC, PRINCE OF TANTUSIUM, SAVIOR OF KOTH!
THREE HUZZAHS FOR HIS ISHTAR-BLESSED VICTORY!
HUZ--

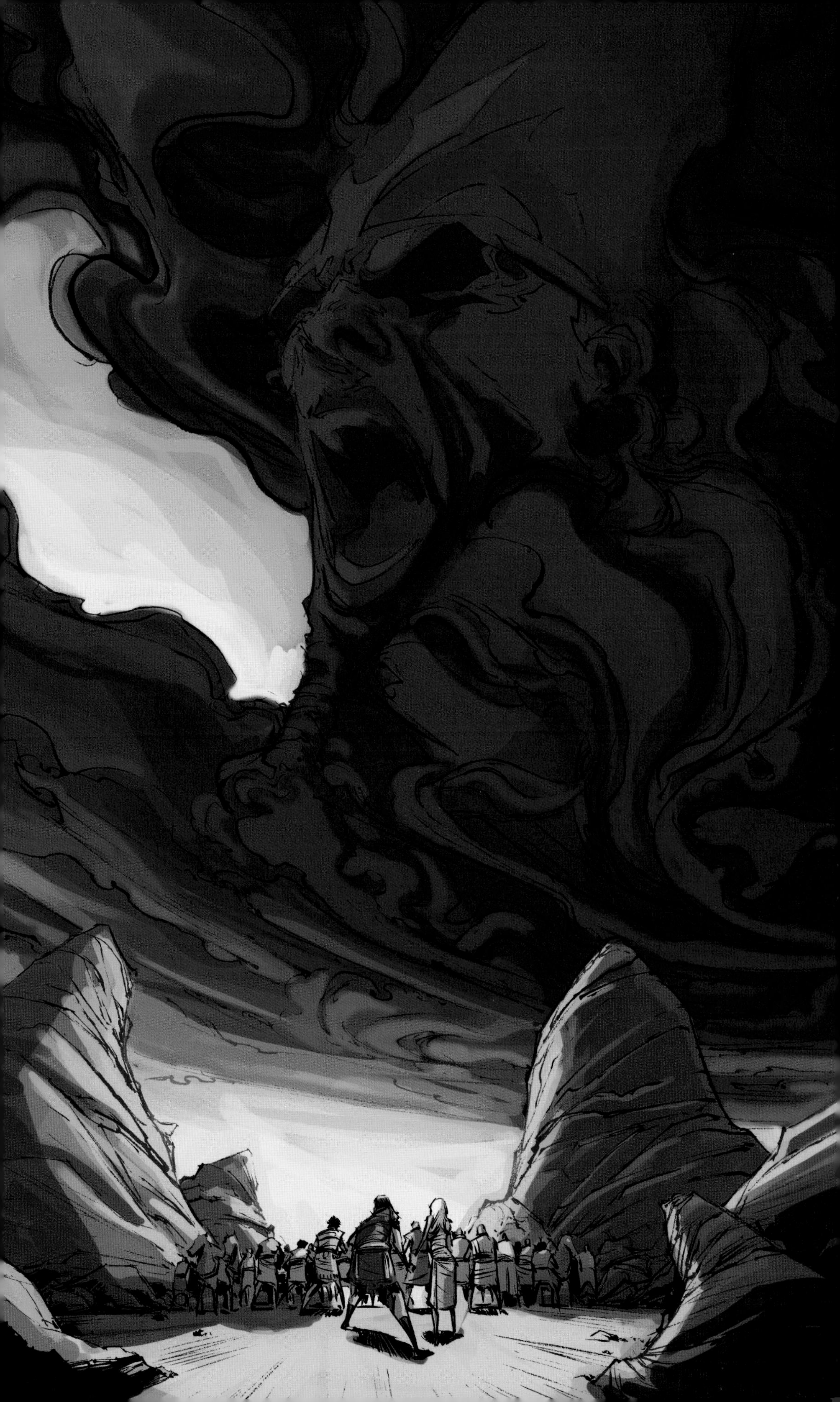

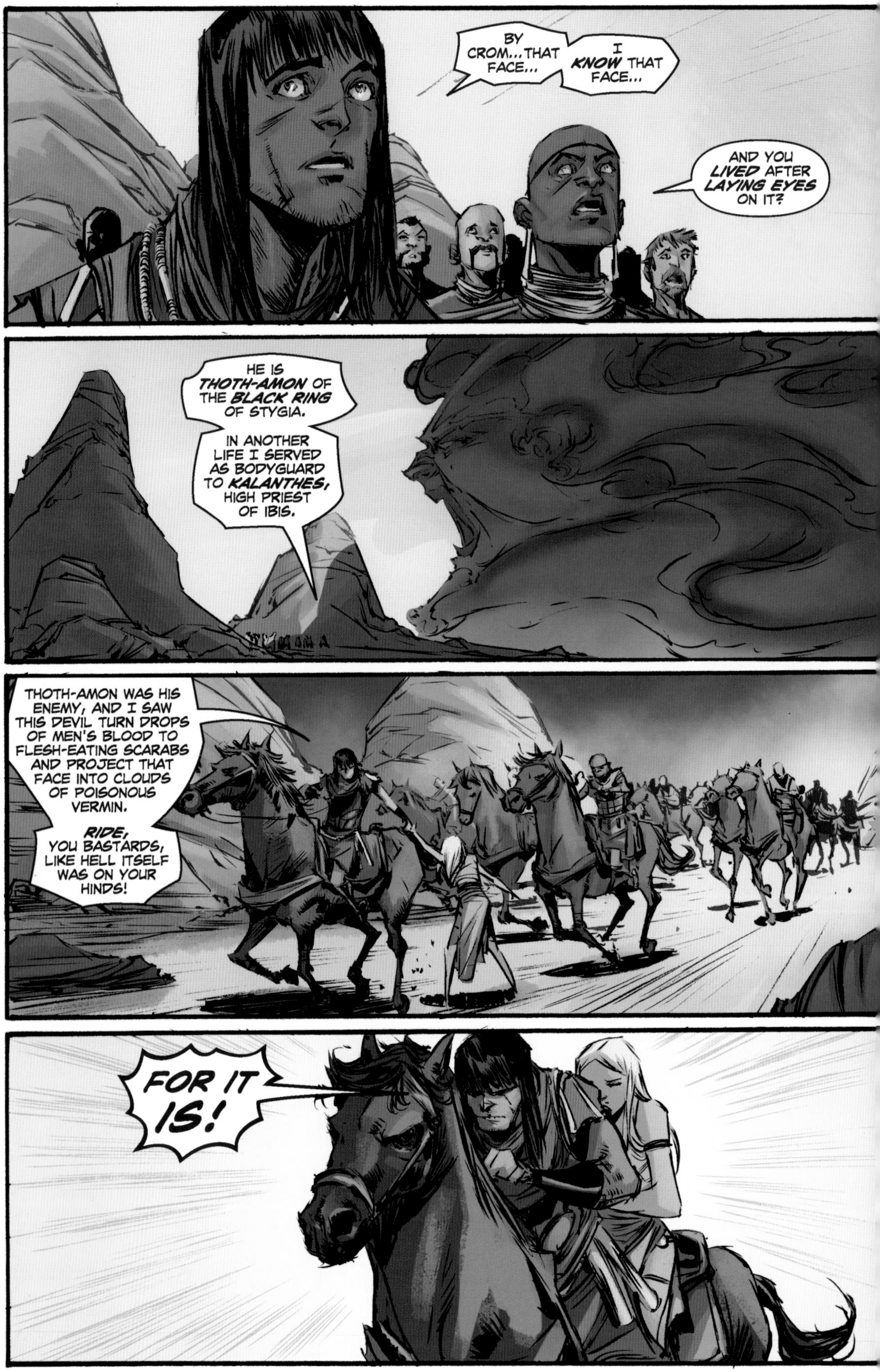

BY CROM... THAT FACE...
I KNOW THAT FACE...
AND YOU LIVED AFTER LAYING EYES ON IT?
HE IS THOTH-AMON OF THE BLACK RING OF STYGIA.
IN ANOTHER LIFE I SERVED AS BODYGUARD TO KALANTHES, HIGH PRIEST OF IBIS.
THOTH-AMON WAS HIS ENEMY, AND I SAW THIS DEVIL TURN DROPS OF MEN'S BLOOD TO FLESH-EATING SCARABS AND PROJECT THAT FACE INTO CLOUDS OF POISONOUS VERMIN.
RIDE, YOU BASTARDS, LIKE HELL ITSELF WAS ON YOUR HINDS!
FOR IT IS!

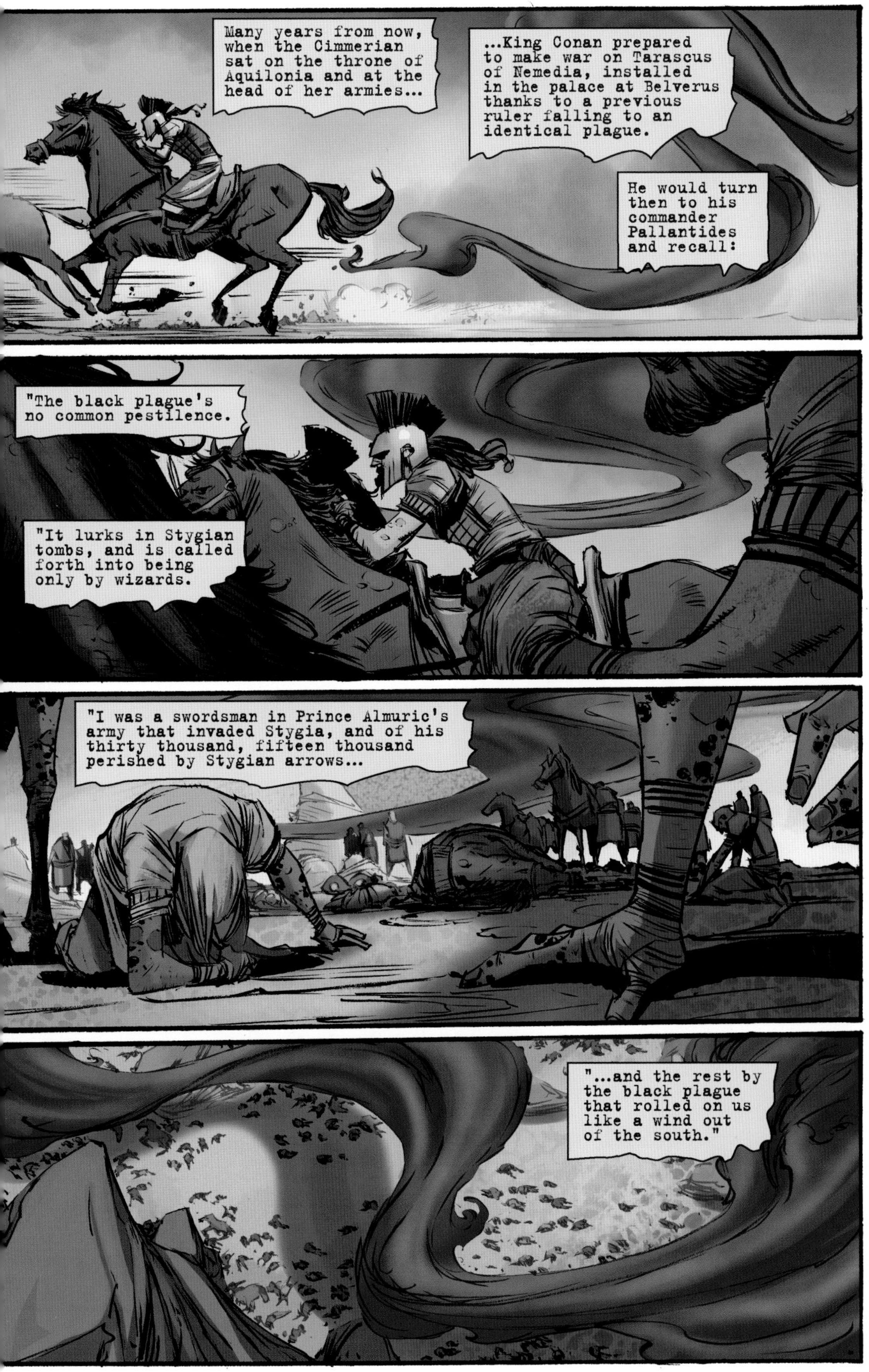
Many years from now, when the Cimmerian sat on the throne of Aquilonia and at the head of her armies...
...King Conan prepared to make war on Tarascus of Nemedia, installed in the palace at Belverus thanks to a previous ruler falling to an identical plague.
He would turn then to his commander Pallantides and recall:
"The black plague's no common pestilence.
"It lurks in Stygian tombs, and is called forth into being only by wizards.
"I was a swordsman in Prince Almuric's army that invaded Stygia, and of his thirty thousand, fifteen thousand perished by Stygian arrows...
"...and the rest by the black plague that rolled on us like a wind out of the south."

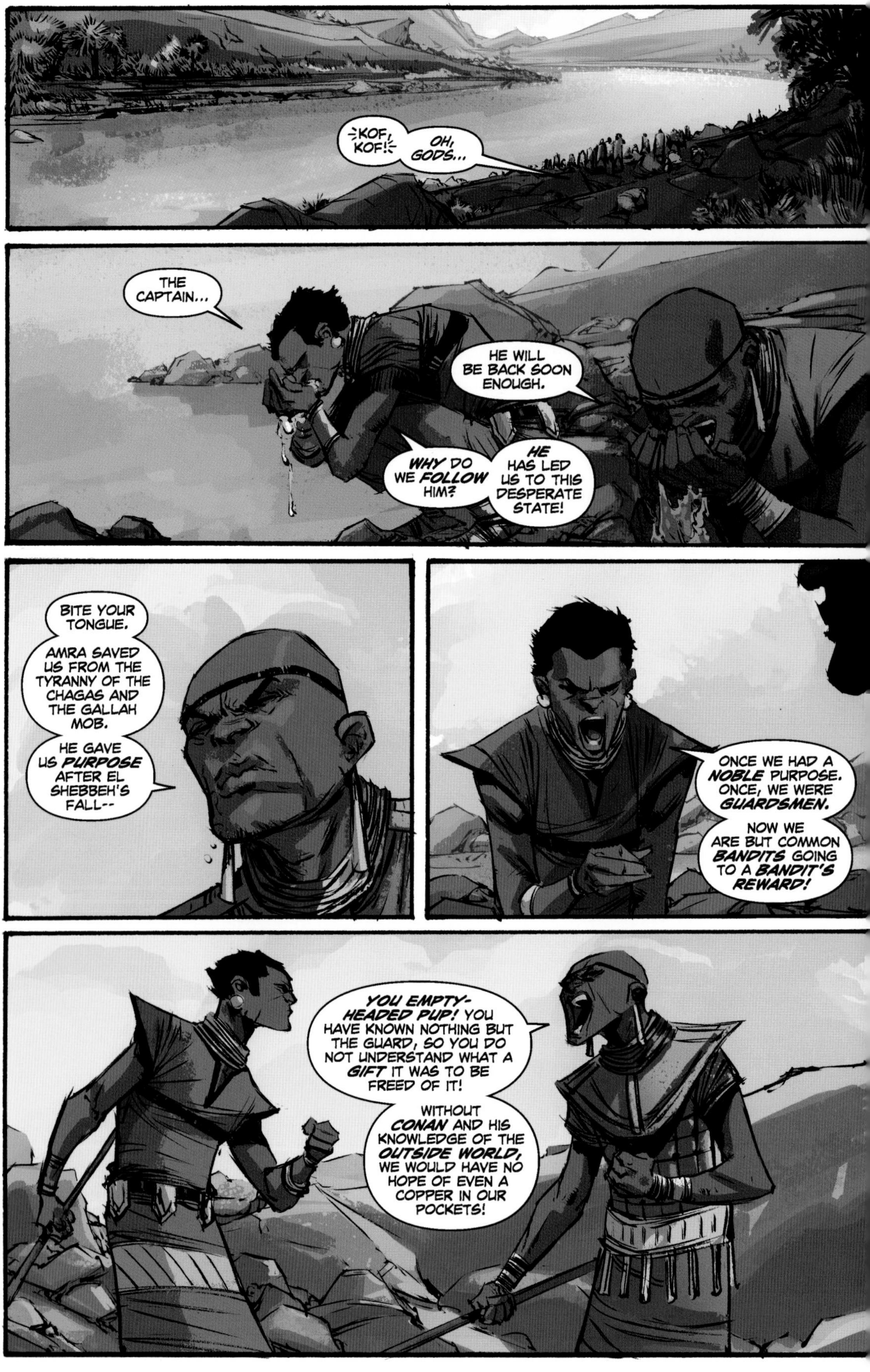

KOF, KOF!
OH, GODS...
THE CAPTAIN...
HE WILL BE BACK SOON ENOUGH.
WHY DO WE FOLLOW HIM?
HE HAS LED US TO THIS DESPERATE STATE!
BITE YOUR TONGUE.
AMRA SAVED US FROM THE TYRANNY OF THE CHAGAS AND THE GALLAH MOB.
HE GAVE US PURPOSE AFTER EL SHEBBEH'S FALL--
ONCE WE HAD A NOBLE PURPOSE. ONCE, WE WERE GUARDSMEN.
NOW WE ARE BUT COMMON BANDITS GOING TO A BANDIT'S REWARD!
YOU EMPTY-HEADED PUP! YOU HAVE KNOWN NOTHING BUT THE GUARD, SO YOU DO NOT UNDERSTAND WHAT A GIFT IT WAS TO BE FREED OF IT!
WITHOUT CONAN AND HIS KNOWLEDGE OF THE OUTSIDE WORLD, WE WOULD HAVE NO HOPE OF EVEN A COPPER IN OUR POCKETS!

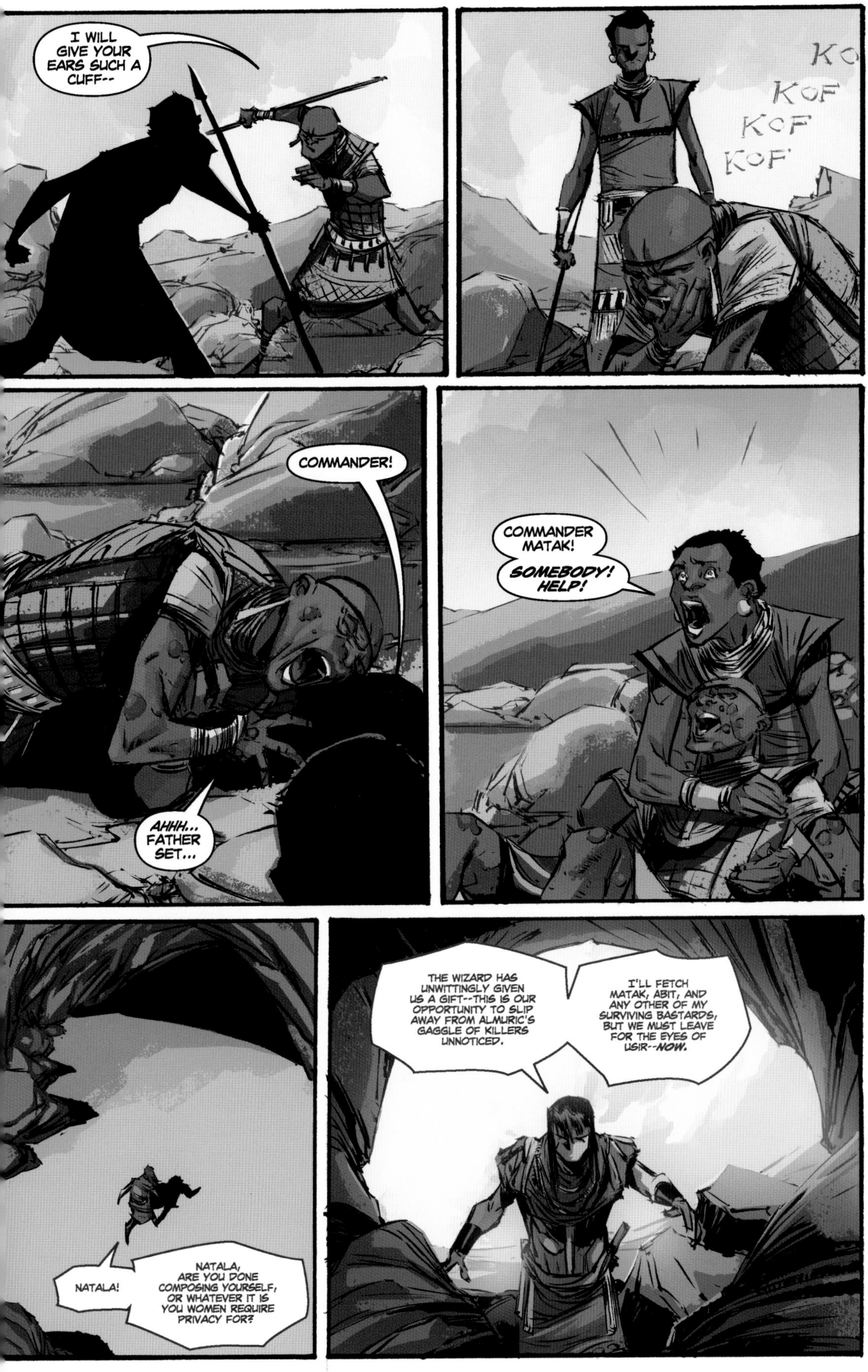
I WILL GIVE YOUR EARS SUCH A CUFF--
KOF KOF KOF KOF
COMMANDER!
AHHH... FATHER SET...
COMMANDER MATAK!
SOMEBODY! HELP!
NATALA!
NATALA, ARE YOU DONE COMPOSING YOURSELF, OR WHATEVER IT IS YOU WOMEN REQUIRE PRIVACY FOR?
THE WIZARD HAS UNWITTINGLY GIVEN US A GIFT--THIS IS OUR OPPORTUNITY TO SLIP AWAY FROM ALMURIC'S GAGGLE OF KILLERS UNNOTICED.
I'LL FETCH MATAK, ABIT, AND ANY OTHER OF MY SURVIVING BASTARDS, BUT WE MUST LEAVE FOR THE EYES OF USIR--NOW.

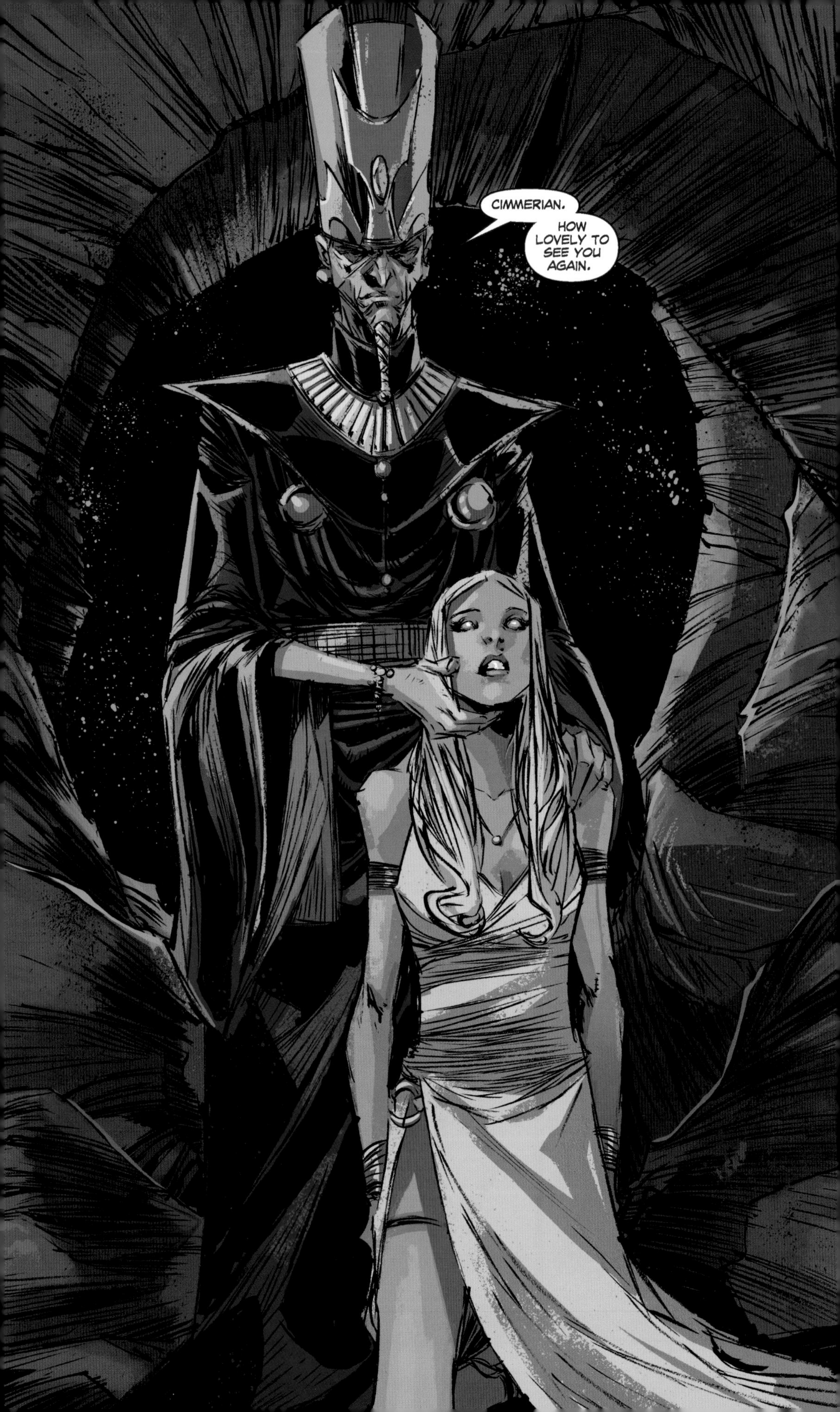
CIMMERIAN.
HOW LOVELY TO SEE YOU AGAIN.

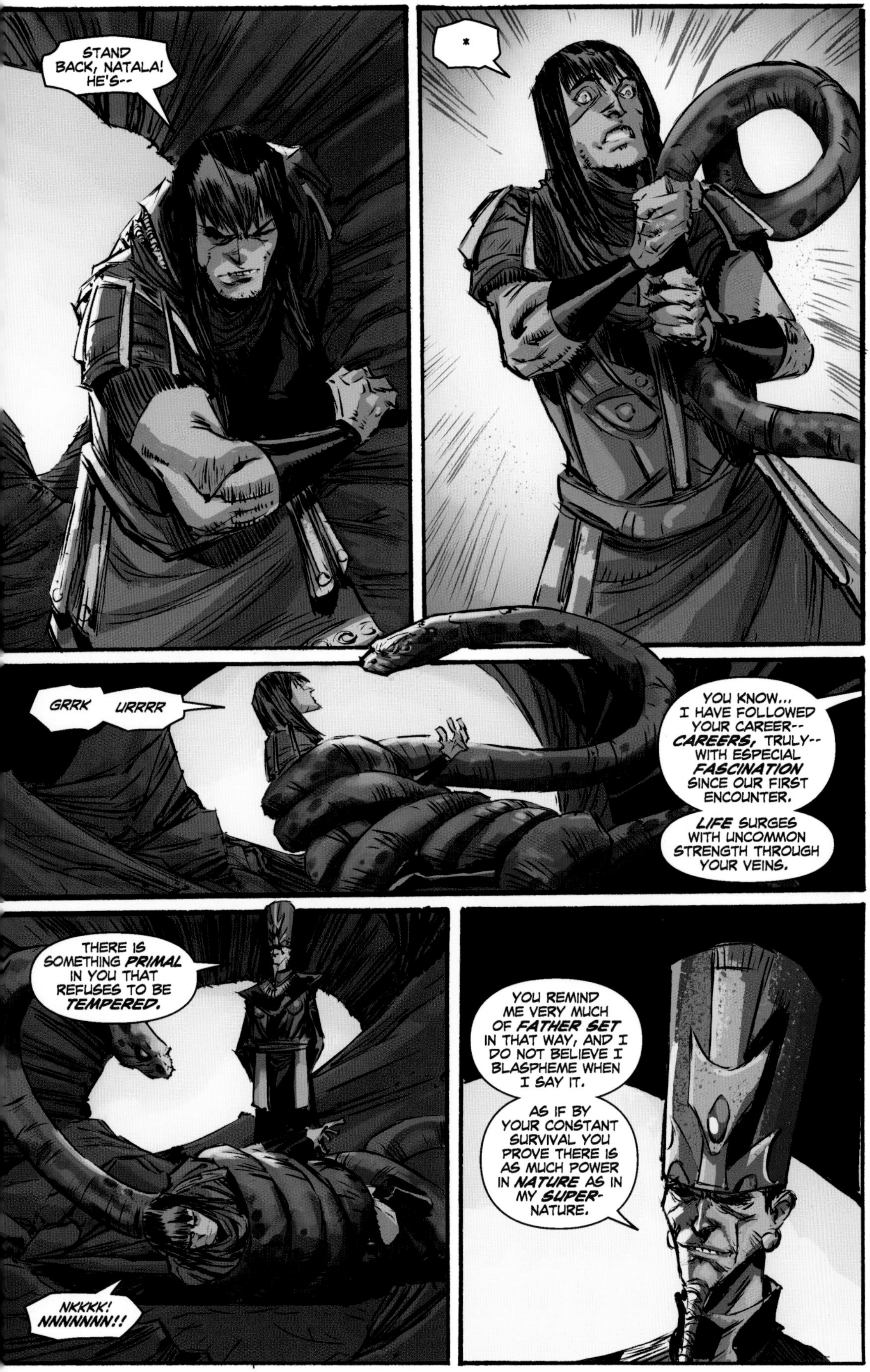
STAND BACK, NATALA! HE'S--
*
GRRK URRRR
YOU KNOW... I HAVE FOLLOWED YOUR CAREER-- CAREERS, TRULY-- WITH ESPECIAL FASCINATION SINCE OUR FIRST ENCOUNTER.
LIFE SURGES WITH UNCOMMON STRENGTH THROUGH YOUR VEINS.
THERE IS SOMETHING PRIMAL IN YOU THAT REFUSES TO BE TEMPERED.
NKKKK! NNNNNNN!!
YOU REMIND ME VERY MUCH OF FATHER SET IN THAT WAY, AND I DO NOT BELIEVE I BLASPHEME WHEN I SAY IT.
AS IF BY YOUR CONSTANT SURVIVAL YOU PROVE THERE IS AS MUCH POWER IN NATURE AS IN MY SUPER-NATURE.

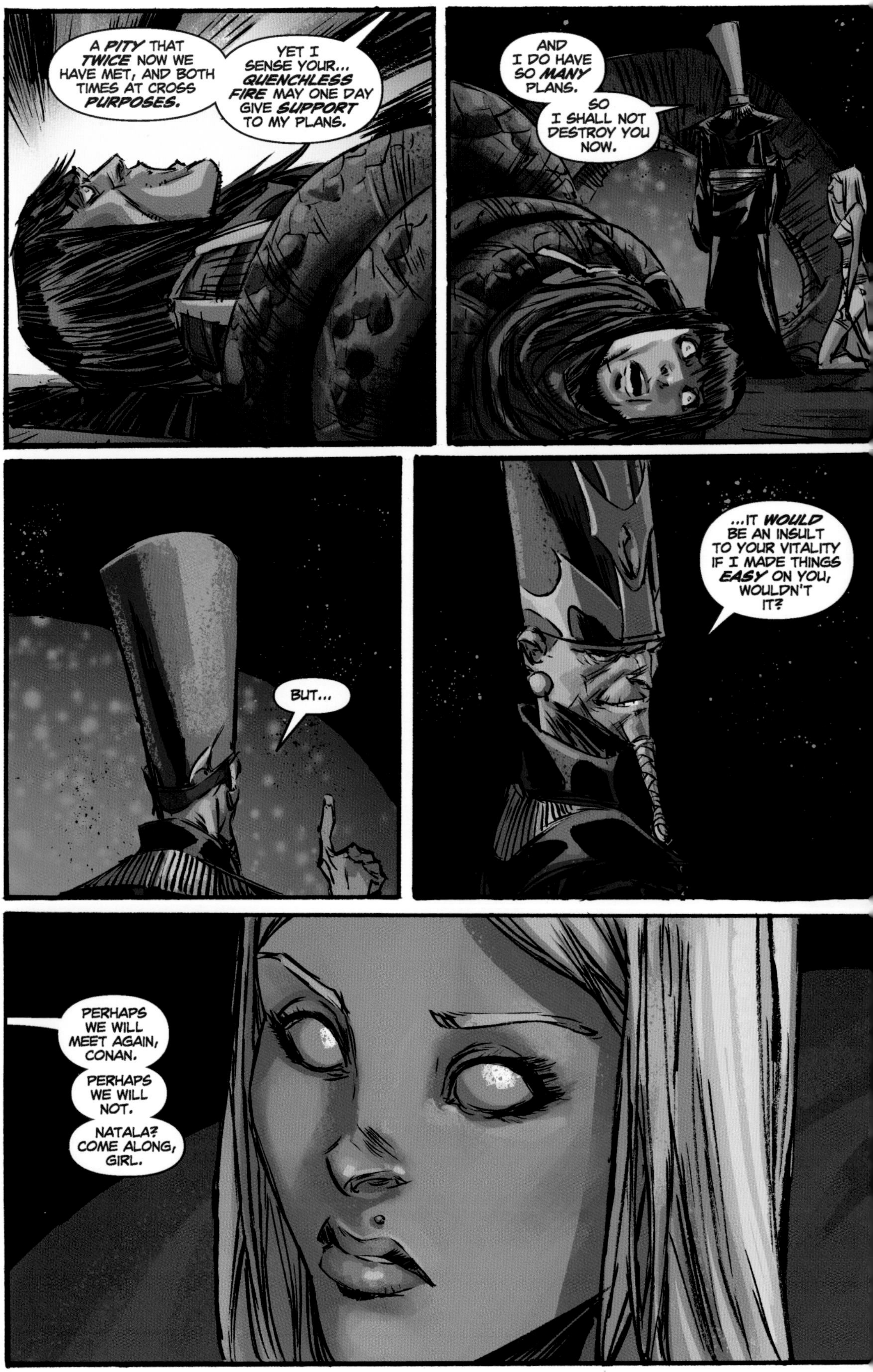
A PITY THAT TWICE NOW WE HAVE MET, AND BOTH TIMES AT CROSS PURPOSES.
YET I SENSE YOUR... QUENCHLESS FIRE MAY ONE DAY GIVE SUPPORT TO MY PLANS.
AND I DO HAVE SO MANY PLANS.
SO I SHALL NOT DESTROY YOU NOW.
BUT...
...IT WOULD BE AN INSULT TO YOUR VITALITY IF I MADE THINGS EASY ON YOU, WOULDN'T IT?
PERHAPS WE WILL MEET AGAIN, CONAN.
PERHAPS WE WILL NOT.
NATALA? COME ALONG, GIRL.

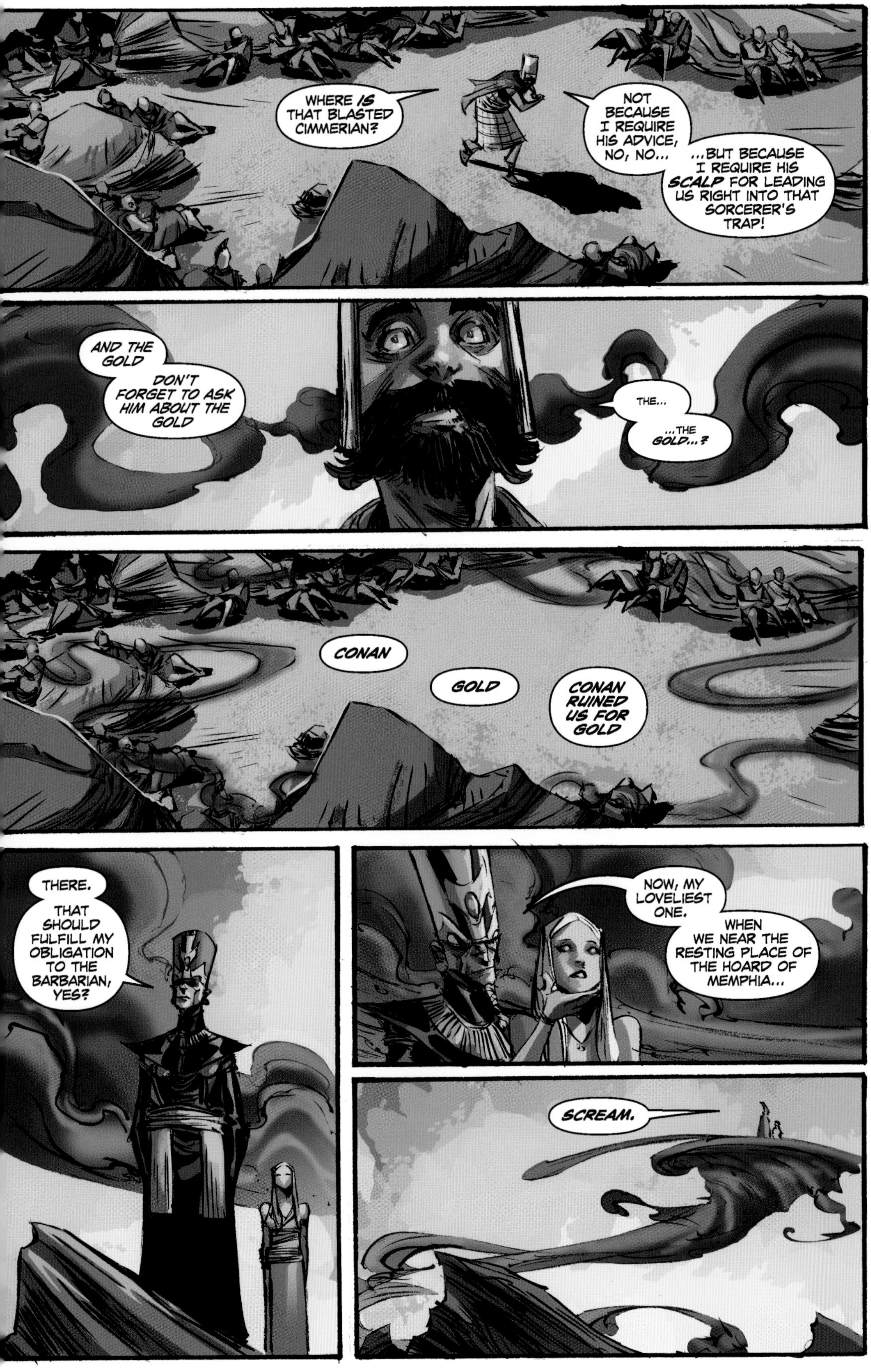
WHERE IS THAT BLASTED CIMMERIAN?
NOT BECAUSE I REQUIRE HIS ADVICE, NO, NO...
...BUT BECAUSE I REQUIRE HIS SCALP FOR LEADING US RIGHT INTO THAT SORCERER'S TRAP!
AND THE GOLD
DON'T FORGET TO ASK HIM ABOUT THE GOLD
THE...
...THE GOLD...?
CONAN
GOLD
CONAN RUINED US FOR GOLD
THERE.
THAT SHOULD FULFILL MY OBLIGATION TO THE BARBARIAN, YES?
NOW, MY LOVELIEST ONE.
WHEN WE NEAR THE RESTING PLACE OF THE HOARD OF MEMPHIA...
SCREAM.

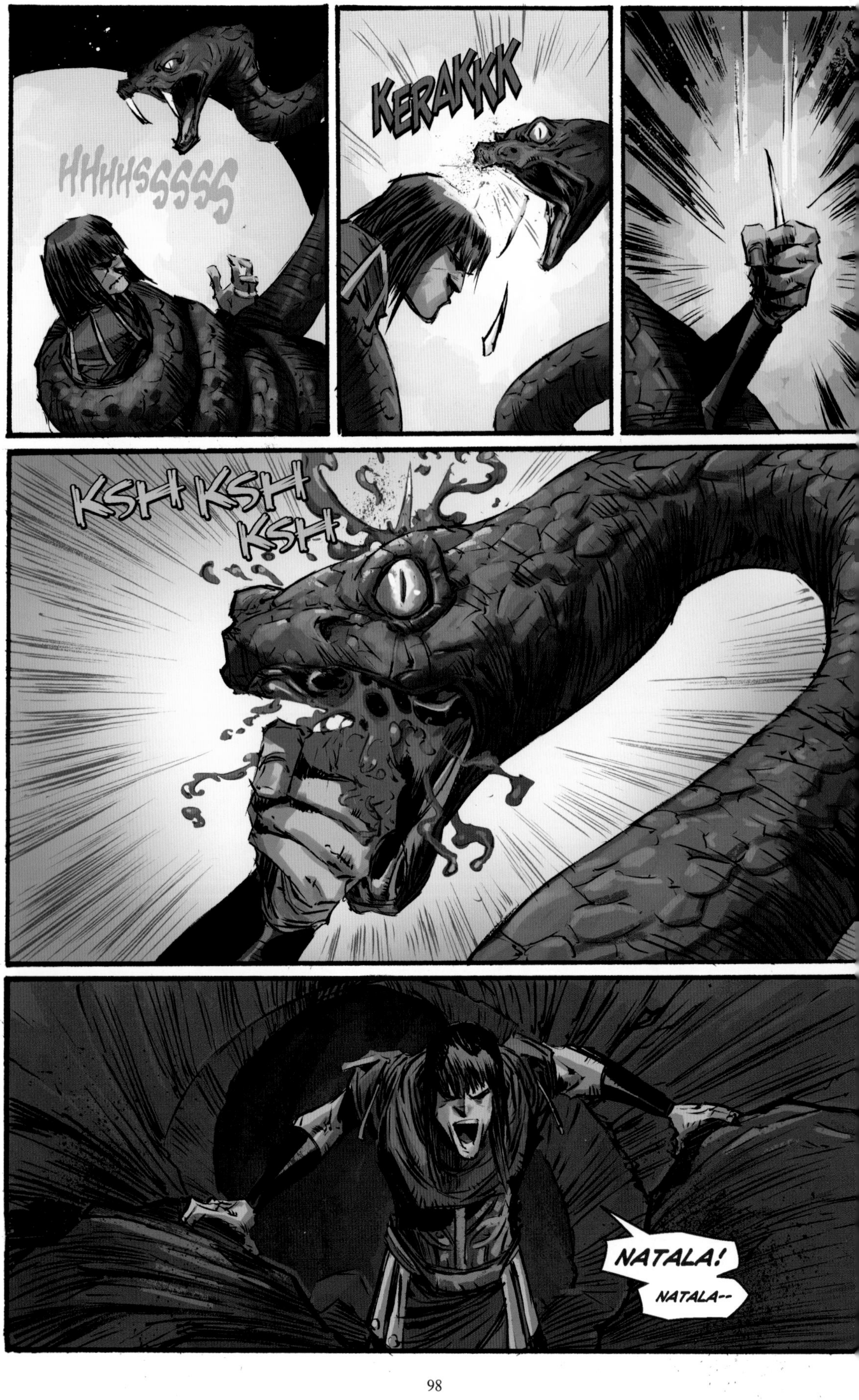
HHHHSSSSS
KERAKKK
KSH KSH KSH
NATALA!
NATALA--

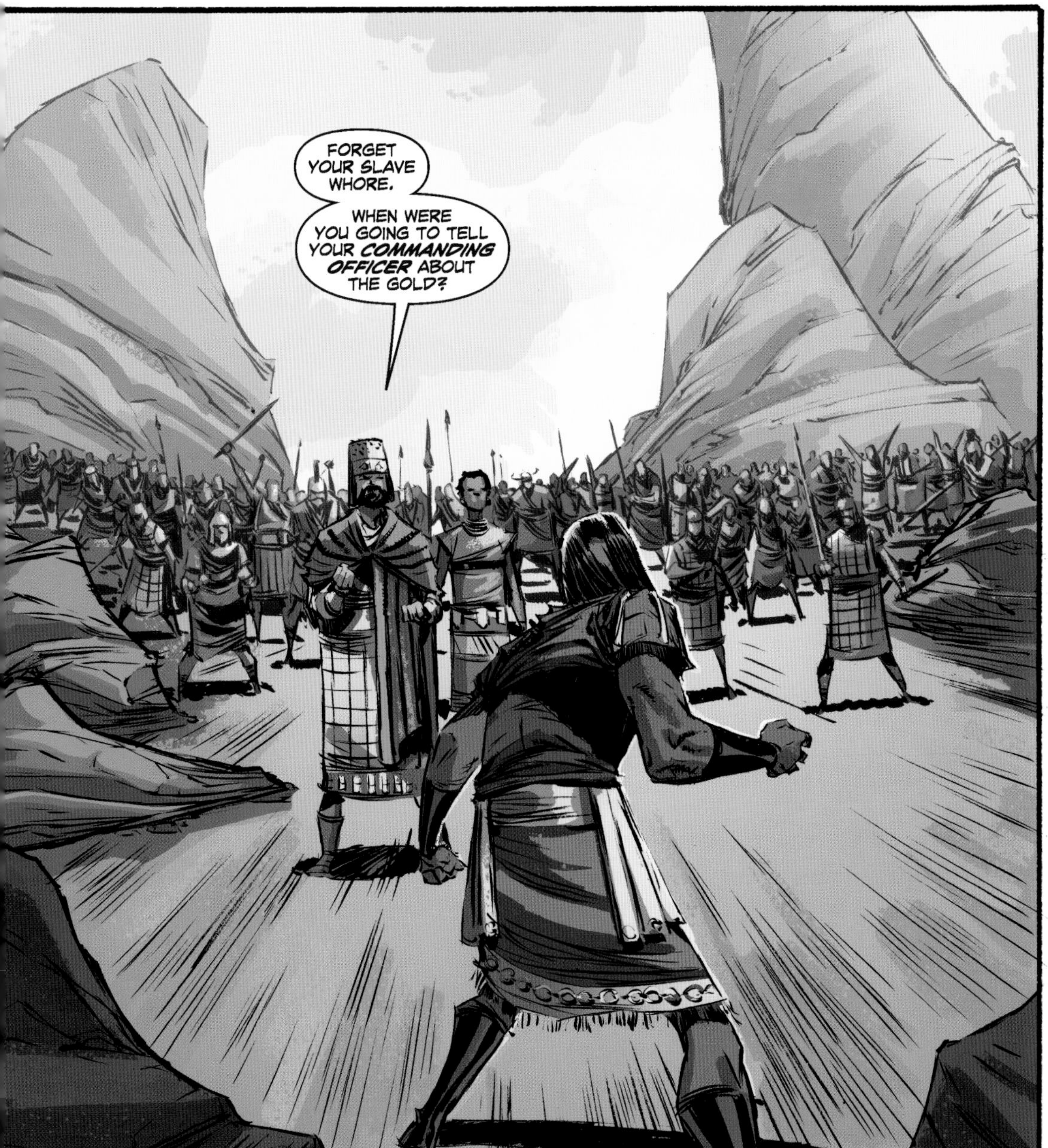
FORGET YOUR SLAVE WHORE.
WHEN WERE YOU GOING TO TELL YOUR COMMANDING OFFICER ABOUT THE GOLD?

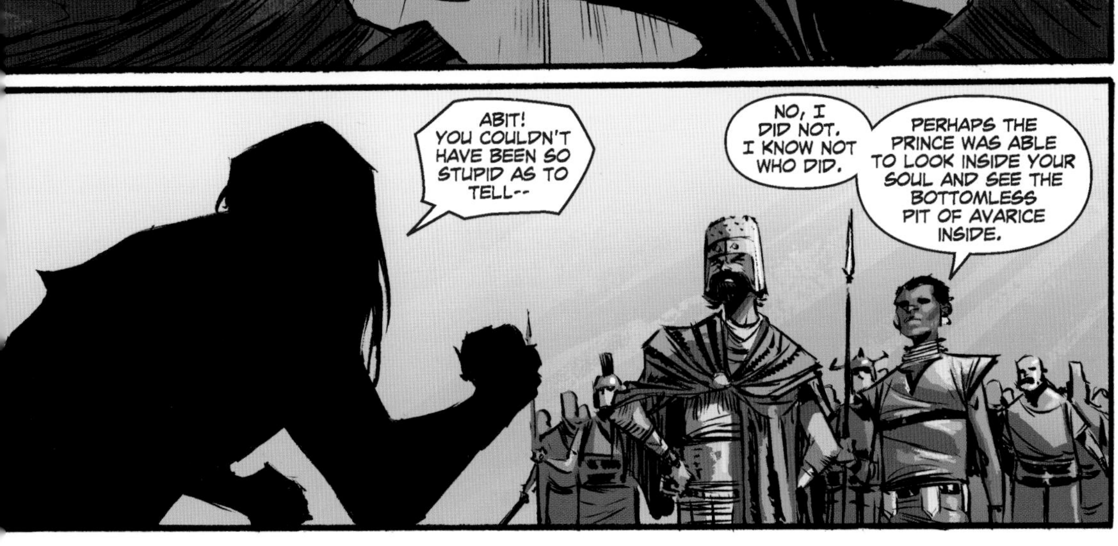
ABIT! YOU COULDN'T HAVE BEEN SO STUPID AS TO TELL--
NO, I DID NOT. I KNOW NOT WHO DID.
PERHAPS THE PRINCE WAS ABLE TO LOOK INSIDE YOUR SOUL AND SEE THE BOTTOMLESS PIT OF AVARICE INSIDE.

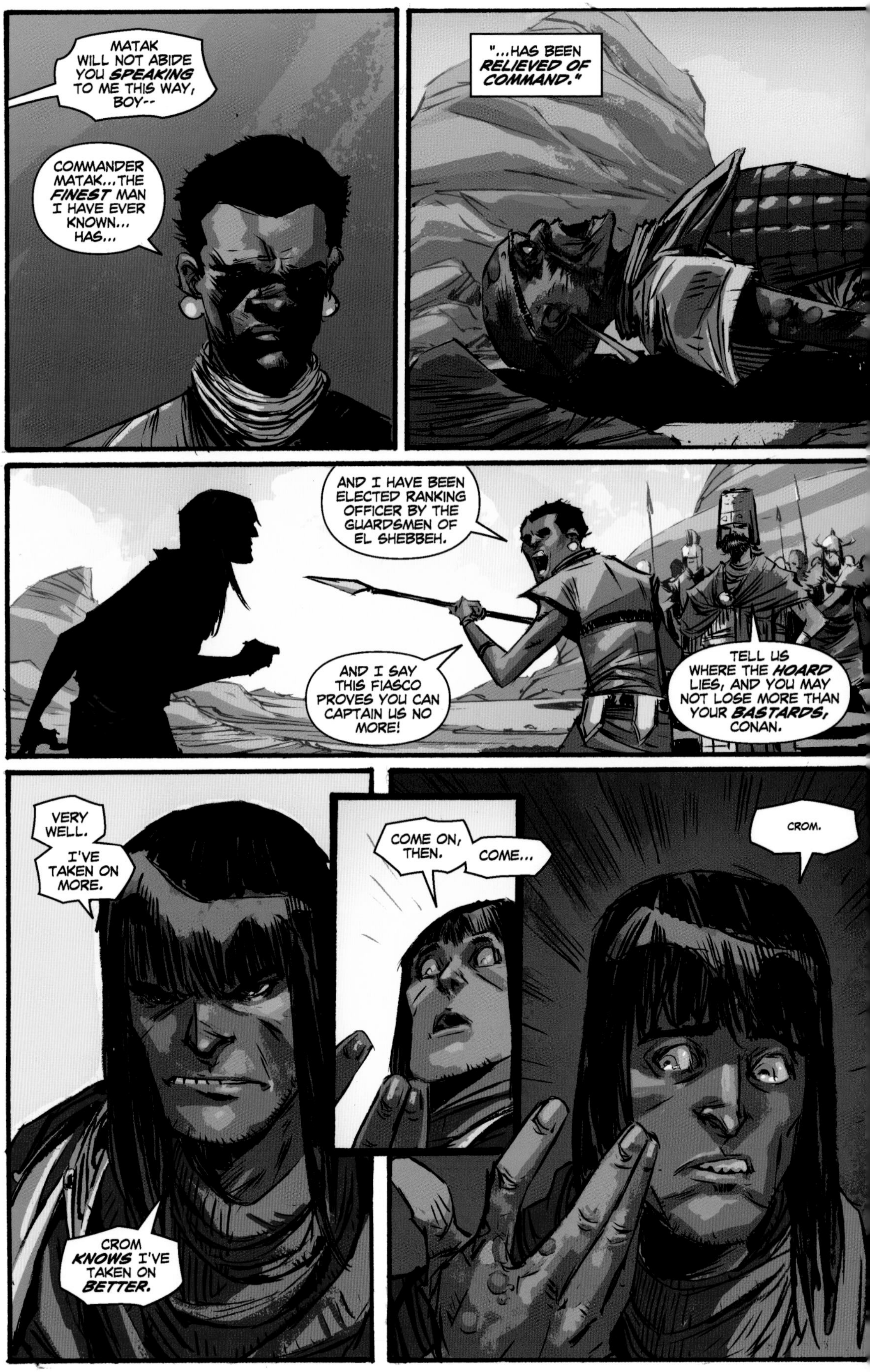
MATAK WILL NOT ABIDE YOU SPEAKING TO ME THIS WAY, BOY--
COMMANDER MATAK...THE FINEST MAN I HAVE EVER KNOWN... HAS...
"...HAS BEEN RELIEVED OF COMMAND."
AND I HAVE BEEN ELECTED RANKING OFFICER BY THE GUARDSMEN OF EL SHEBBEH.
AND I SAY THIS FIASCO PROVES YOU CAN CAPTAIN US NO MORE!
TELL US WHERE THE HOARD LIES, AND YOU MAY NOT LOSE MORE THAN YOUR BASTARDS, CONAN.
VERY WELL.
I'VE TAKEN ON MORE.
CROM KNOWS I'VE TAKEN ON BETTER.
COME ON, THEN.
COME...
CROM.

CHAPTER FIVE

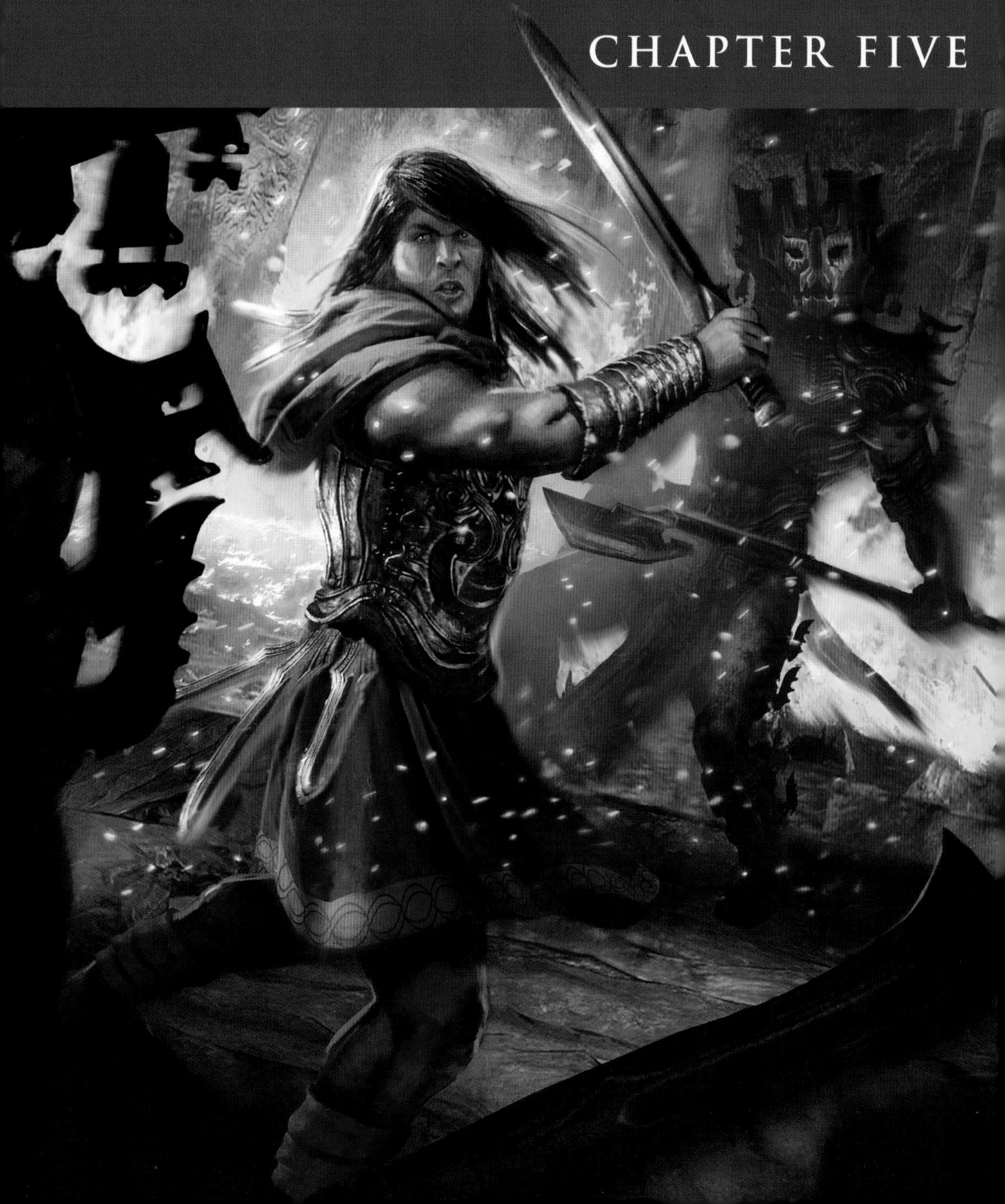

"Believe me, wizard, if *I* insulted you, you'd *know* it."

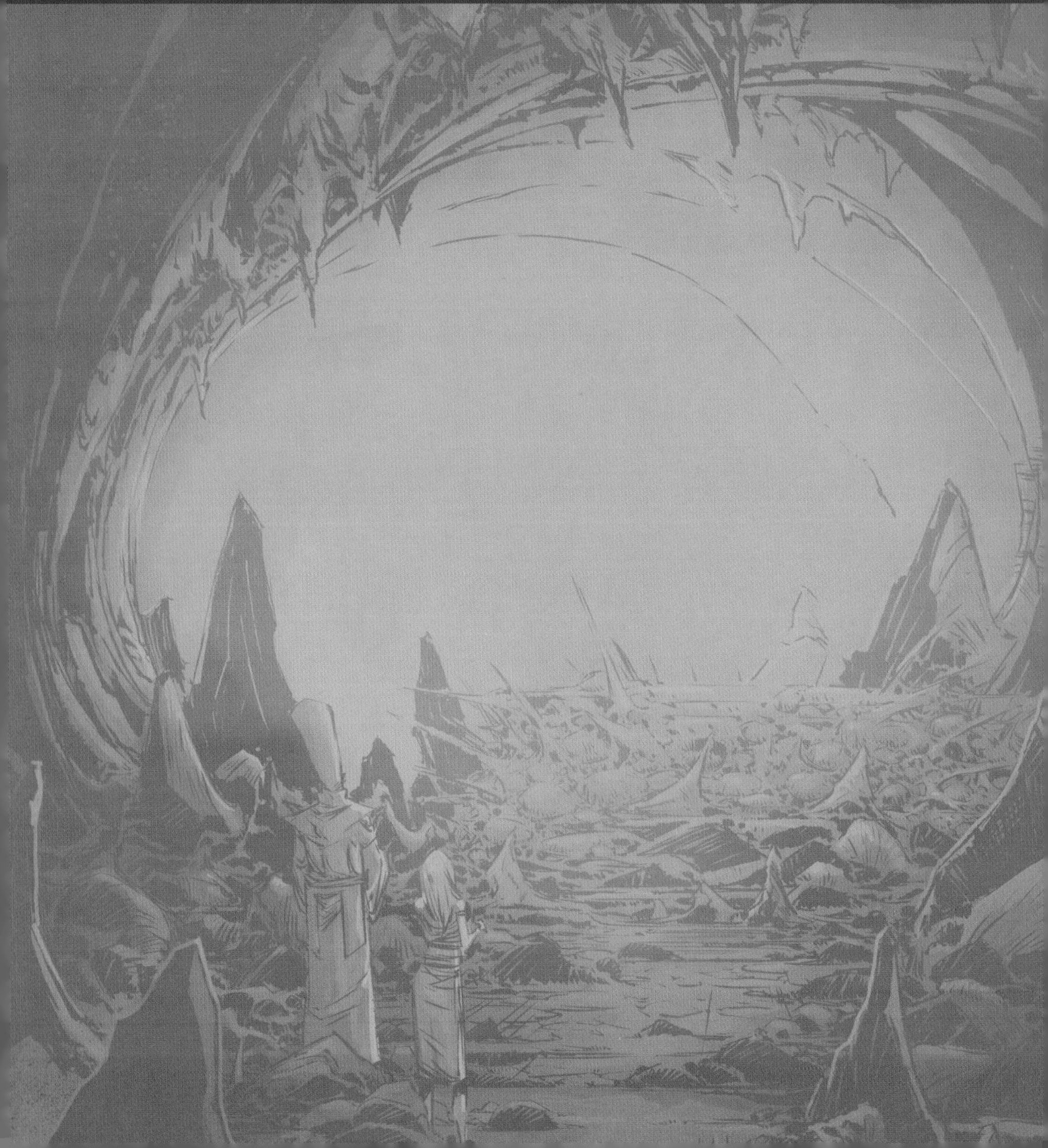

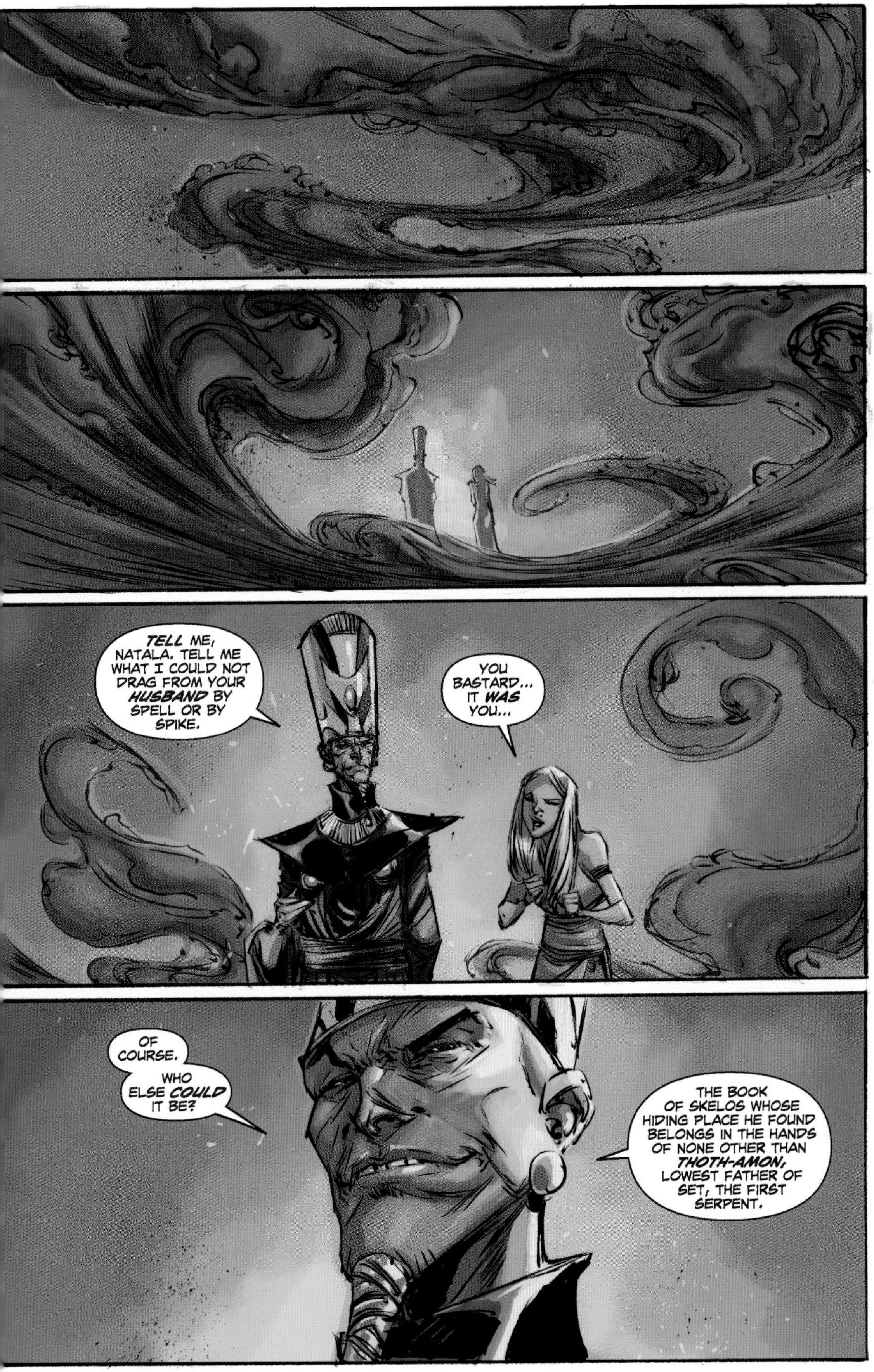

TELL ME, NATALA. TELL ME WHAT I COULD NOT DRAG FROM YOUR HUSBAND BY SPELL OR BY SPIKE.
YOU BASTARD... IT WAS YOU...
OF COURSE.
WHO ELSE COULD IT BE?
THE BOOK OF SKELOS WHOSE HIDING PLACE HE FOUND BELONGS IN THE HANDS OF NONE OTHER THAN THOTH-AMON, LOWEST FATHER OF SET, THE FIRST SERPENT.

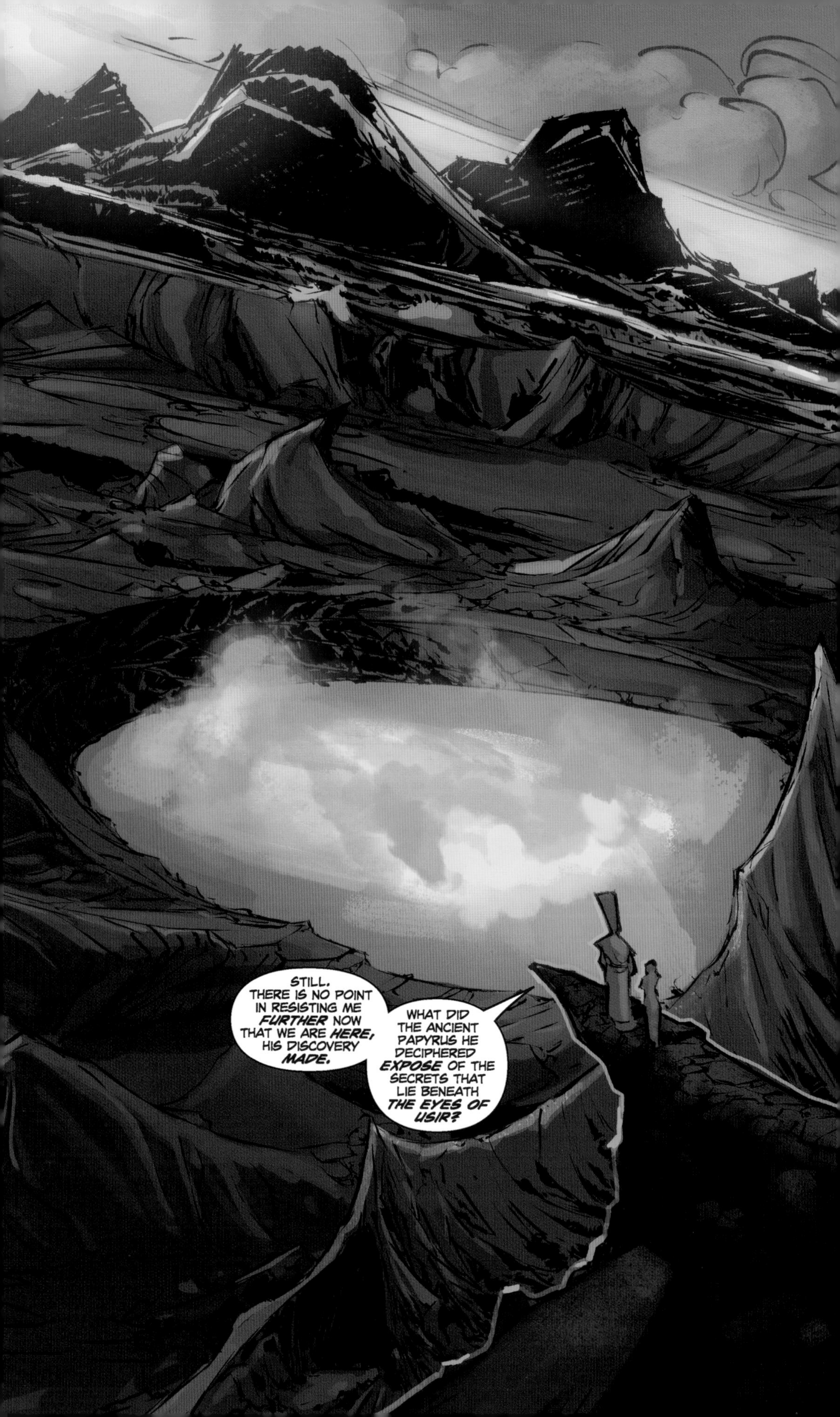
STILL. THERE IS NO POINT IN RESISTING ME FURTHER NOW THAT WE ARE HERE, HIS DISCOVERY MADE.
WHAT DID THE ANCIENT PAPYRUS HE DECIPHERED EXPOSE OF THE SECRETS THAT LIE BENEATH THE EYES OF USIR?

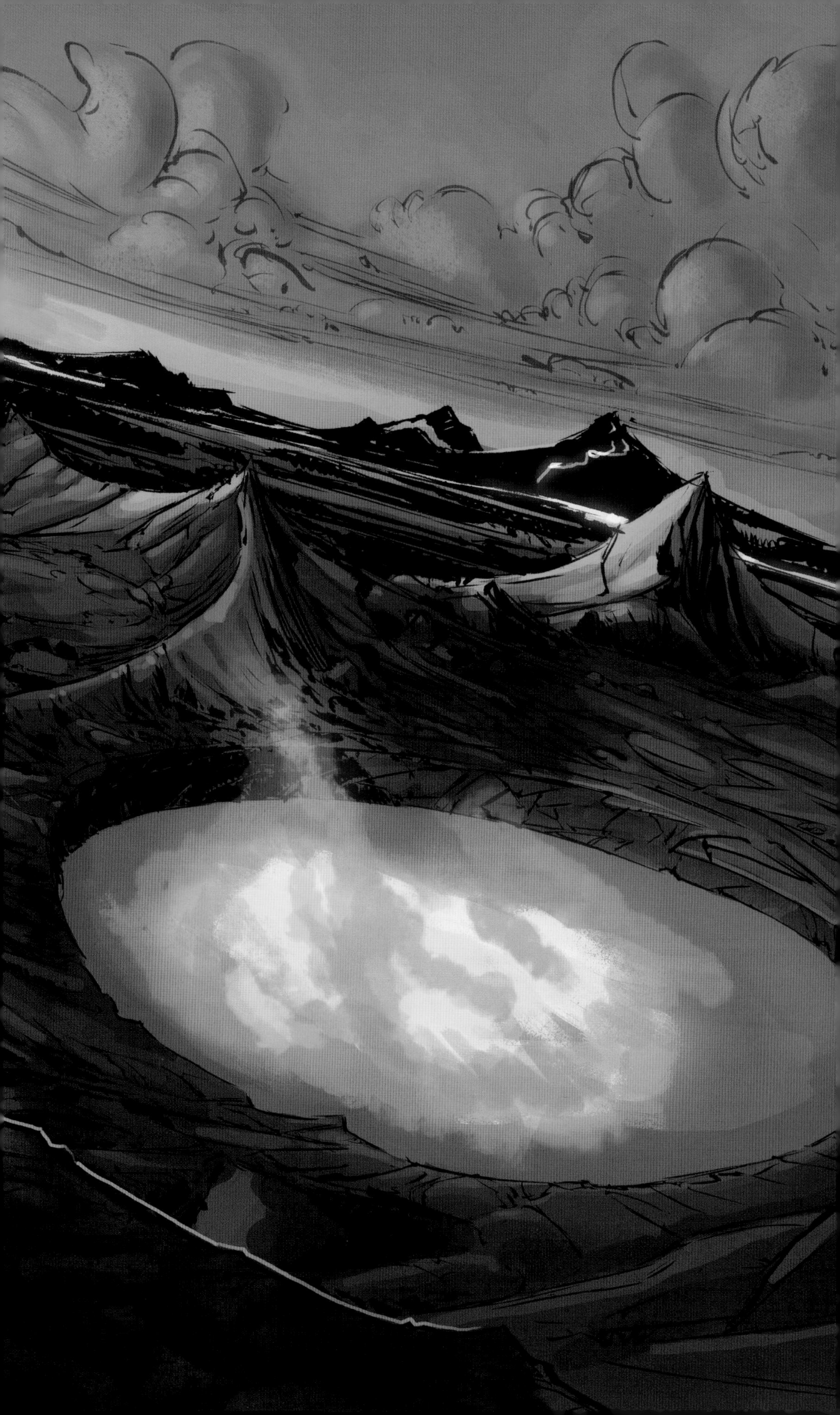

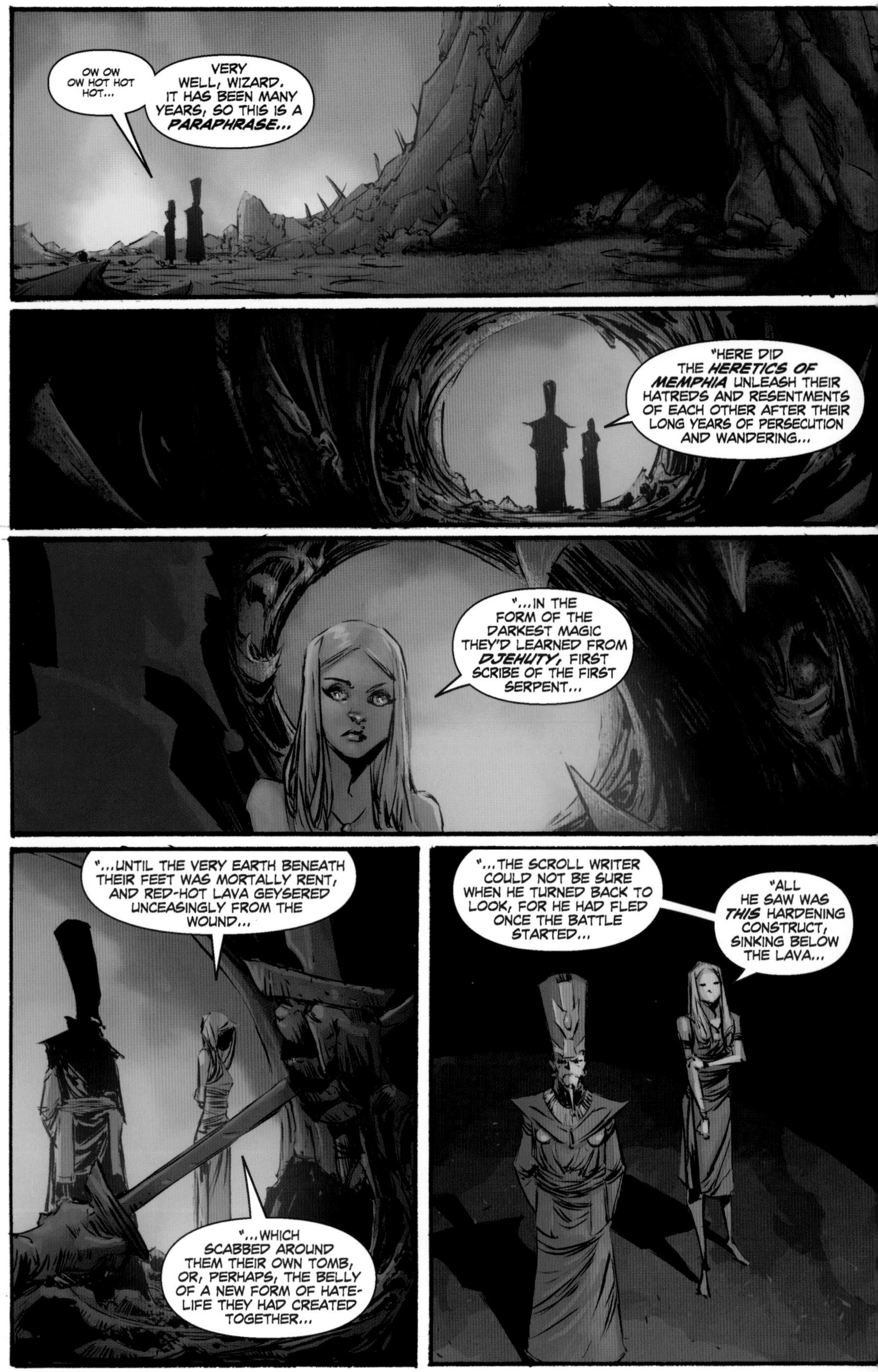
OW OW OW HOT HOT HOT...
VERY WELL, WIZARD. IT HAS BEEN MANY YEARS, SO THIS IS A PARAPHRASE...
"HERE DID THE HERETICS OF MEMPHIA UNLEASH THEIR HATREDS AND RESENTMENTS OF EACH OTHER AFTER THEIR LONG YEARS OF PERSECUTION AND WANDERING...
"...IN THE FORM OF THE DARKEST MAGIC THEY'D LEARNED FROM DJEHUTY, FIRST SCRIBE OF THE FIRST SERPENT...
"...UNTIL THE VERY EARTH BENEATH THEIR FEET WAS MORTALLY RENT, AND RED-HOT LAVA GEYSERED UNCEASINGLY FROM THE WOUND...
"...WHICH SCABBED AROUND THEM THEIR OWN TOMB, OR, PERHAPS, THE BELLY OF A NEW FORM OF HATE-LIFE THEY HAD CREATED TOGETHER...
"...THE SCROLL WRITER COULD NOT BE SURE WHEN HE TURNED BACK TO LOOK, FOR HE HAD FLED ONCE THE BATTLE STARTED...
"ALL HE SAW WAS THIS HARDENING CONSTRUCT, SINKING BELOW THE LAVA...

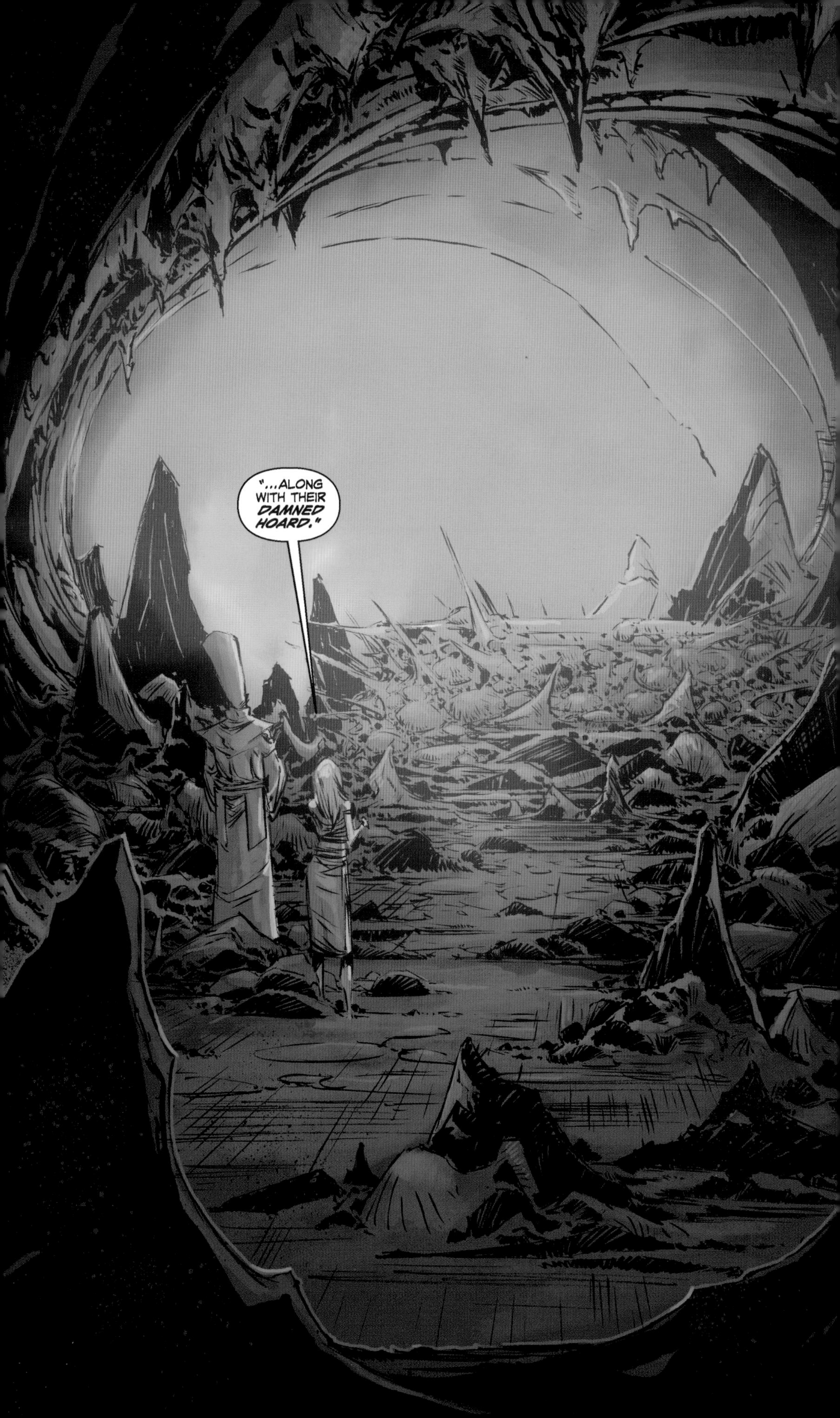
"...ALONG WITH THEIR DAMNED HOARD."

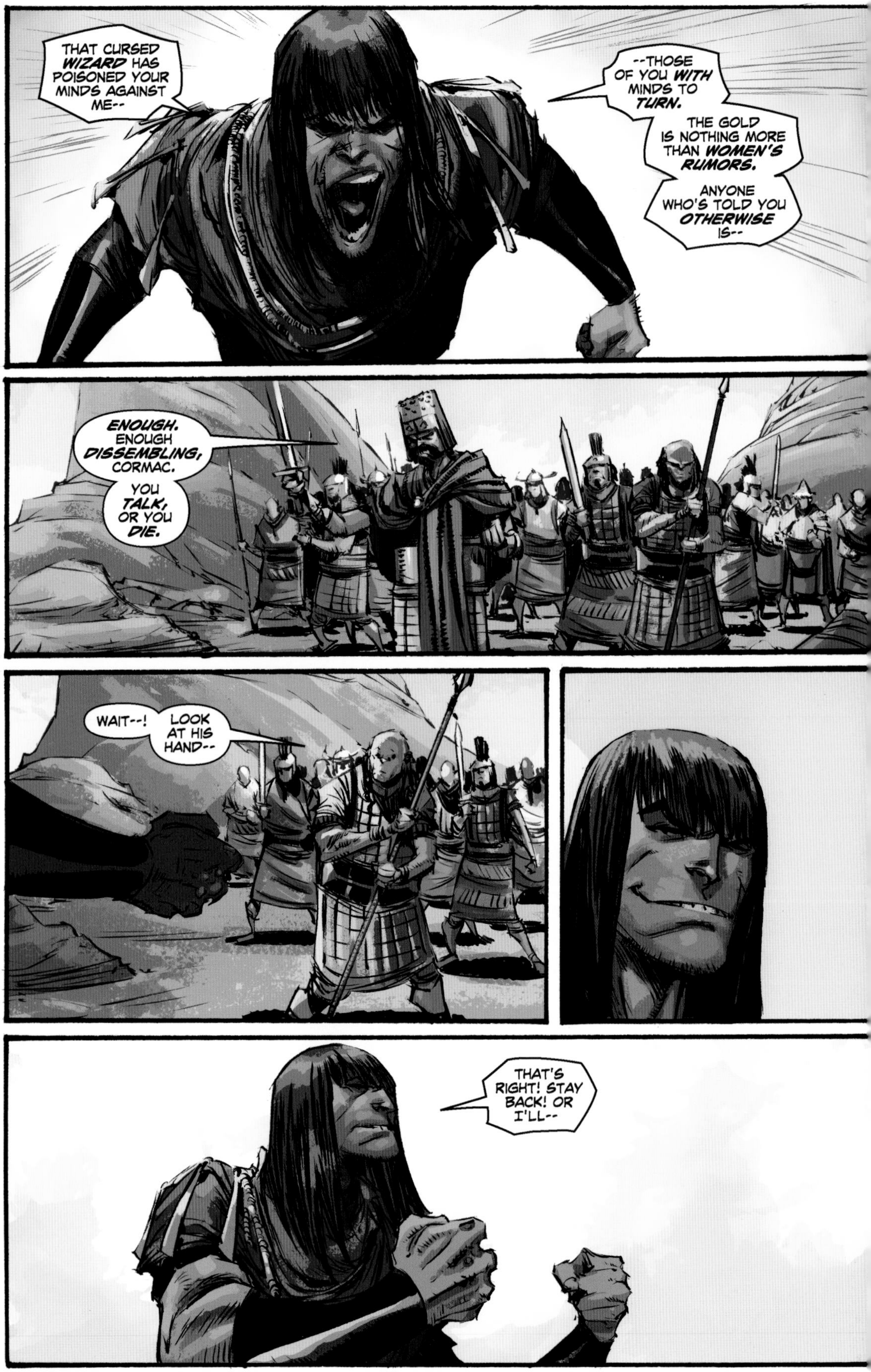
THAT CURSED WIZARD HAS POISONED YOUR MINDS AGAINST ME--
--THOSE OF YOU WITH MINDS TO TURN.
THE GOLD IS NOTHING MORE THAN WOMEN'S RUMORS.
ANYONE WHO'S TOLD YOU OTHERWISE IS--
ENOUGH. ENOUGH DISSEMBLING, CORMAC.
YOU TALK, OR YOU DIE.
WAIT--!
LOOK AT HIS HAND--
THAT'S RIGHT! STAY BACK! OR I'LL--

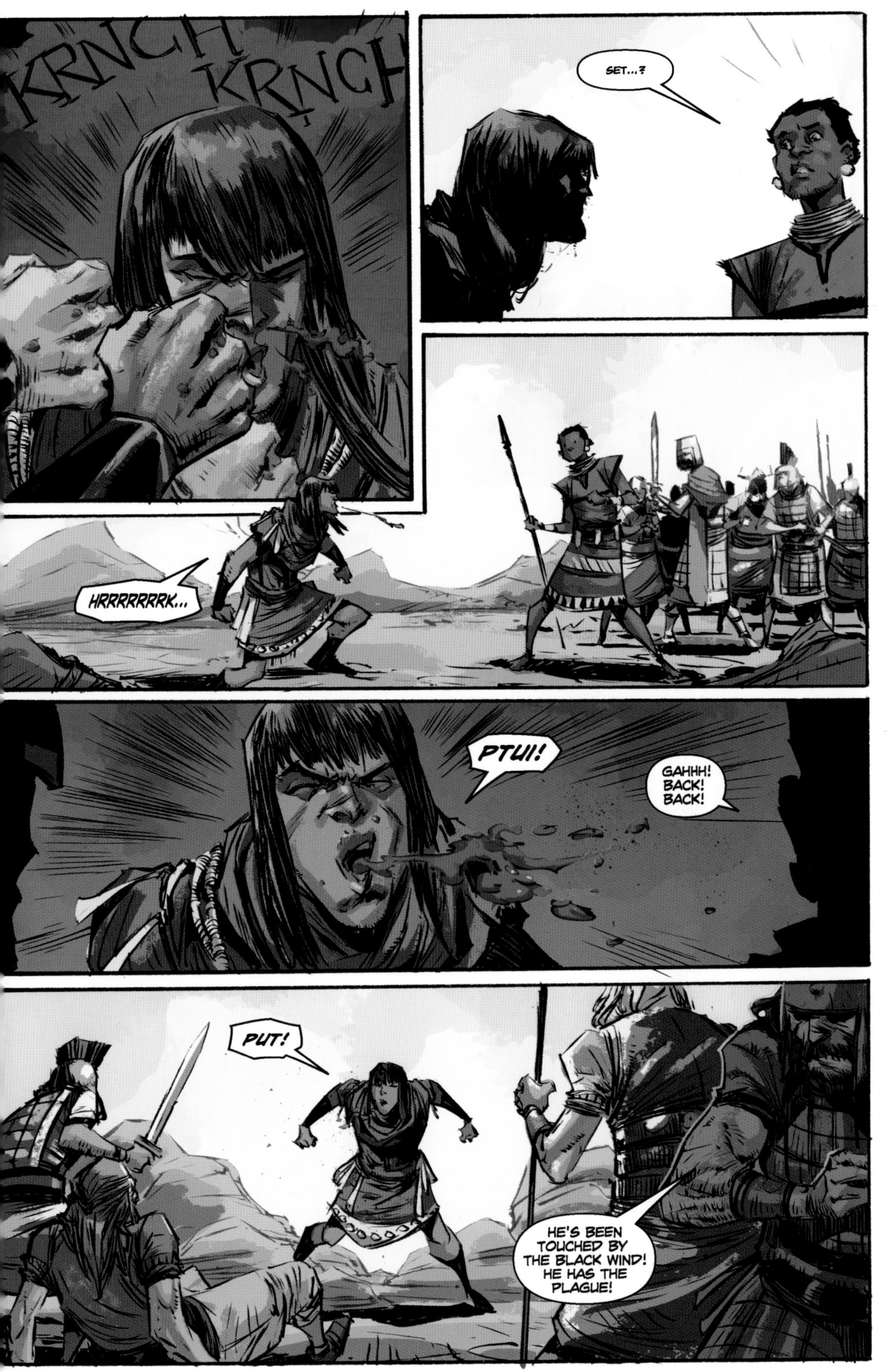
KRNCH KRNCH
SET...?
HRRRRRRRK...
PTUI!
GAHHH! BACK! BACK!
PUT!
HE'S BEEN TOUCHED BY THE BLACK WIND! HE HAS THE PLAGUE!

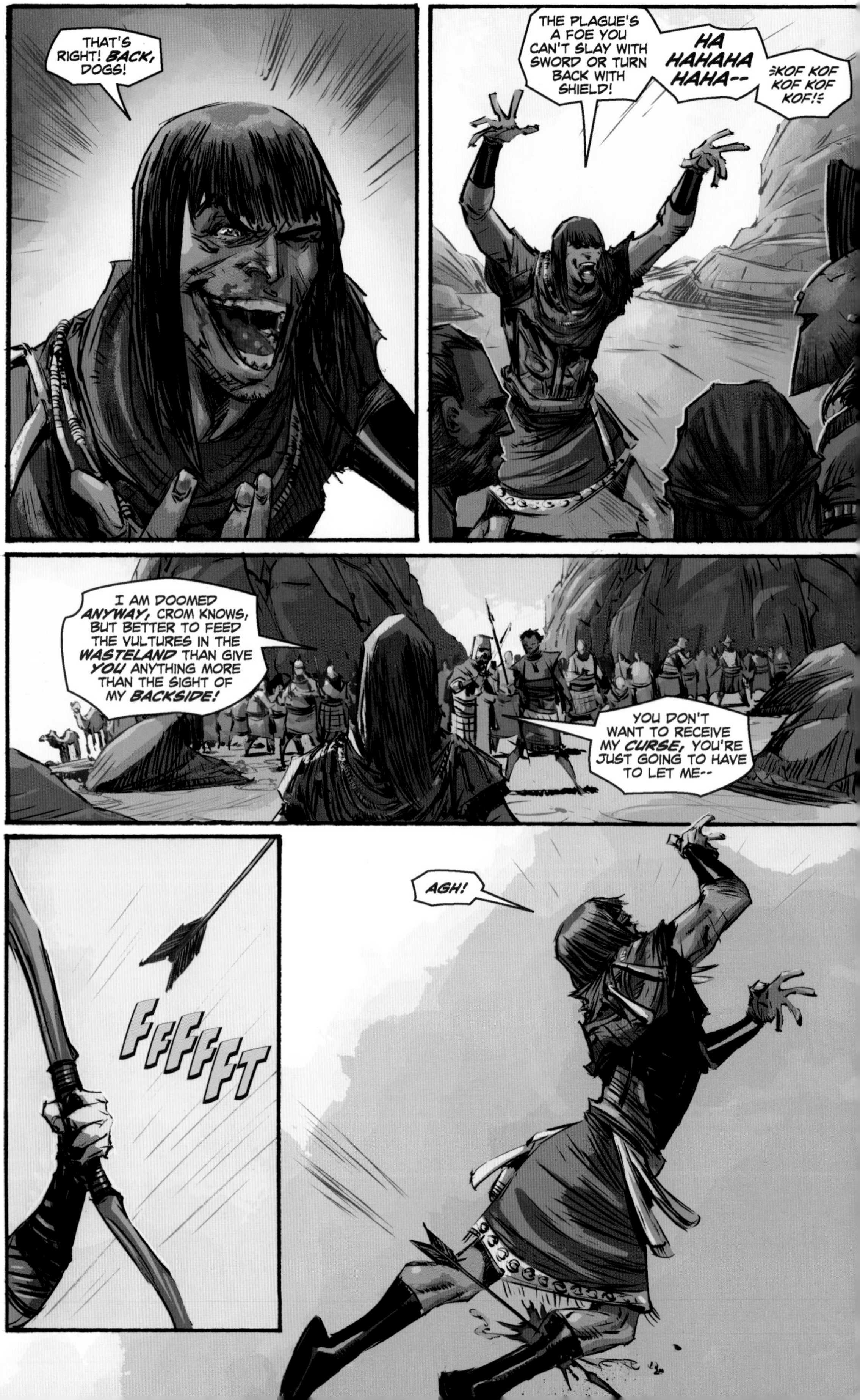
THAT'S RIGHT! BACK, DOGS!
THE PLAGUE'S A FOE YOU CAN'T SLAY WITH SWORD OR TURN BACK WITH SHIELD!
HA HAHAHA HAHA--
KOF KOF KOF KOF KOF!
I AM DOOMED ANYWAY, CROM KNOWS, BUT BETTER TO FEED THE VULTURES IN THE WASTELAND THAN GIVE YOU ANYTHING MORE THAN THE SIGHT OF MY BACKSIDE!
YOU DON'T WANT TO RECEIVE MY CURSE, YOU'RE JUST GOING TO HAVE TO LET ME--
FFFFFT
AGH!

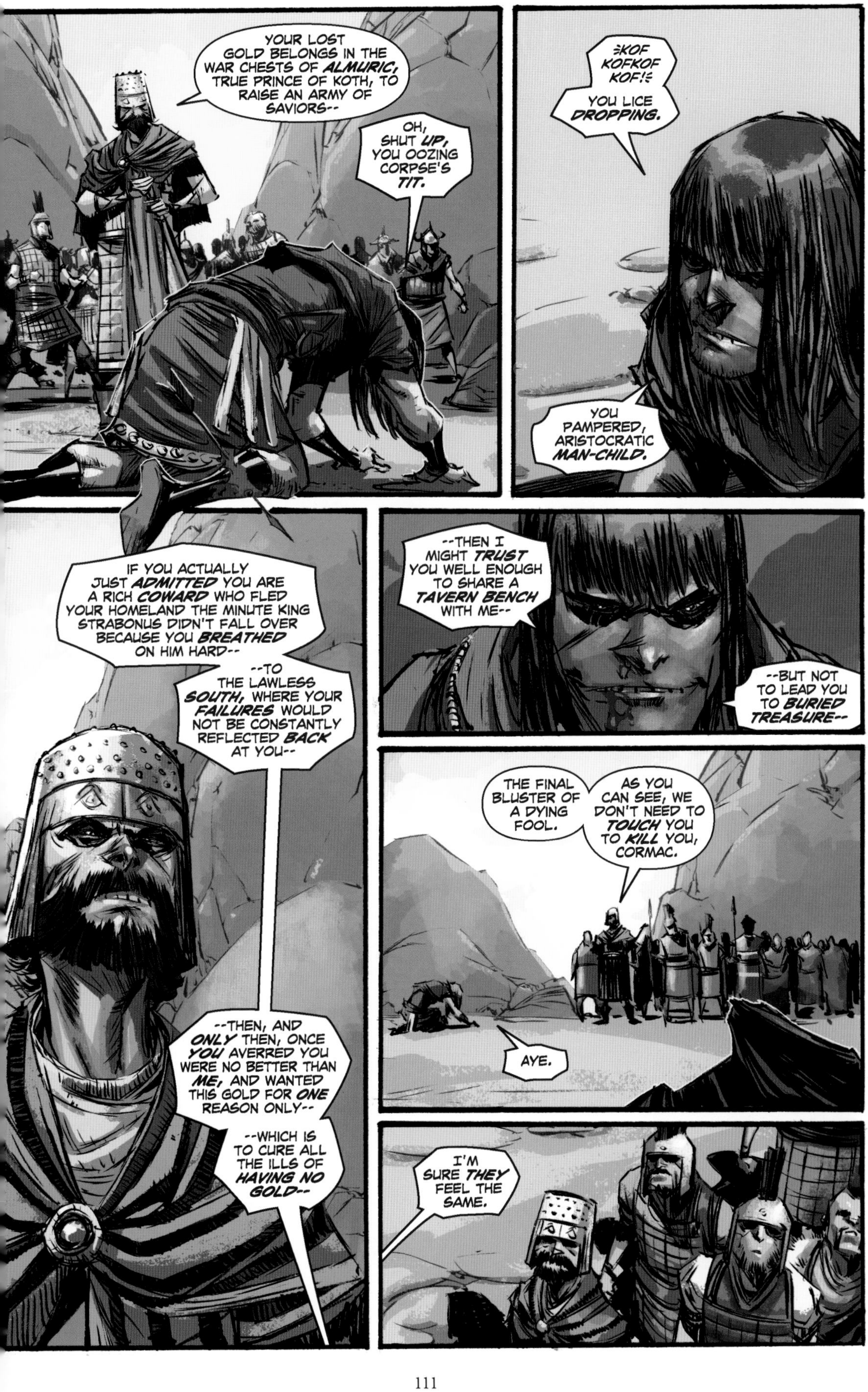
YOUR LOST GOLD BELONGS IN THE WAR CHESTS OF ALMURIC, TRUE PRINCE OF KOTH, TO RAISE AN ARMY OF SAVIORS--
OH, SHUT UP, YOU OOZING CORPSE'S TIT.
ƸKOF KOFKOF KOF!Ʒ
YOU LICE DROPPING.
YOU PAMPERED, ARISTOCRATIC MAN-CHILD.
IF YOU ACTUALLY JUST ADMITTED YOU ARE A RICH COWARD WHO FLED YOUR HOMELAND THE MINUTE KING STRABONUS DIDN'T FALL OVER BECAUSE YOU BREATHED ON HIM HARD--
--TO THE LAWLESS SOUTH, WHERE YOUR FAILURES WOULD NOT BE CONSTANTLY REFLECTED BACK AT YOU--
--THEN, AND ONLY THEN, ONCE YOU AVERRED YOU WERE NO BETTER THAN ME, AND WANTED THIS GOLD FOR ONE REASON ONLY--
--WHICH IS TO CURE ALL THE ILLS OF HAVING NO GOLD--
--THEN I MIGHT TRUST YOU WELL ENOUGH TO SHARE A TAVERN BENCH WITH ME--
--BUT NOT TO LEAD YOU TO BURIED TREASURE--
THE FINAL BLUSTER OF A DYING FOOL.
AS YOU CAN SEE, WE DON'T NEED TO TOUCH YOU TO KILL YOU, CORMAC.
AYE.
I'M SURE THEY FEEL THE SAME.

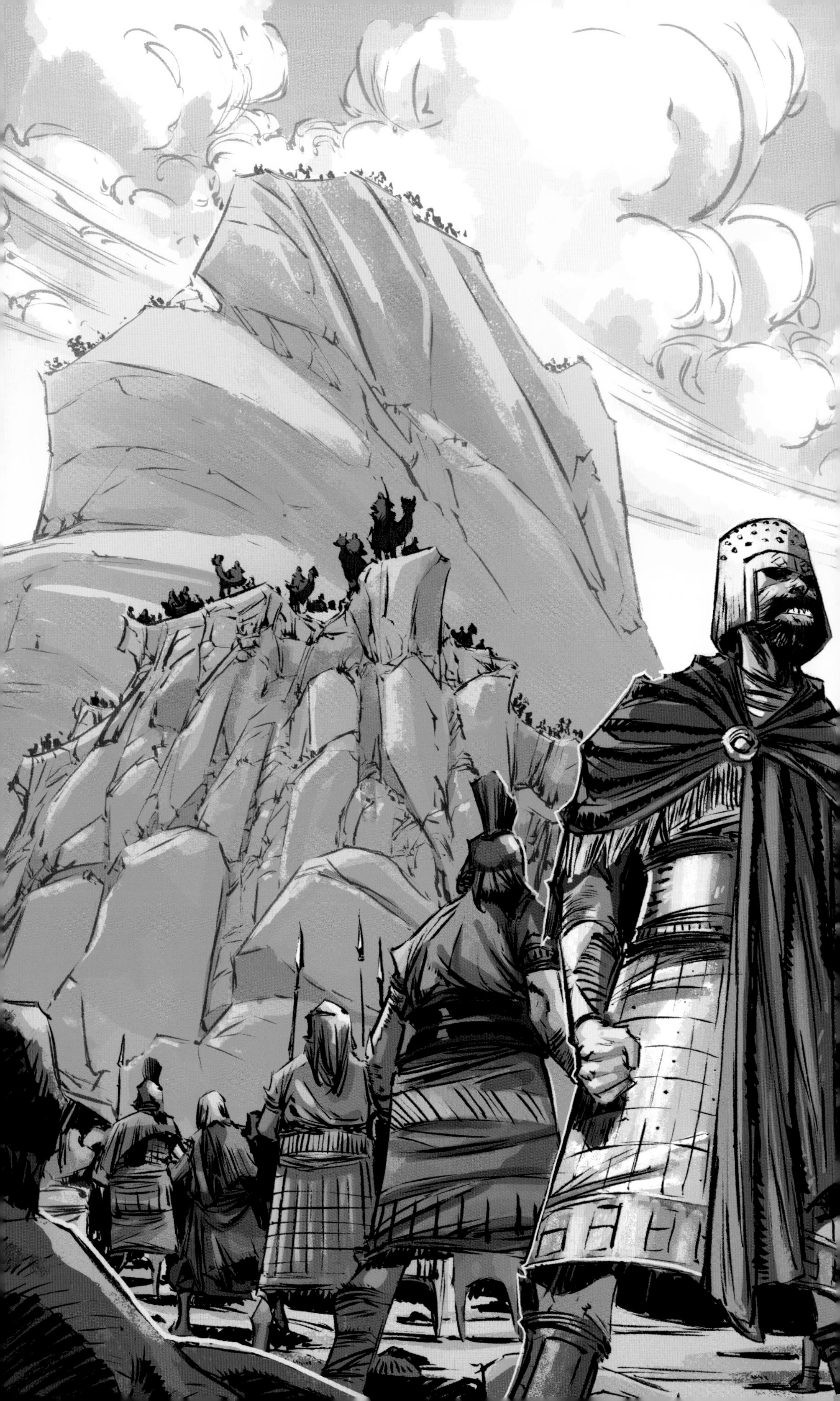

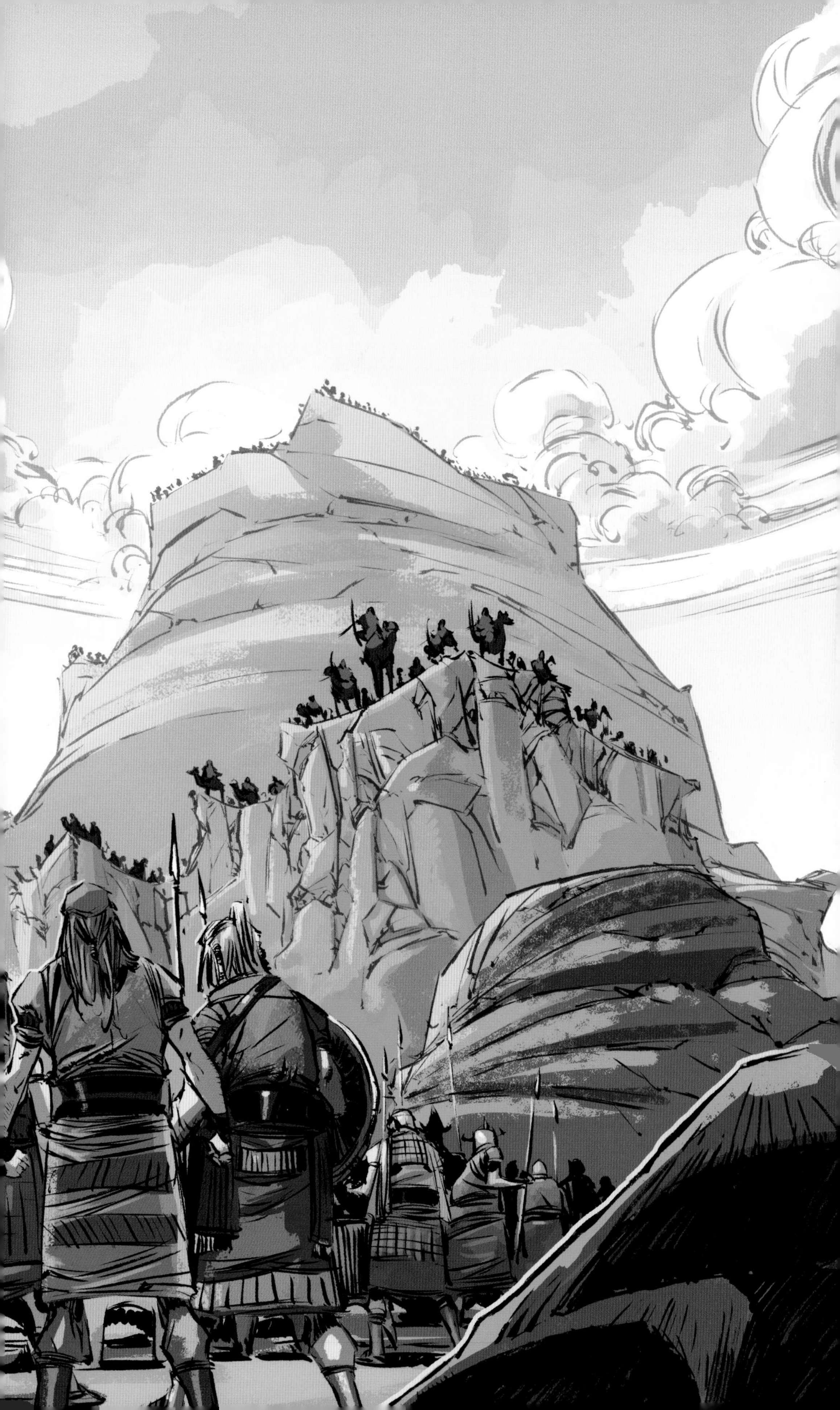

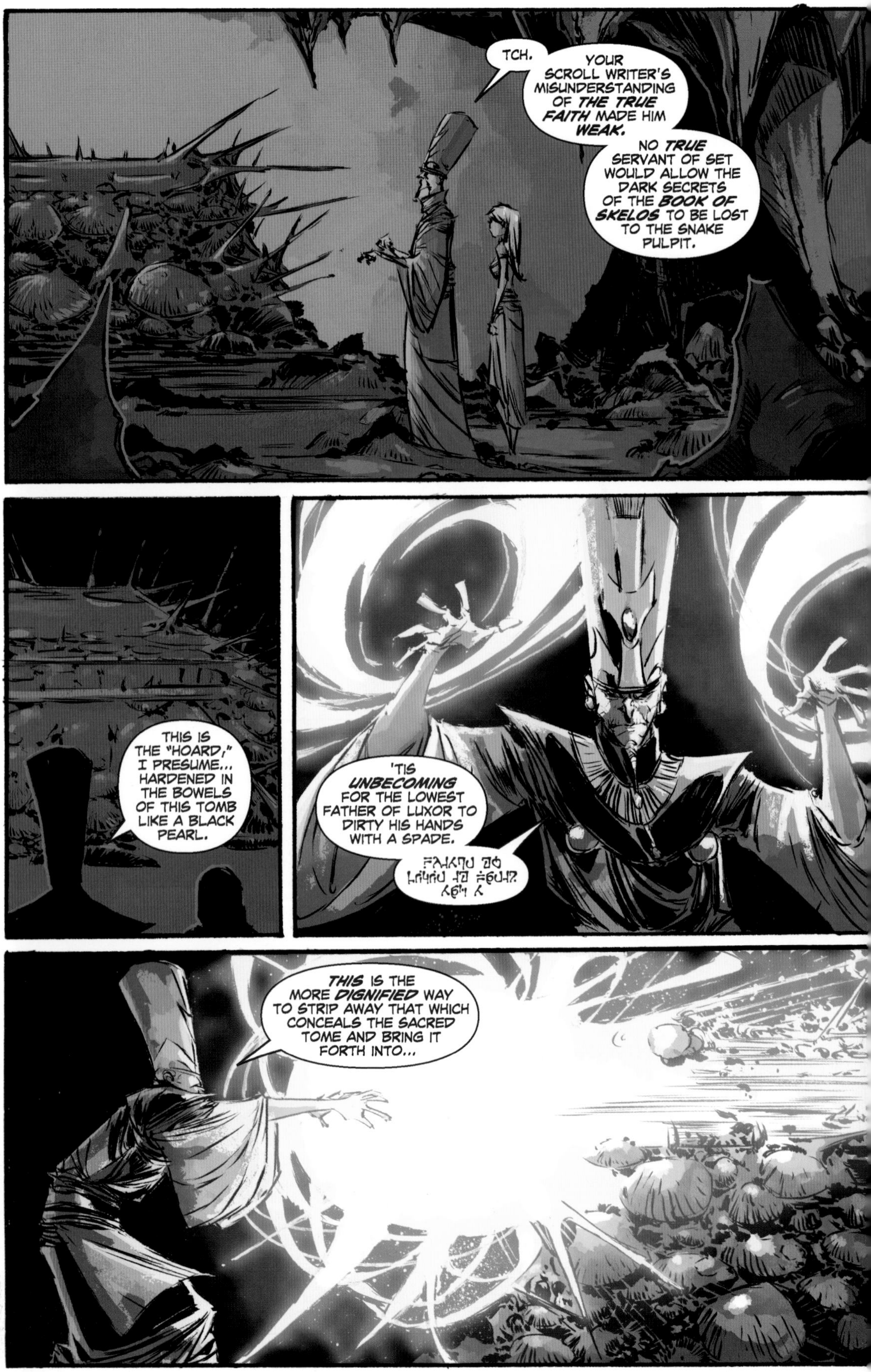
TCH.
YOUR SCROLL WRITER'S MISUNDERSTANDING OF THE TRUE FAITH MADE HIM WEAK.
NO TRUE SERVANT OF SET WOULD ALLOW THE DARK SECRETS OF THE BOOK OF SKELOS TO BE LOST TO THE SNAKE PULPIT.
THIS IS THE "HOARD," I PRESUME... HARDENED IN THE BOWELS OF THIS TOMB LIKE A BLACK PEARL.
'TIS UNBECOMING FOR THE LOWEST FATHER OF LUXOR TO DIRTY HIS HANDS WITH A SPADE.
THIS IS THE MORE DIGNIFIED WAY TO STRIP AWAY THAT WHICH CONCEALS THE SACRED TOME AND BRING IT FORTH INTO...

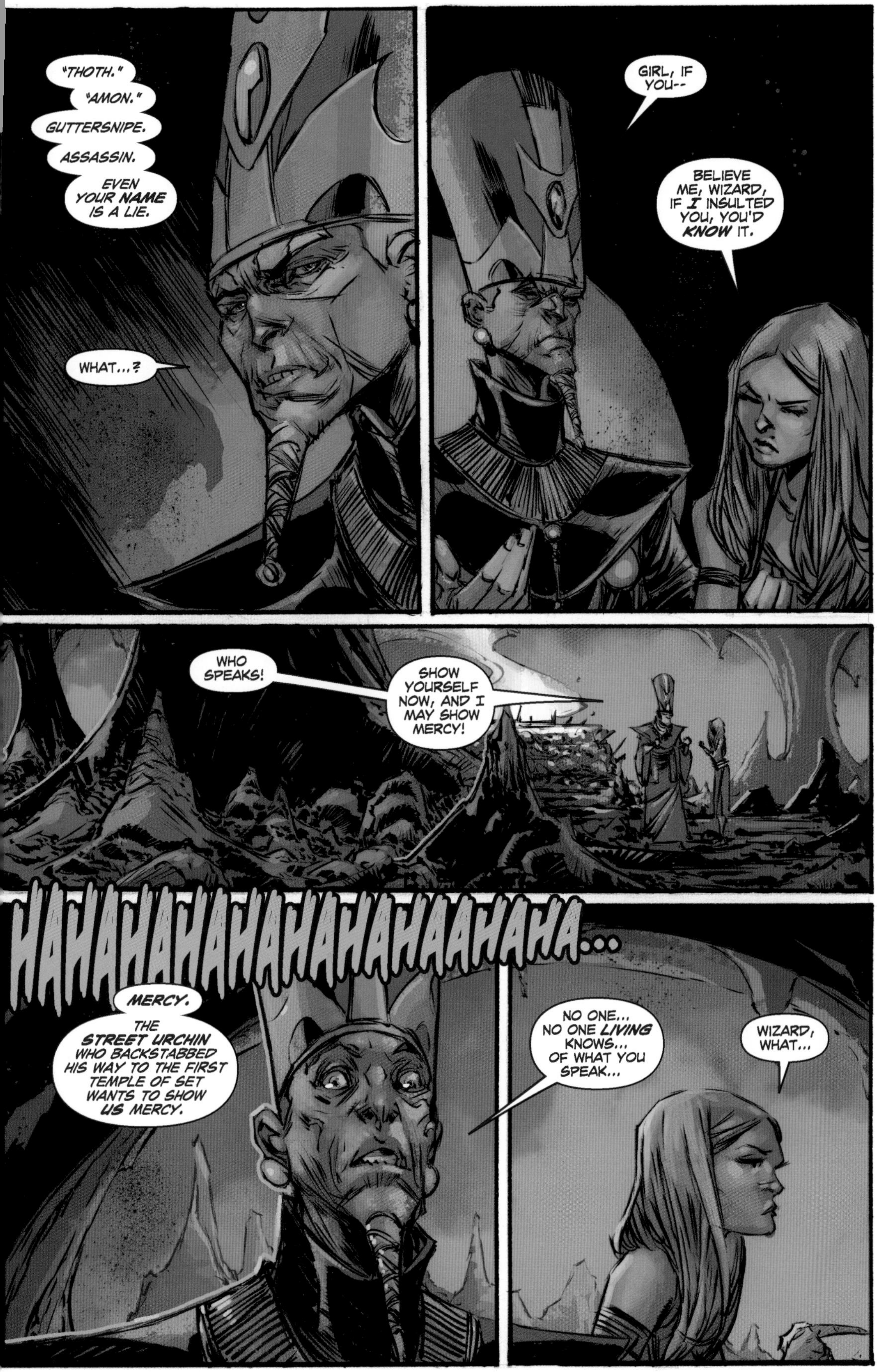
"THOTH."
"AMON."
GUTTERSNIPE.
ASSASSIN.
EVEN YOUR NAME IS A LIE.
WHAT...?
GIRL, IF YOU--
BELIEVE ME, WIZARD, IF I INSULTED YOU, YOU'D KNOW IT.
WHO SPEAKS!
SHOW YOURSELF NOW, AND I MAY SHOW MERCY!
HAHAHAHAHAHAHAHAHAAHAHA...
MERCY.
THE STREET URCHIN WHO BACKSTABBED HIS WAY TO THE FIRST TEMPLE OF SET WANTS TO SHOW US MERCY.
NO ONE... NO ONE LIVING KNOWS... OF WHAT YOU SPEAK...
WIZARD, WHAT...

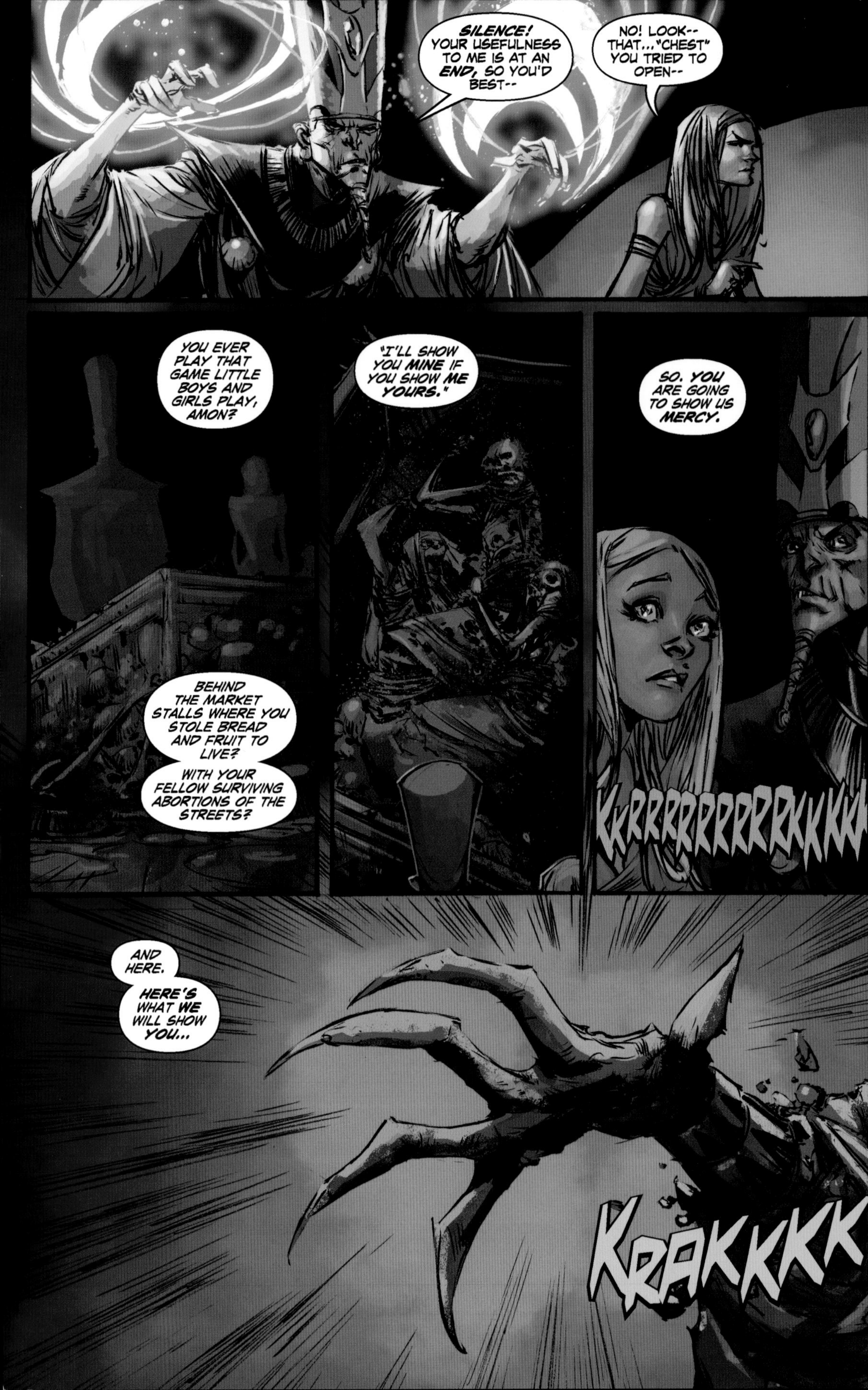

SILENCE! YOUR USEFULNESS TO ME IS AT AN END, SO YOU'D BEST--
NO! LOOK-- THAT... "CHEST" YOU TRIED TO OPEN--
YOU EVER PLAY THAT GAME LITTLE BOYS AND GIRLS PLAY, AMON?
BEHIND THE MARKET STALLS WHERE YOU STOLE BREAD AND FRUIT TO LIVE?
WITH YOUR FELLOW SURVIVING ABORTIONS OF THE STREETS?
"I'LL SHOW YOU MINE IF YOU SHOW ME YOURS."
SO. YOU ARE GOING TO SHOW US MERCY.
KKRRRRRRRRRKKKK
AND HERE.
HERE'S WHAT WE WILL SHOW YOU...
KRAKKKK

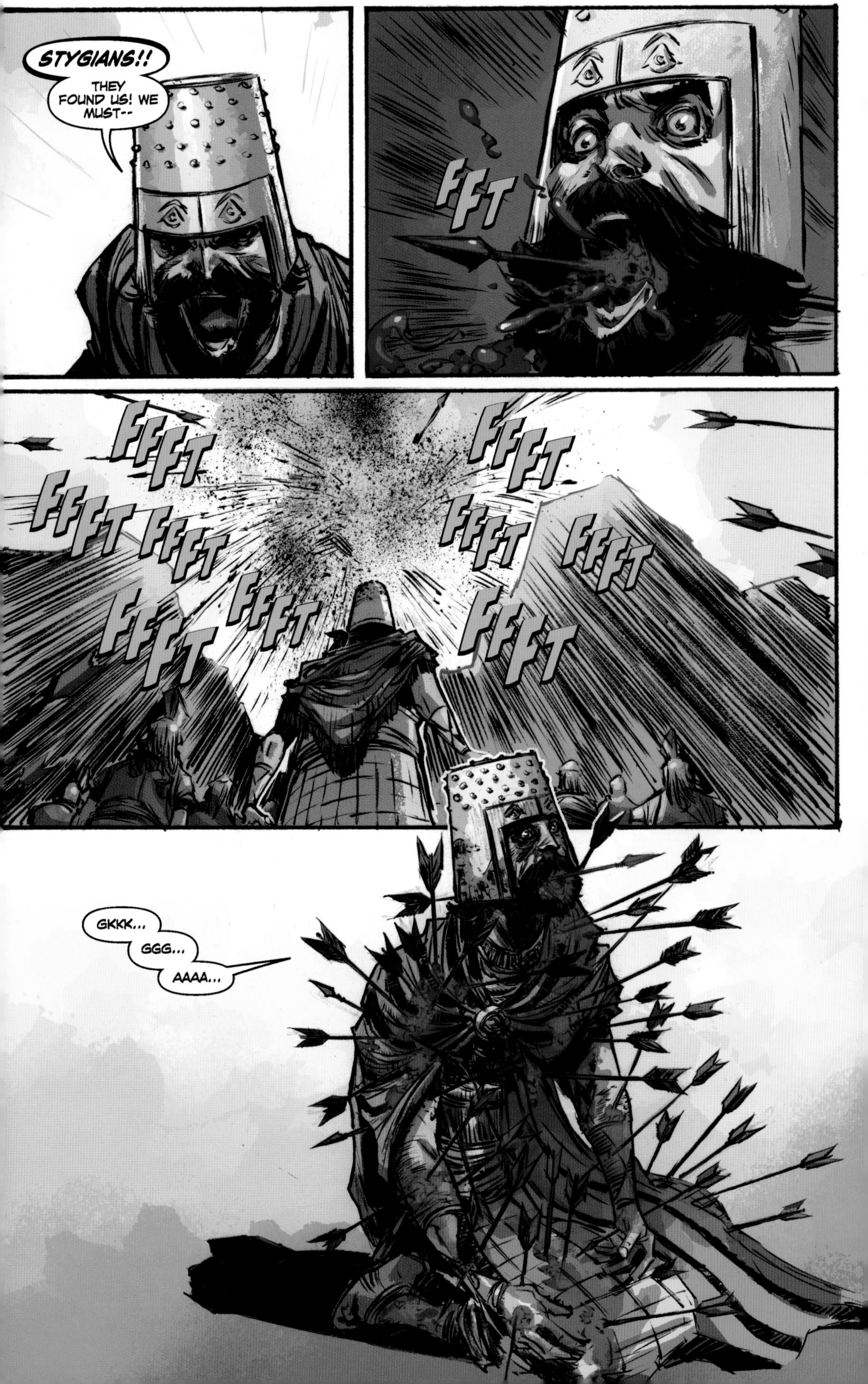
STYGIANS!!
THEY FOUND US! WE MUST--
FFT
FFFT
FFFT
FFFT
FFFT
FFFT
FFFT
FFFT
FFFT
GKKK...
GGG...
AAAA...

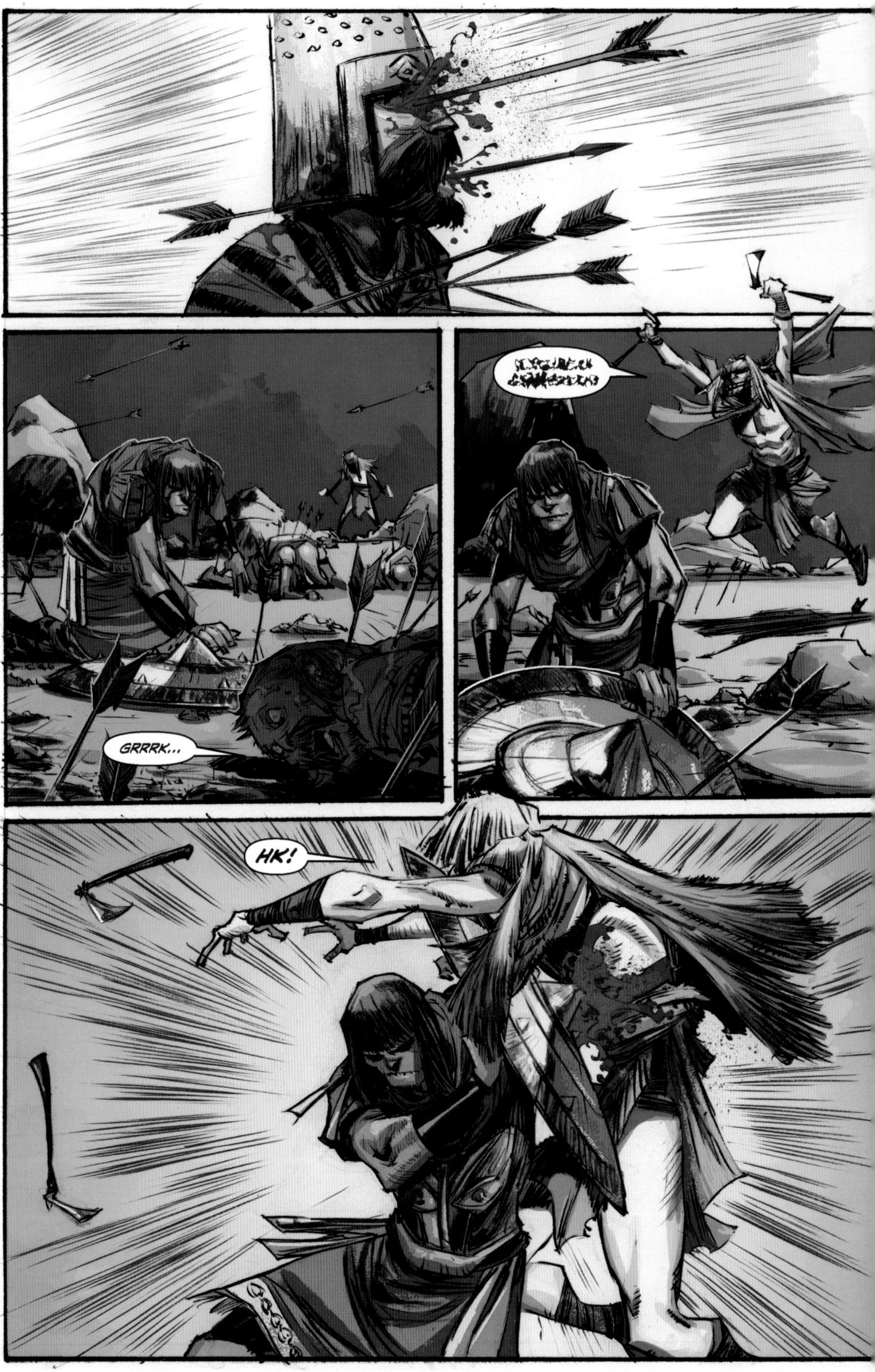
GRRRK...
HK!

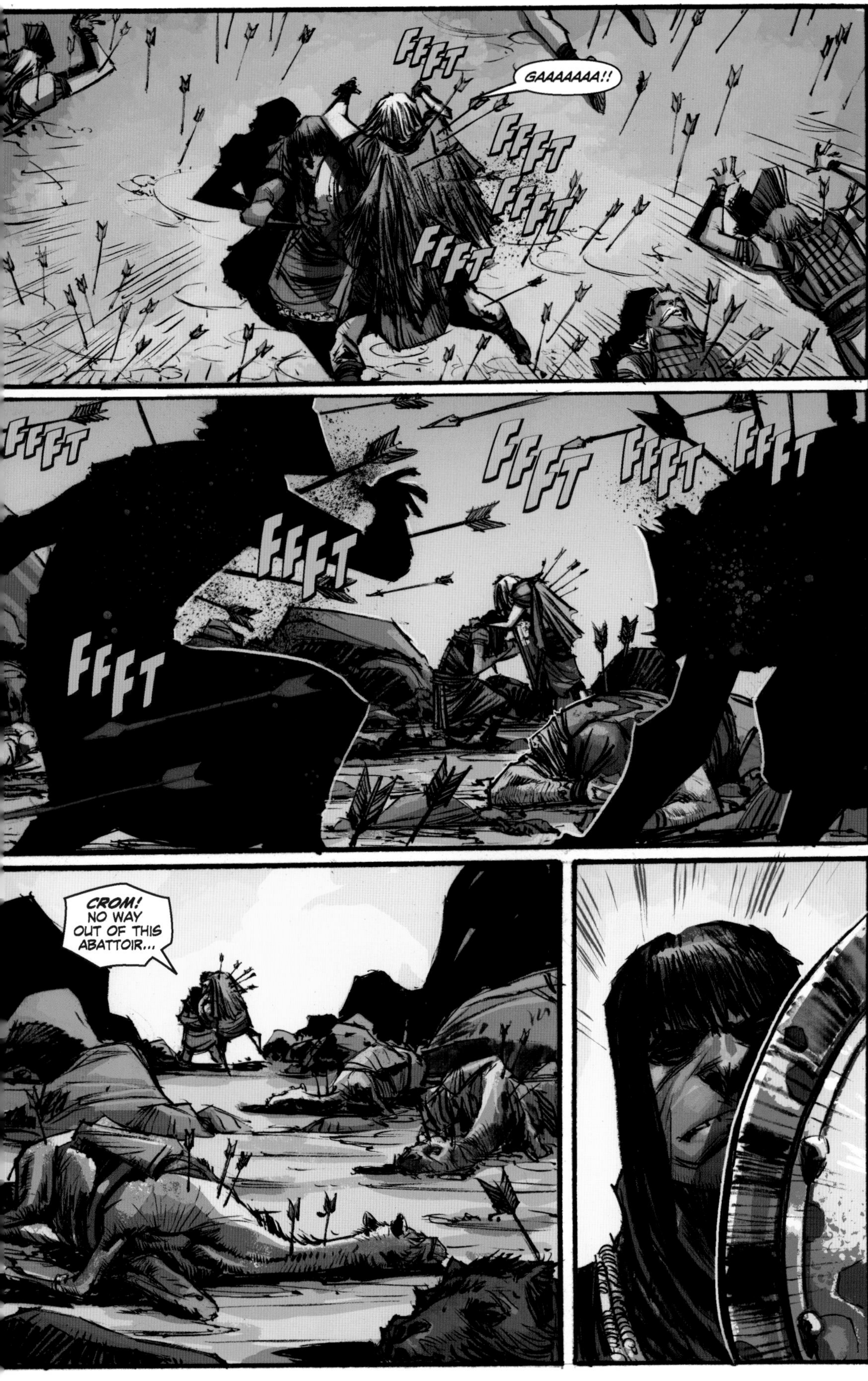
FFFT
GAAAAAAA!!
FFFT
FFFT
FFFT
FFFT
FFFT
FFFT
FFFT
FFFT
FFFT
CROM! NO WAY OUT OF THIS ABATTOIR...

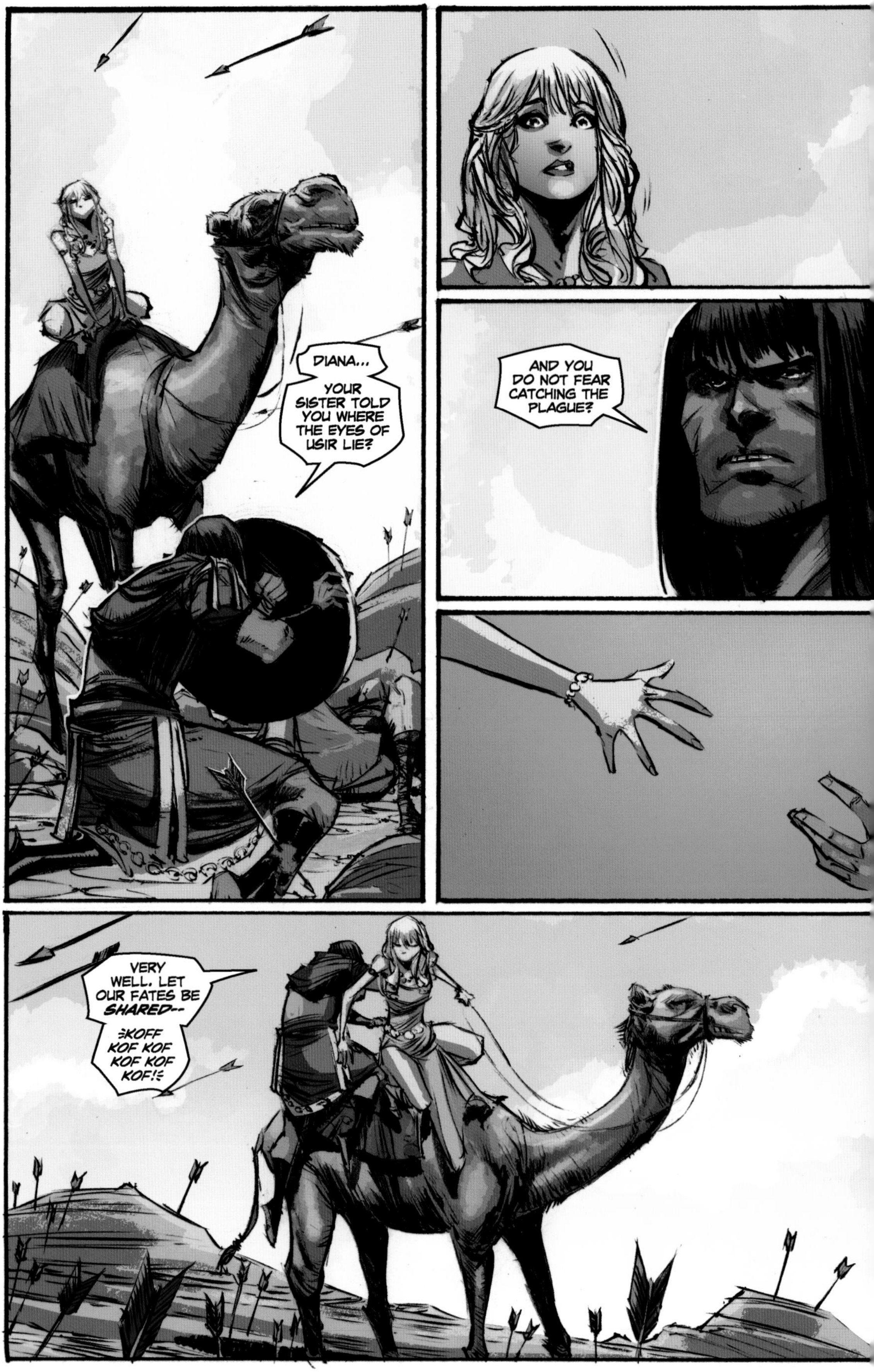

DIANA... YOUR SISTER TOLD YOU WHERE THE EYES OF USIR LIE?
AND YOU DO NOT FEAR CATCHING THE PLAGUE?
VERY WELL. LET OUR FATES BE SHARED--
⁼KOFF KOF KOF KOF KOF KOF!⁼

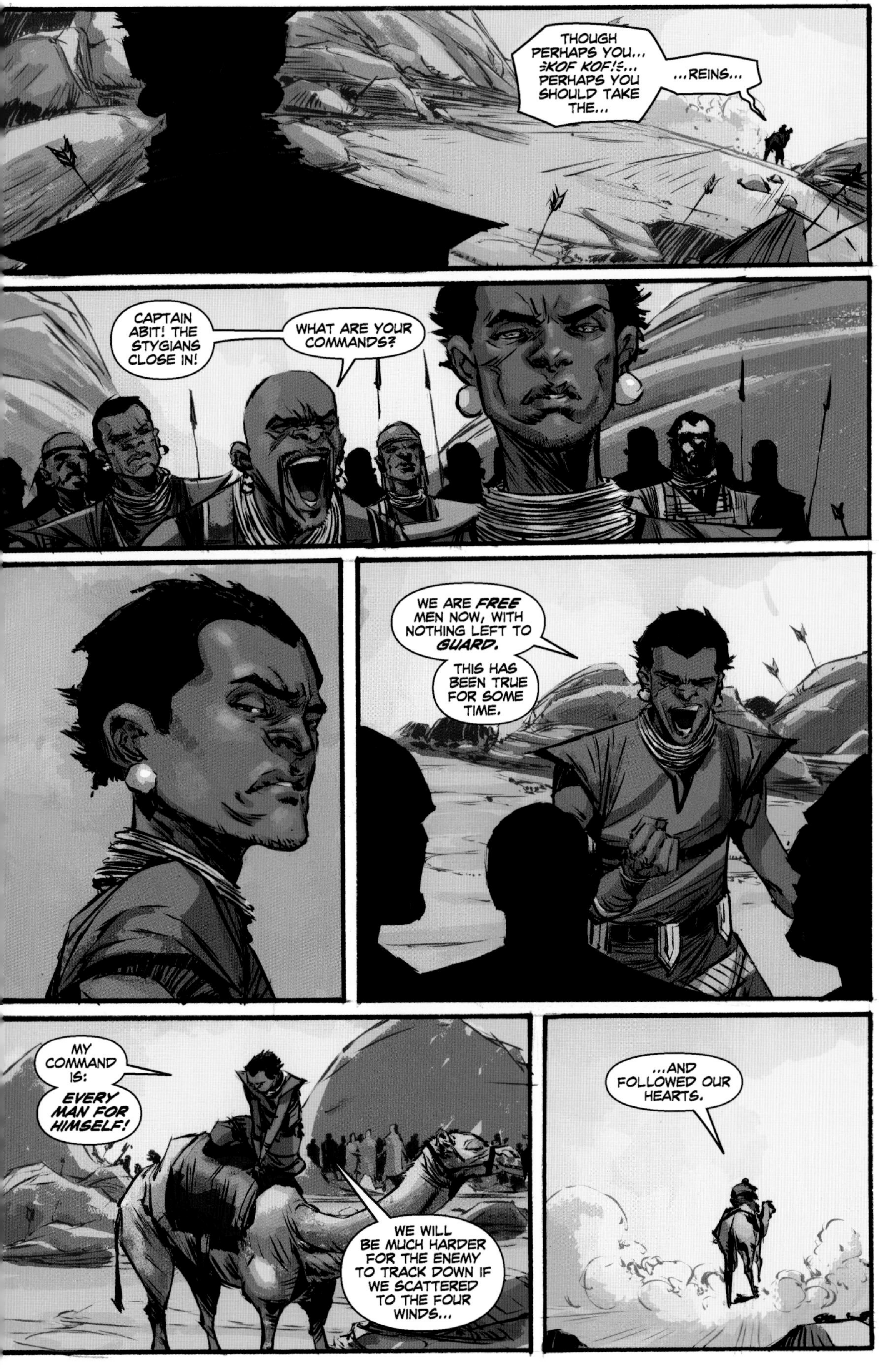
THOUGH PERHAPS YOU... *KOF KOF!*... PERHAPS YOU SHOULD TAKE THE...
...REINS...
CAPTAIN ABIT! THE STYGIANS CLOSE IN!
WHAT ARE YOUR COMMANDS?
WE ARE *FREE* MEN NOW, WITH NOTHING LEFT TO *GUARD.*
THIS HAS BEEN TRUE FOR SOME TIME.
MY COMMAND IS:
EVERY MAN FOR HIMSELF!
WE WILL BE MUCH HARDER FOR THE ENEMY TO TRACK DOWN IF WE SCATTERED TO THE FOUR WINDS...
...AND FOLLOWED OUR HEARTS.

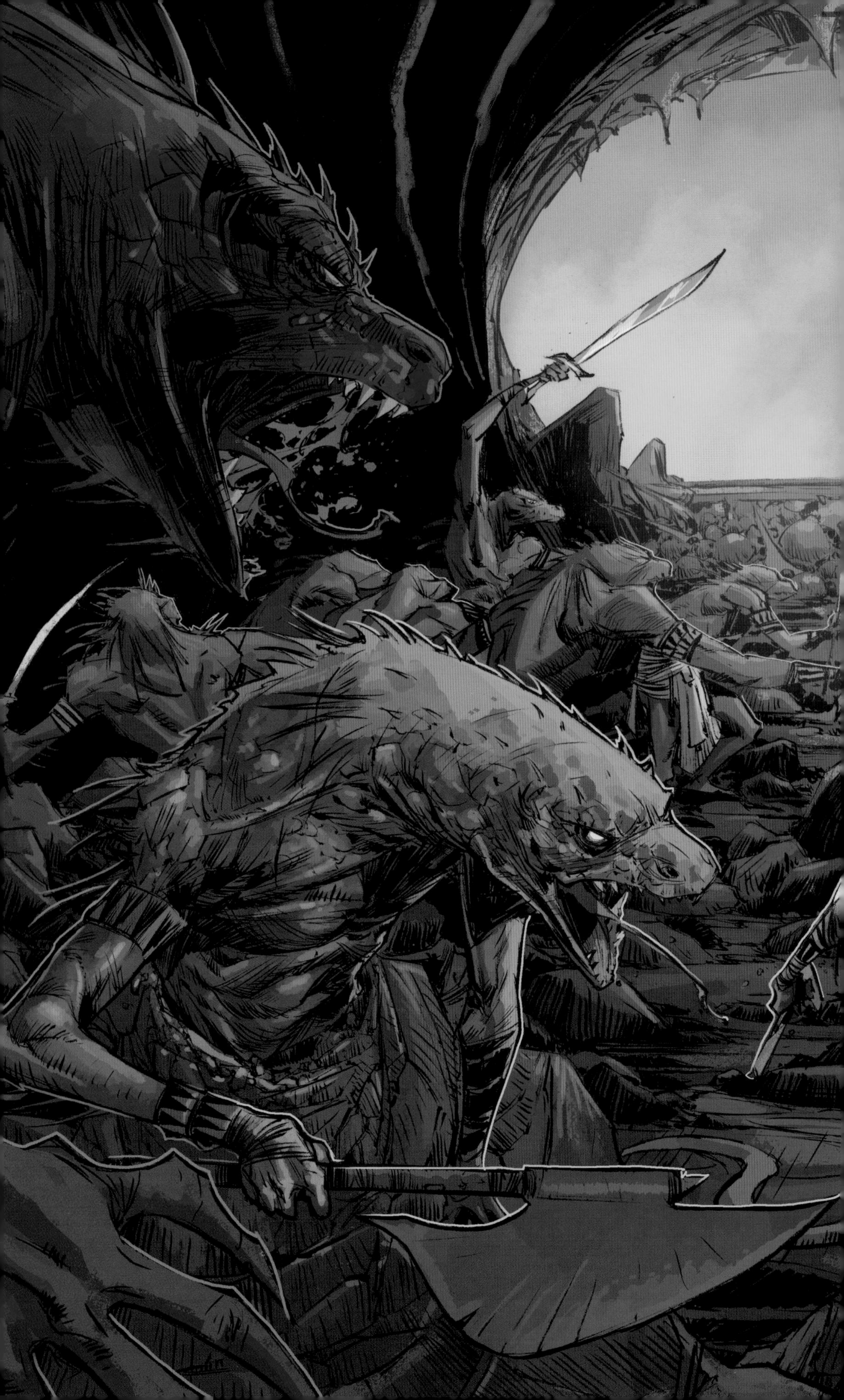

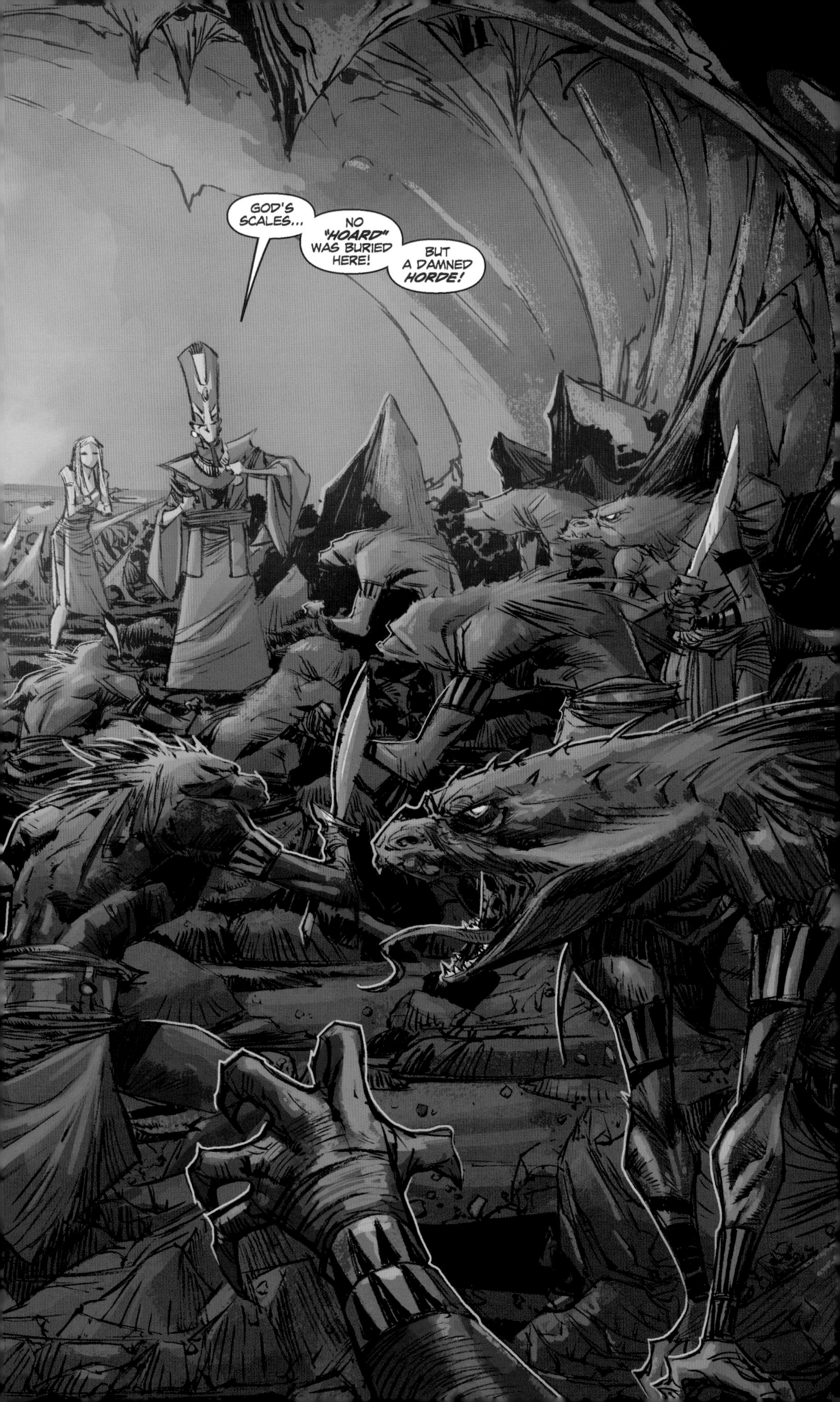
GOD'S SCALES...
NO "HOARD" WAS BURIED HERE!
BUT A DAMNED HORDE!

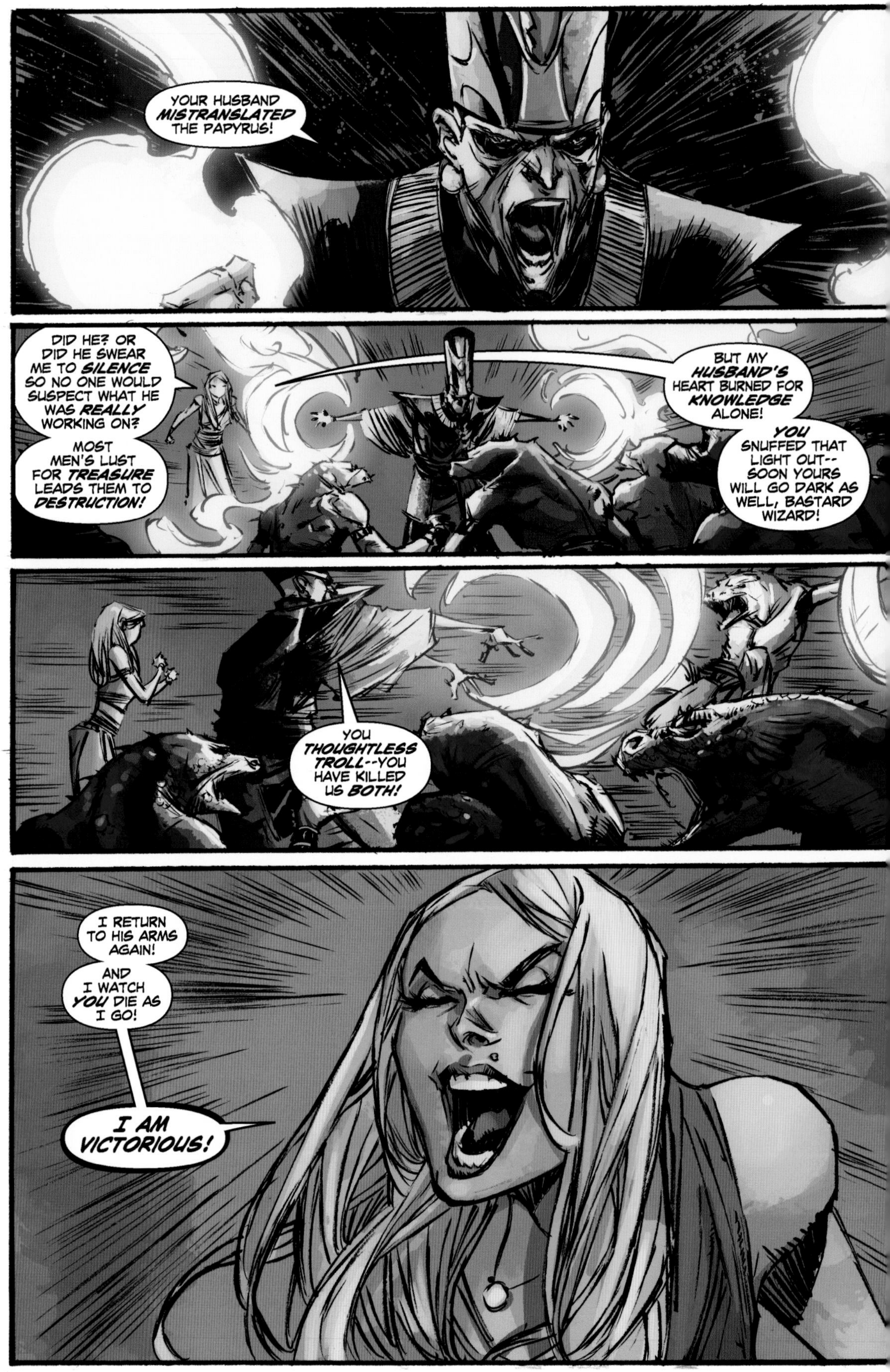
YOUR HUSBAND MISTRANSLATED THE PAPYRUS!
DID HE? OR DID HE SWEAR ME TO SILENCE SO NO ONE WOULD SUSPECT WHAT HE WAS REALLY WORKING ON?
MOST MEN'S LUST FOR TREASURE LEADS THEM TO DESTRUCTION!
BUT MY HUSBAND'S HEART BURNED FOR KNOWLEDGE ALONE!
YOU SNUFFED THAT LIGHT OUT-- SOON YOURS WILL GO DARK AS WELL, BASTARD WIZARD!
YOU THOUGHTLESS TROLL--YOU HAVE KILLED US BOTH!
I RETURN TO HIS ARMS AGAIN!
AND I WATCH YOU DIE AS I GO!
I AM VICTORIOUS!

CHAPTER SIX

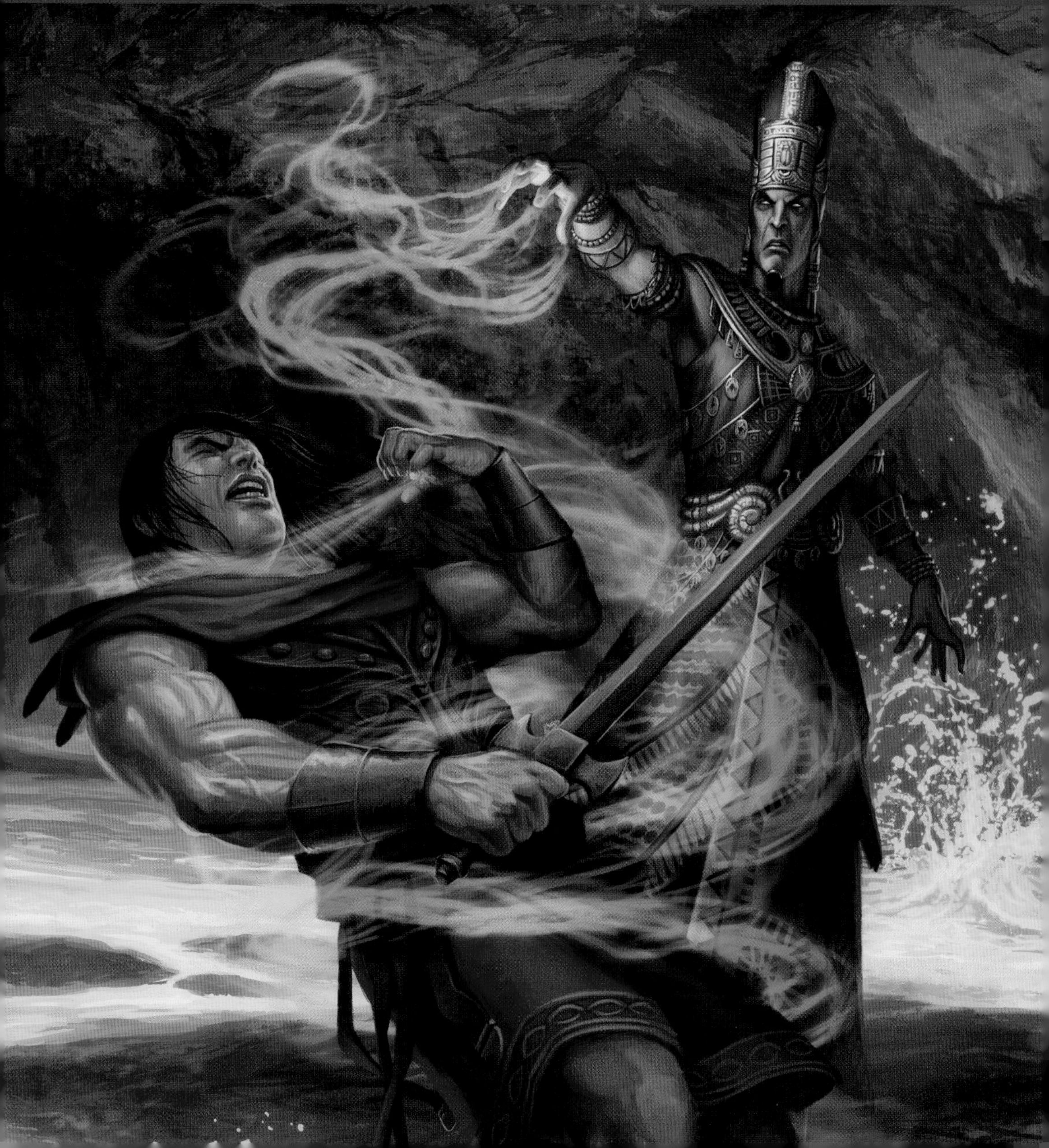

"Stygian scum! Come back here so I can properly murder you!"

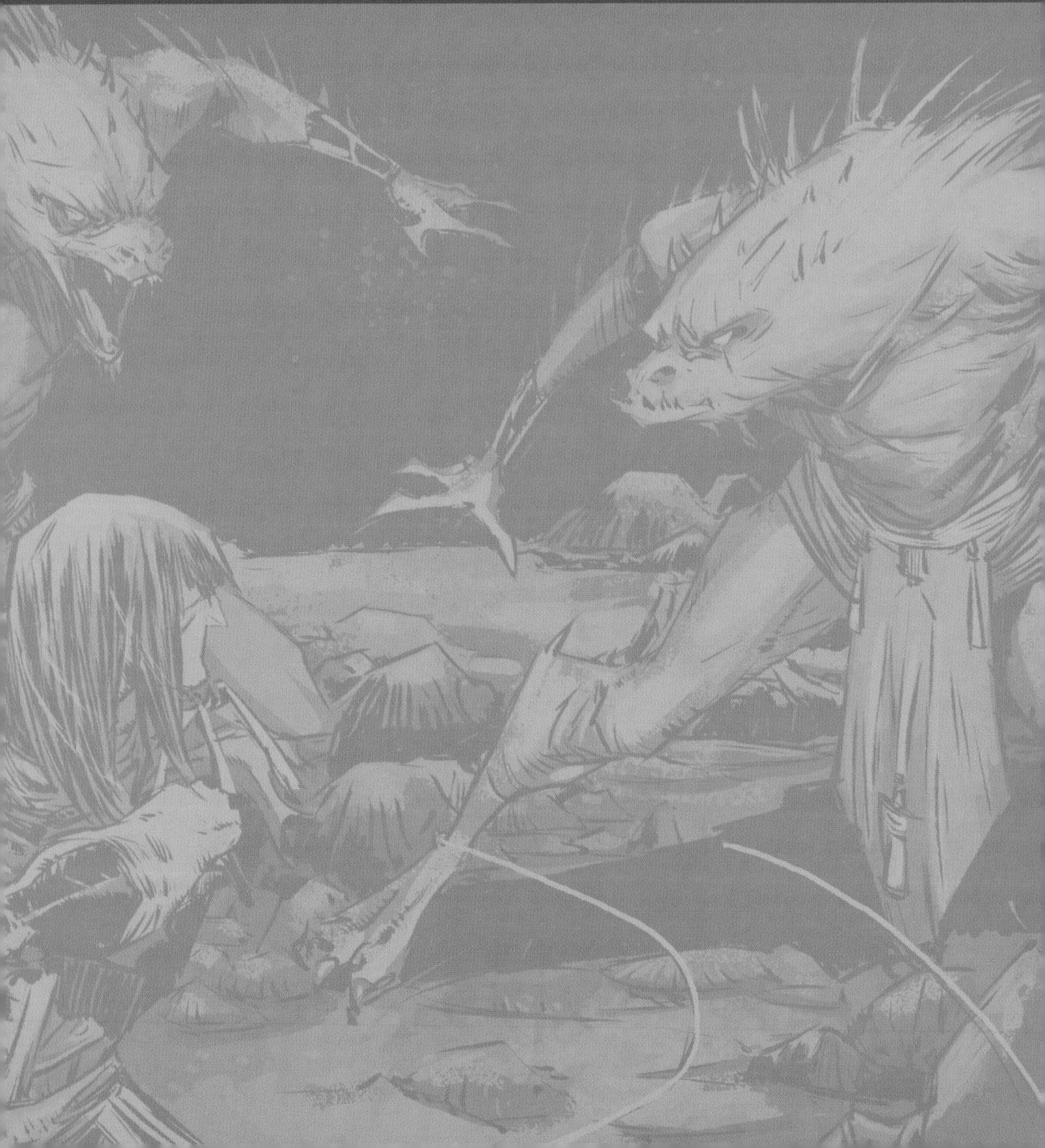

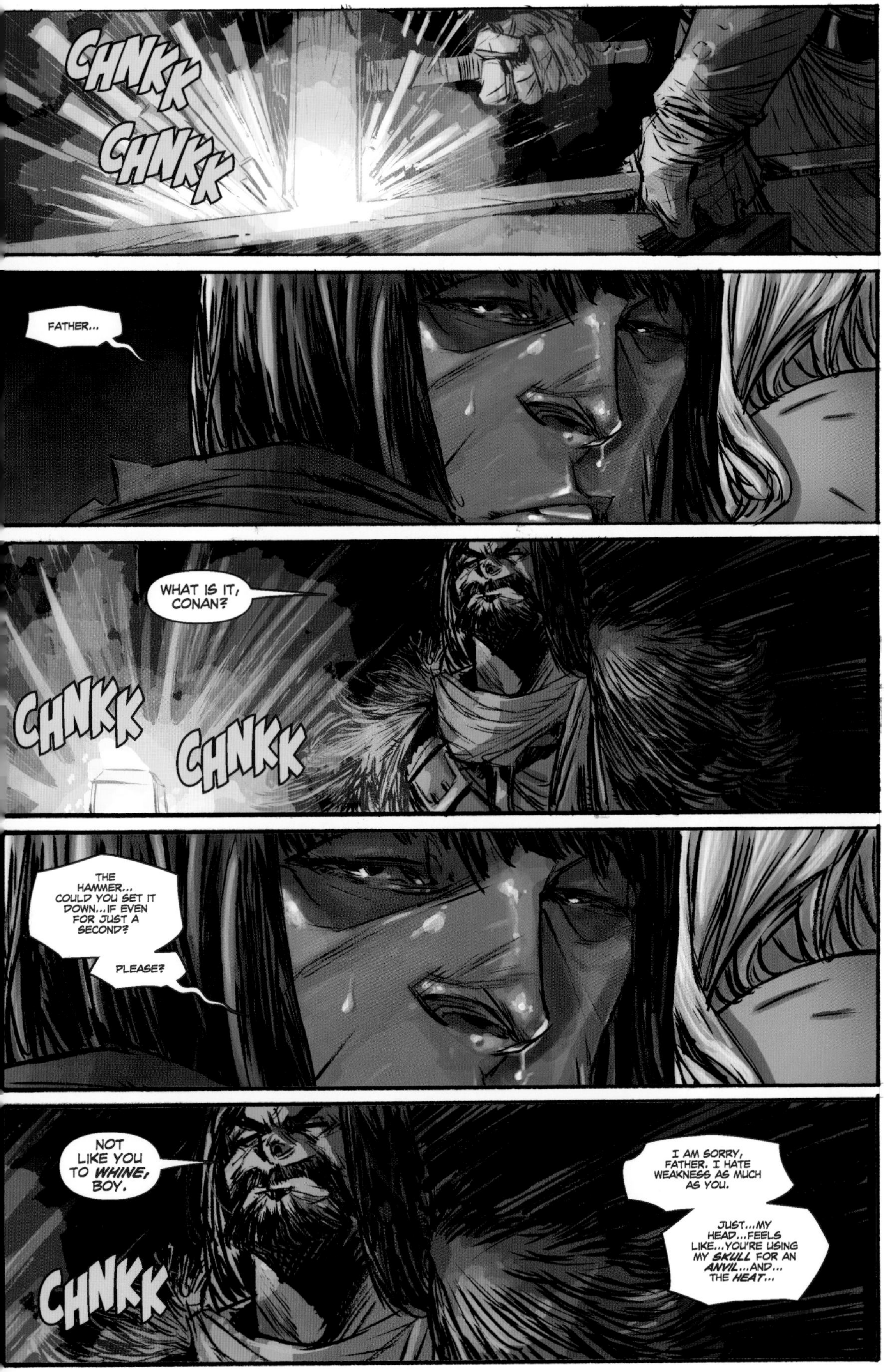
CHNKK
CHNKK
FATHER...
WHAT IS IT, CONAN?
CHNKK
CHNKK
THE HAMMER... COULD YOU SET IT DOWN...IF EVEN FOR JUST A SECOND?
PLEASE?
NOT LIKE YOU TO WHINE, BOY.
CHNKK
I AM SORRY, FATHER. I HATE WEAKNESS AS MUCH AS YOU.
JUST...MY HEAD...FEELS LIKE...YOU'RE USING MY SKULL FOR AN ANVIL...AND... THE HEAT...

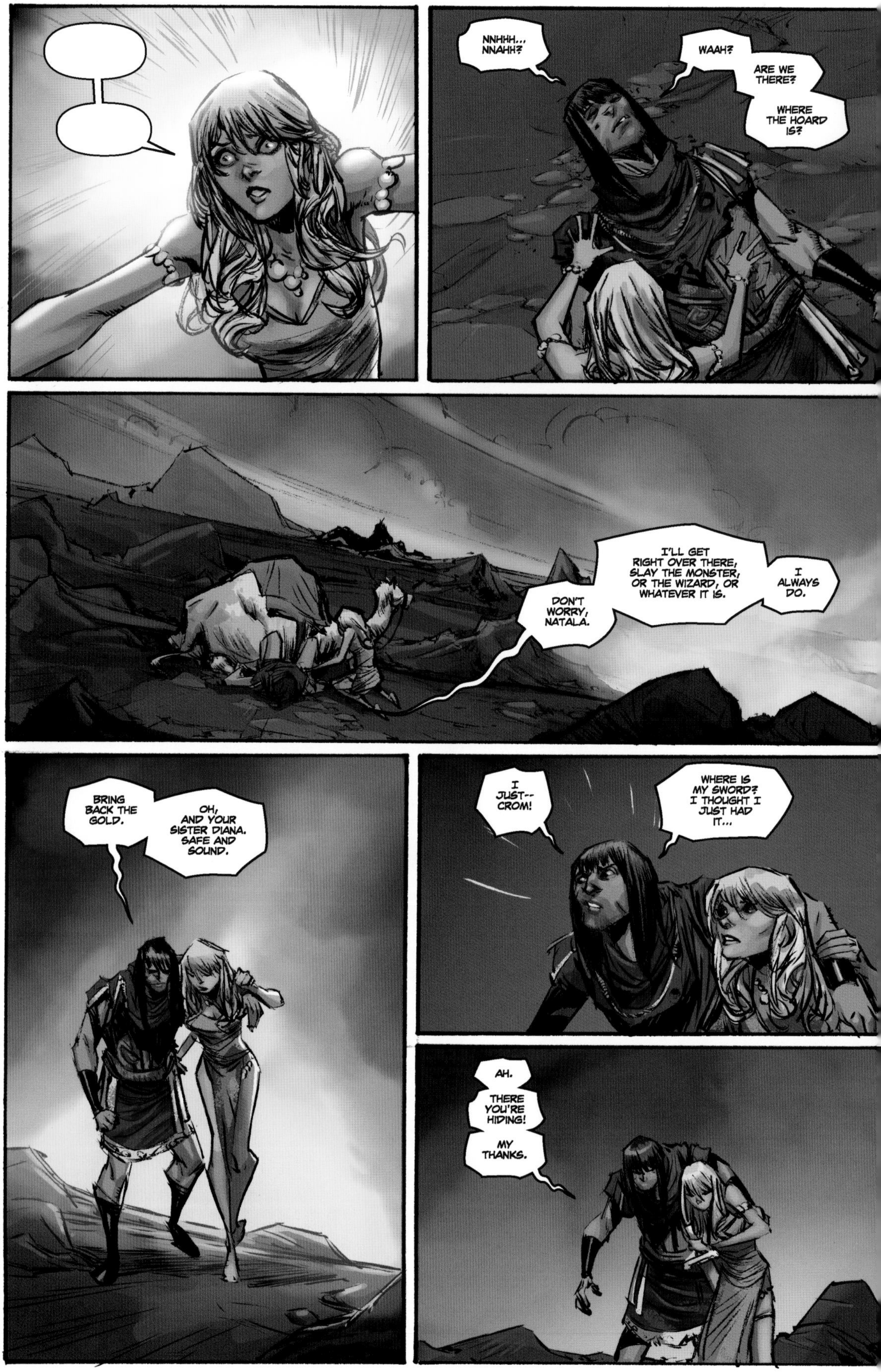
NNHHH... NNAHH?
WAAH?
ARE WE THERE?
WHERE THE HOARD IS?
DON'T WORRY, NATALA.
I'LL GET RIGHT OVER THERE, SLAY THE MONSTER, OR THE WIZARD, OR WHATEVER IT IS.
I ALWAYS DO.
BRING BACK THE GOLD.
OH, AND YOUR SISTER DIANA. SAFE AND SOUND.
I JUST-- CROM!
WHERE IS MY SWORD? I THOUGHT I JUST HAD IT...
AH.
THERE YOU'RE HIDING!
MY THANKS.

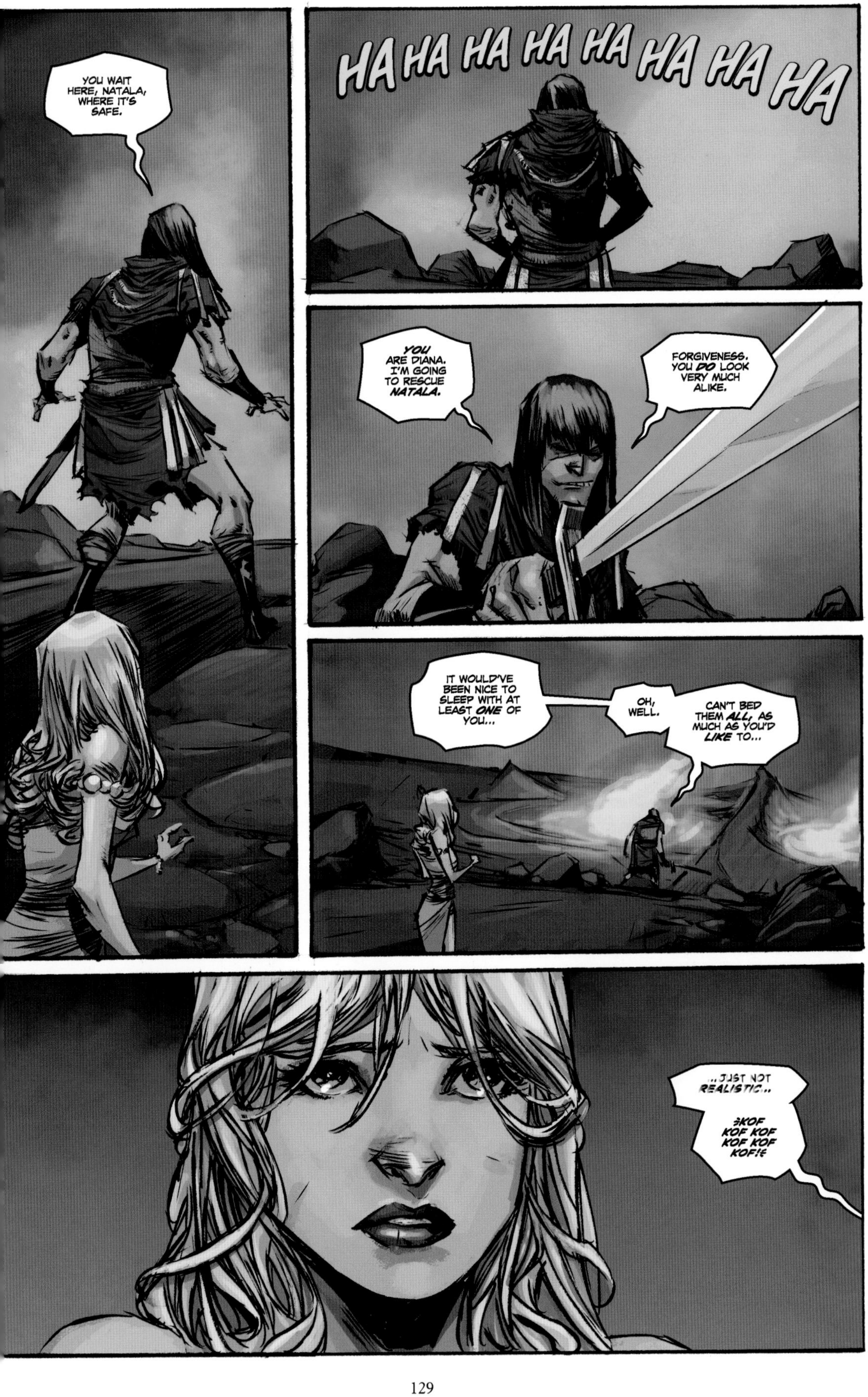
YOU WAIT HERE, NATALA, WHERE IT'S SAFE.
HA HA HA HA HA HA HA HA HA
YOU ARE DIANA. I'M GOING TO RESCUE NATALA.
FORGIVENESS. YOU DO LOOK VERY MUCH ALIKE.
IT WOULD'VE BEEN NICE TO SLEEP WITH AT LEAST ONE OF YOU...
OH, WELL.
CAN'T BED THEM ALL, AS MUCH AS YOU'D LIKE TO...
...JUST NOT REALISTIC...
KOF KOF KOF KOF KOF KOF!

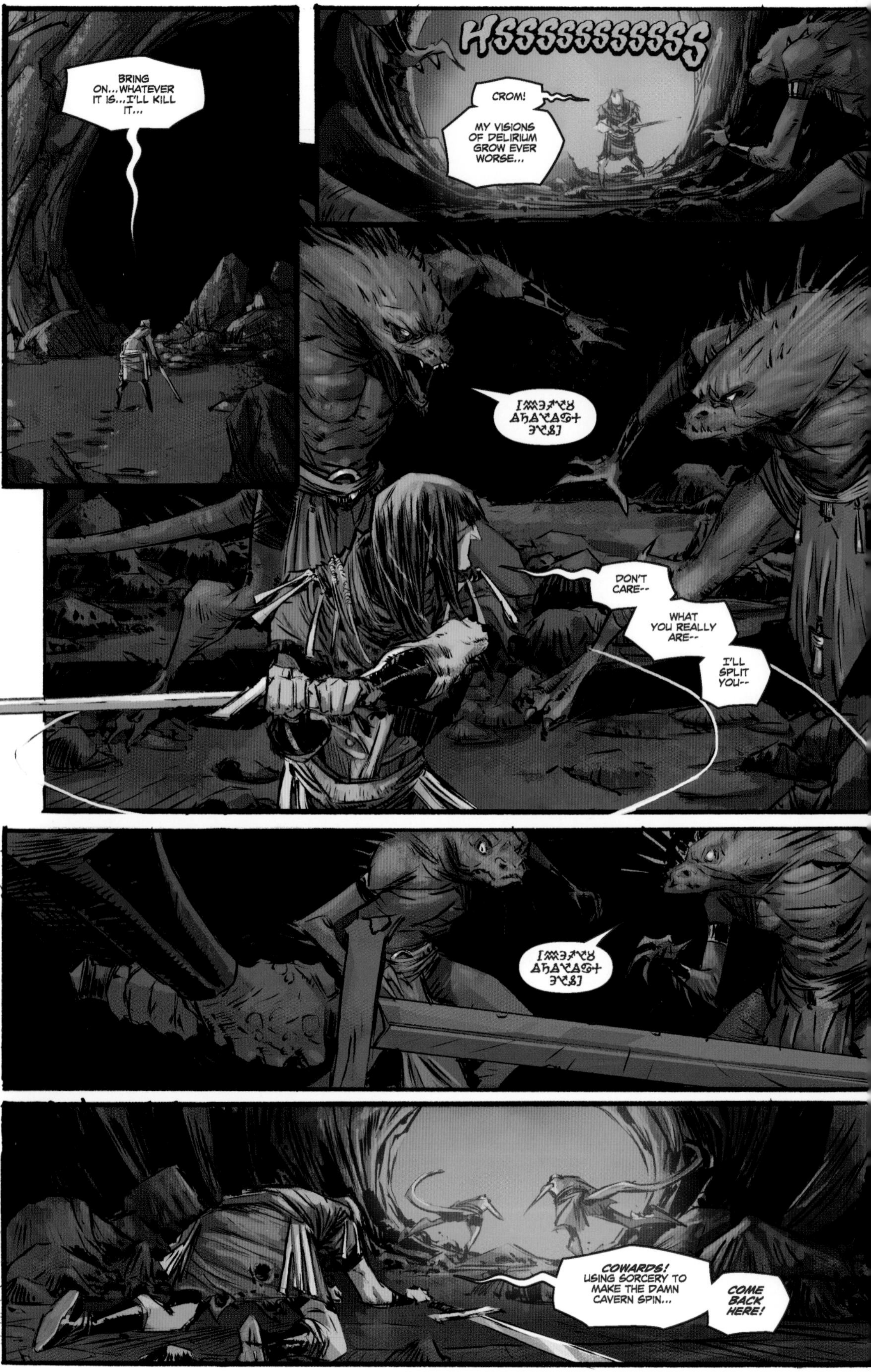
BRING ON...WHATEVER IT IS...I'LL KILL IT...
HSSSSSSSSSSS
CROM!
MY VISIONS OF DELIRIUM GROW EVER WORSE...
DON'T CARE--
WHAT YOU REALLY ARE--
I'LL SPLIT YOU--
COWARDS! USING SORCERY TO MAKE THE DAMN CAVERN SPIN...
COME BACK HERE!

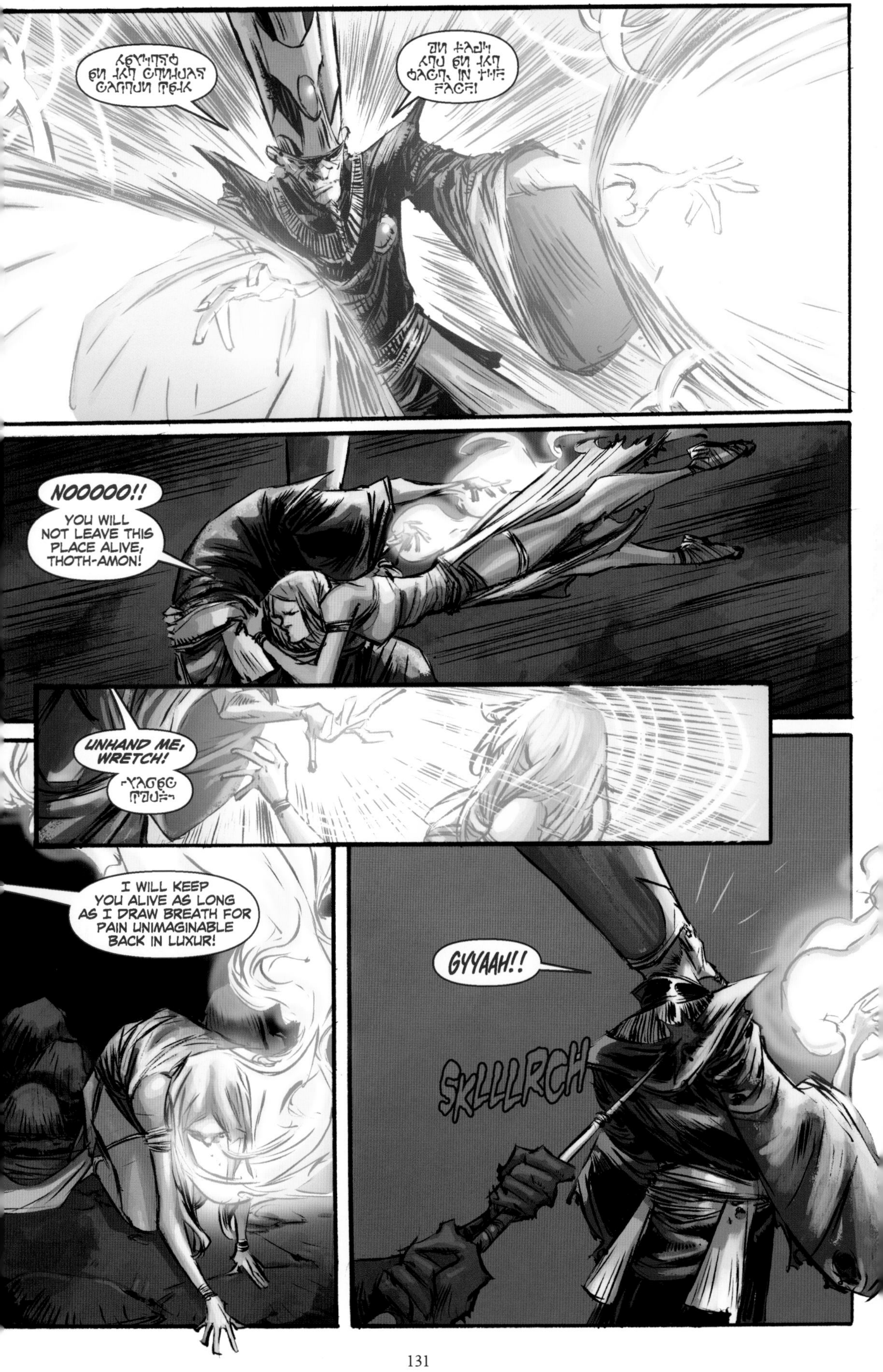
NOOOOO!!
YOU WILL NOT LEAVE THIS PLACE ALIVE, THOTH-AMON!
UNHAND ME, WRETCH!
I WILL KEEP YOU ALIVE AS LONG AS I DRAW BREATH FOR PAIN UNIMAGINABLE BACK IN LUXUR!
GYYAAH!!
SKLLLRCH

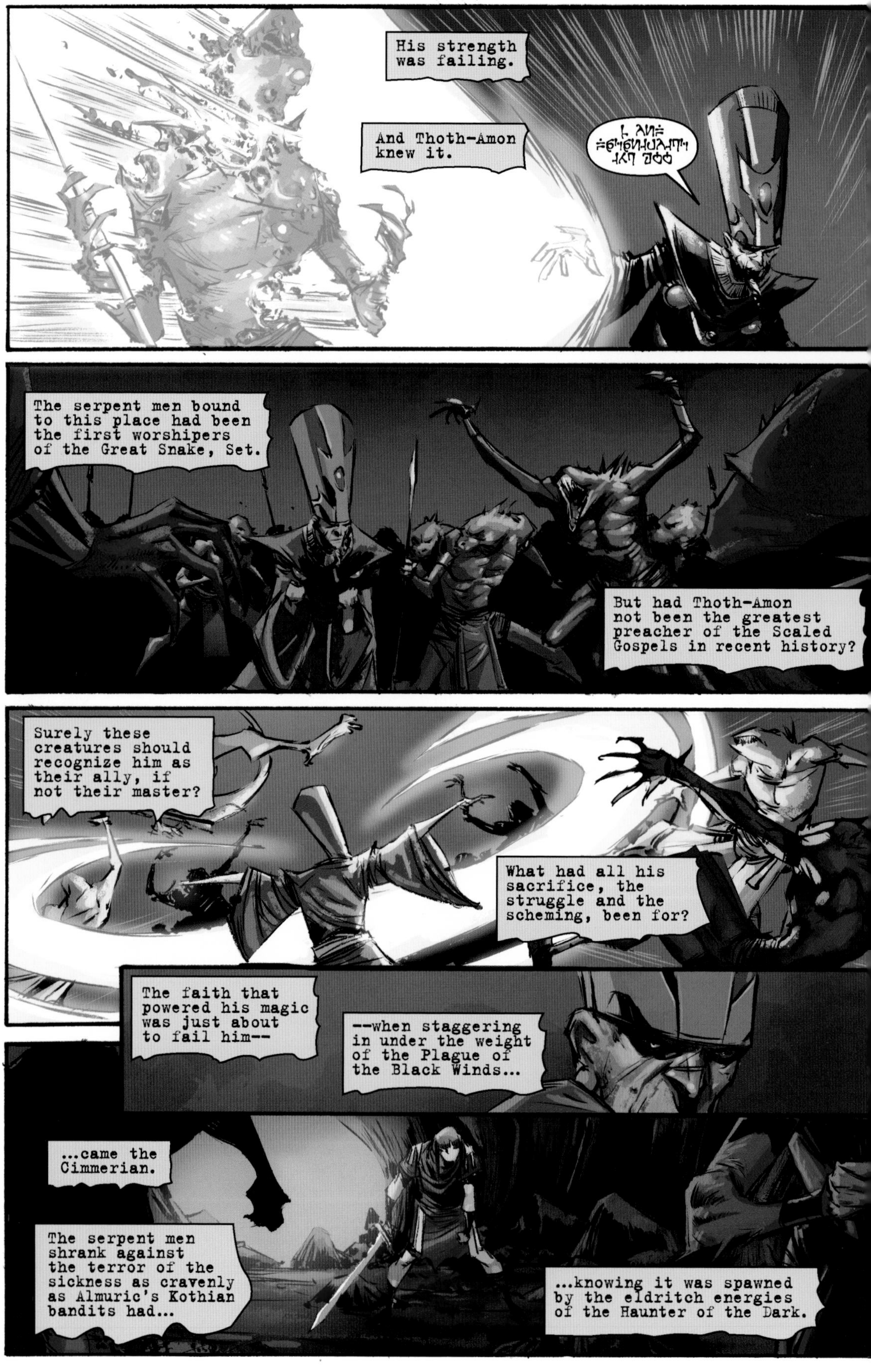
His strength was failing.
And Thoth-Amon knew it.
The serpent men bound to this place had been the first worshipers of the Great Snake, Set.
But had Thoth-Amon not been the greatest preacher of the Scaled Gospels in recent history?
Surely these creatures should recognize him as their ally, if not their master?
What had all his sacrifice, the struggle and the scheming, been for?
The faith that powered his magic was just about to fail him--
--when staggering in under the weight of the Plague of the Black Winds...
...came the Cimmerian.
The serpent men shrank against the terror of the sickness as cravenly as Almuric's Kothian bandits had...
...knowing it was spawned by the eldritch energies of the Haunter of the Dark.

And Thoth-Amon's breast surged with the power and the glory of infernal grace renewed.

ᒧᕮᑕᐟ ᙔᓯᐢᗡ ᗡᑊᕼᓵ ᗡᕳ ᑕᗡᕼᐱᐢᓵᕲ ᕲᗡ

GGGK!

For he recalled that Father Set admired--nay, acknowledged--but one thing, and one thing only:

Power!

POWER!

Alas.

He drew all the energy he could from Conan's mystic sickness.

It was still not enough.

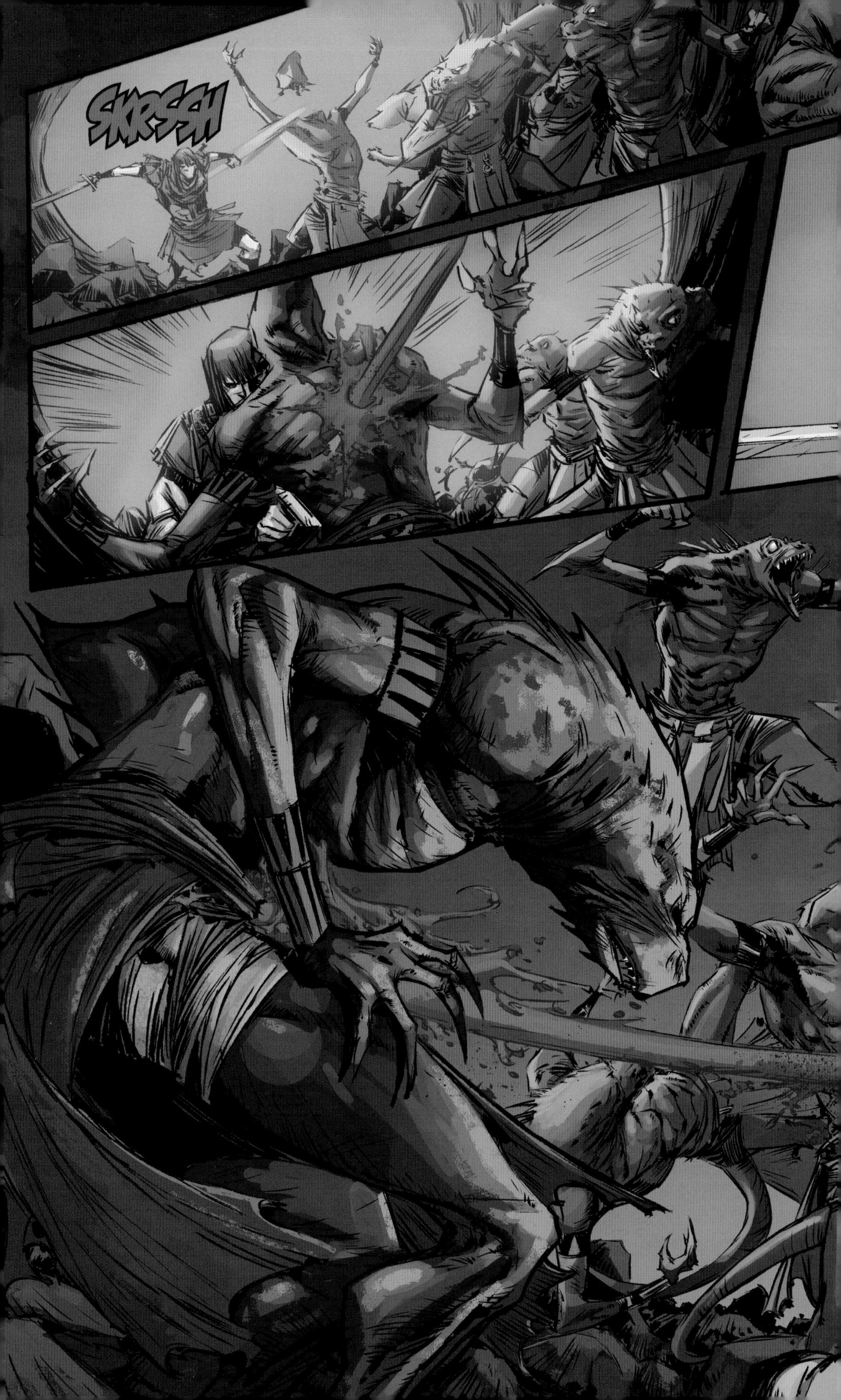
SKRSSH

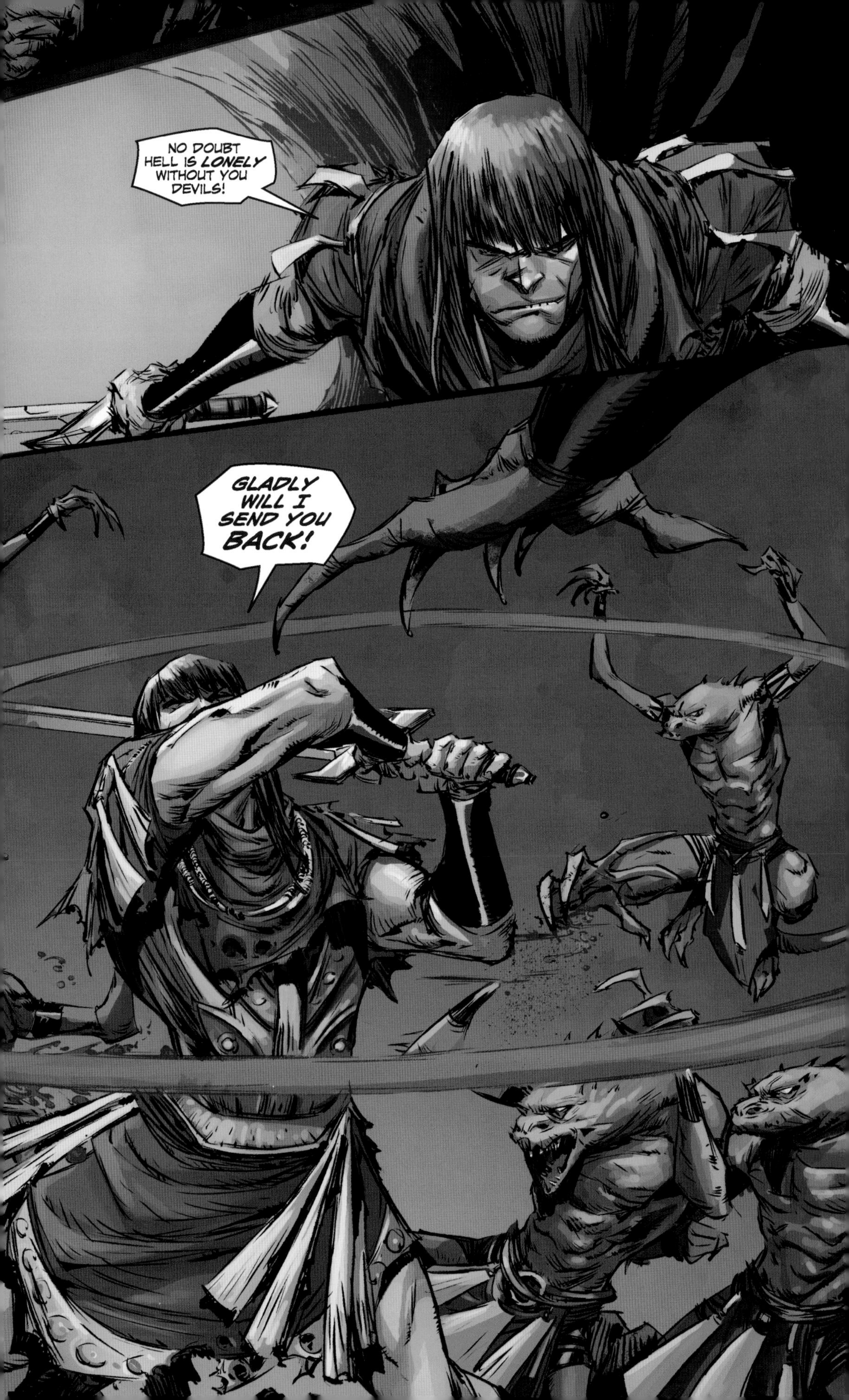
NO DOUBT HELL IS LONELY WITHOUT YOU DEVILS!
GLADLY WILL I SEND YOU BACK!

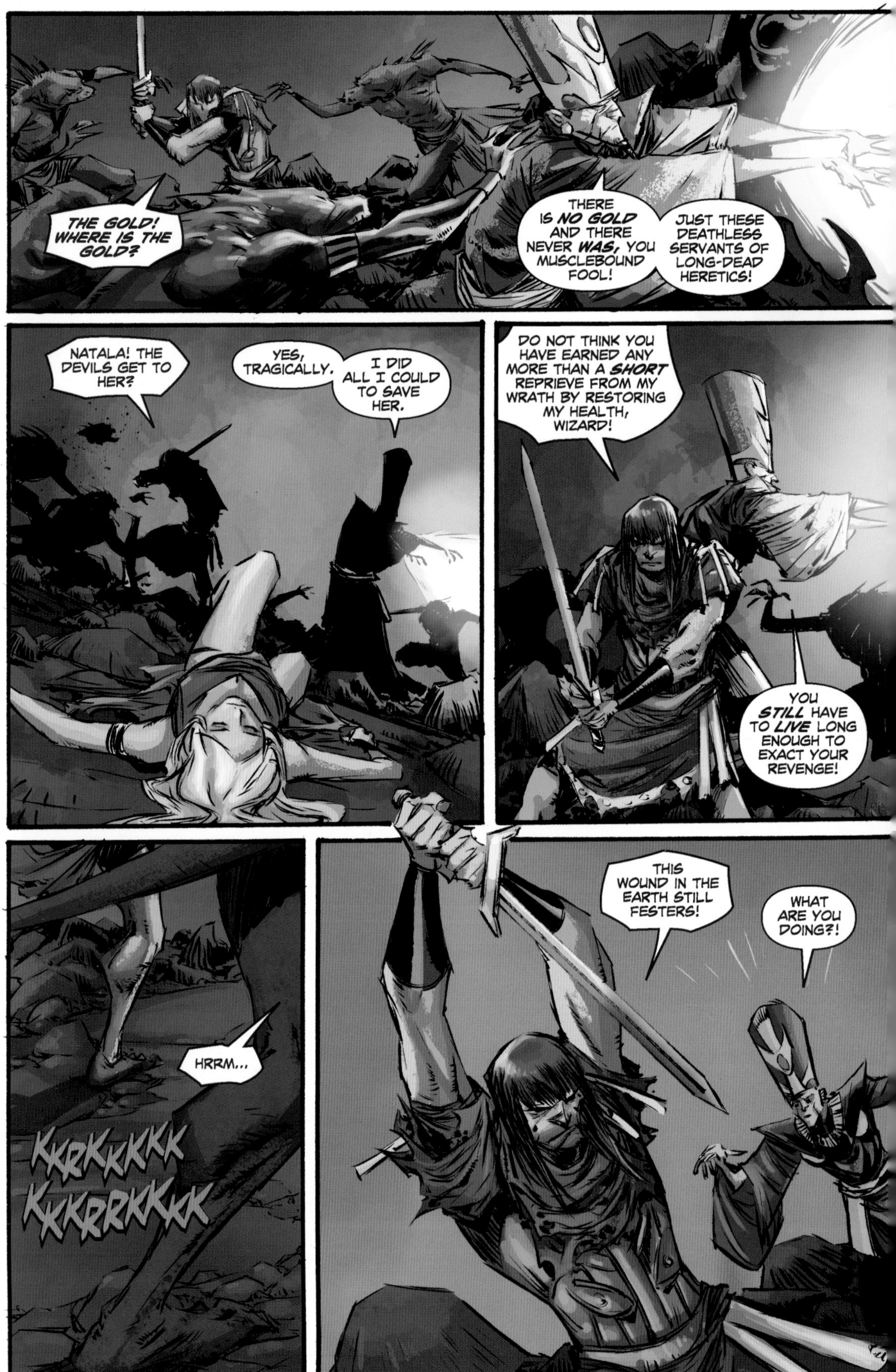
THE GOLD! WHERE IS THE GOLD?
THERE IS NO GOLD AND THERE NEVER WAS, YOU MUSCLEBOUND FOOL!
JUST THESE DEATHLESS SERVANTS OF LONG-DEAD HERETICS!
NATALA! THE DEVILS GET TO HER?
YES, TRAGICALLY.
I DID ALL I COULD TO SAVE HER.
DO NOT THINK YOU HAVE EARNED ANY MORE THAN A SHORT REPRIEVE FROM MY WRATH BY RESTORING MY HEALTH, WIZARD!
YOU STILL HAVE TO LIVE LONG ENOUGH TO EXACT YOUR REVENGE!
HRRM...
KKRKKKKK
KKKRRKKKK
THIS WOUND IN THE EARTH STILL FESTERS!
WHAT ARE YOU DOING?!

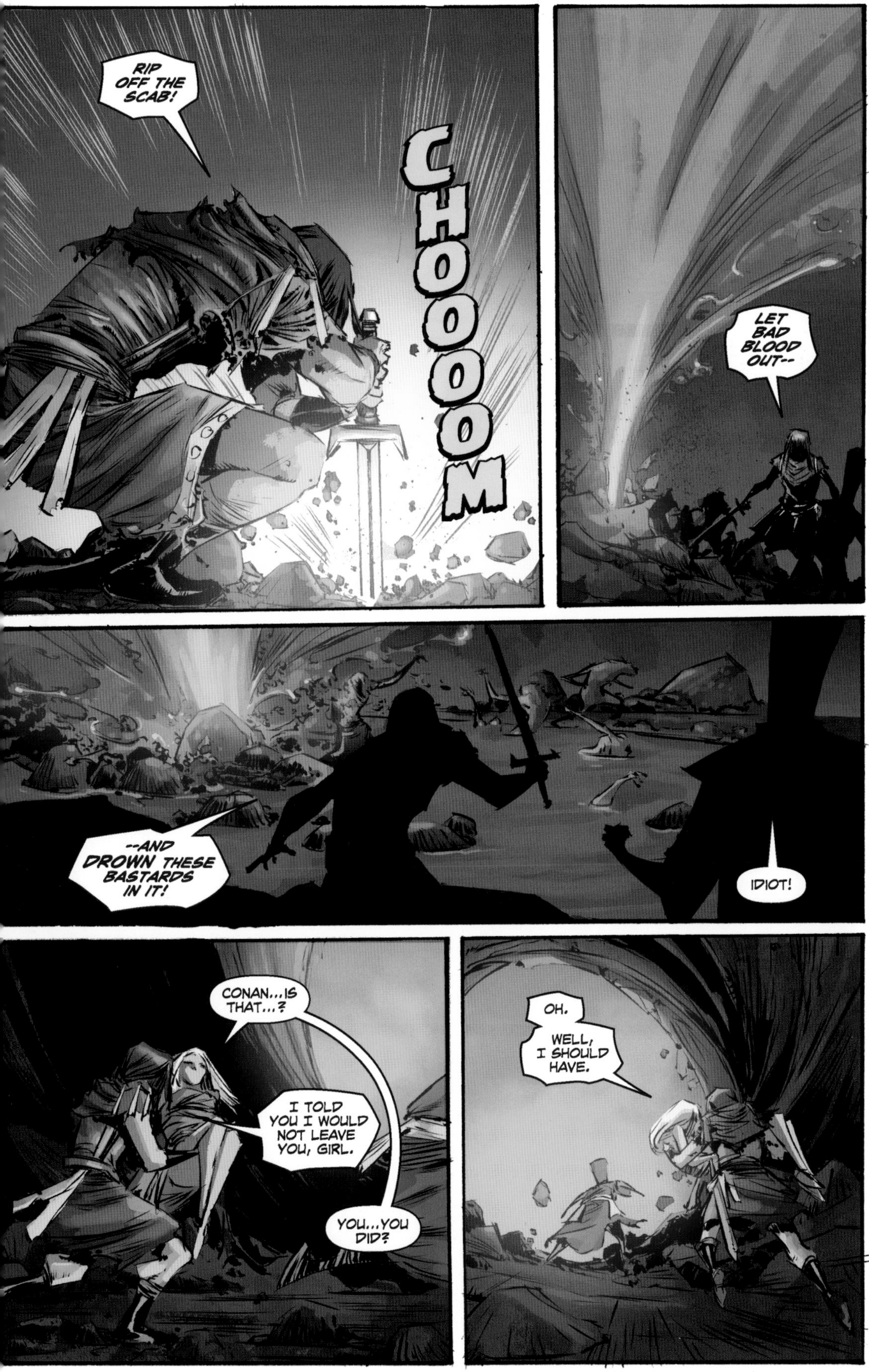
RIP OFF THE SCAB!
CHOOOOM
LET BAD BLOOD OUT--
--AND DROWN THESE BASTARDS IN IT!
IDIOT!
CONAN...IS THAT...?
I TOLD YOU I WOULD NOT LEAVE YOU, GIRL.
YOU...YOU DID?
OH.
WELL, I SHOULD HAVE.

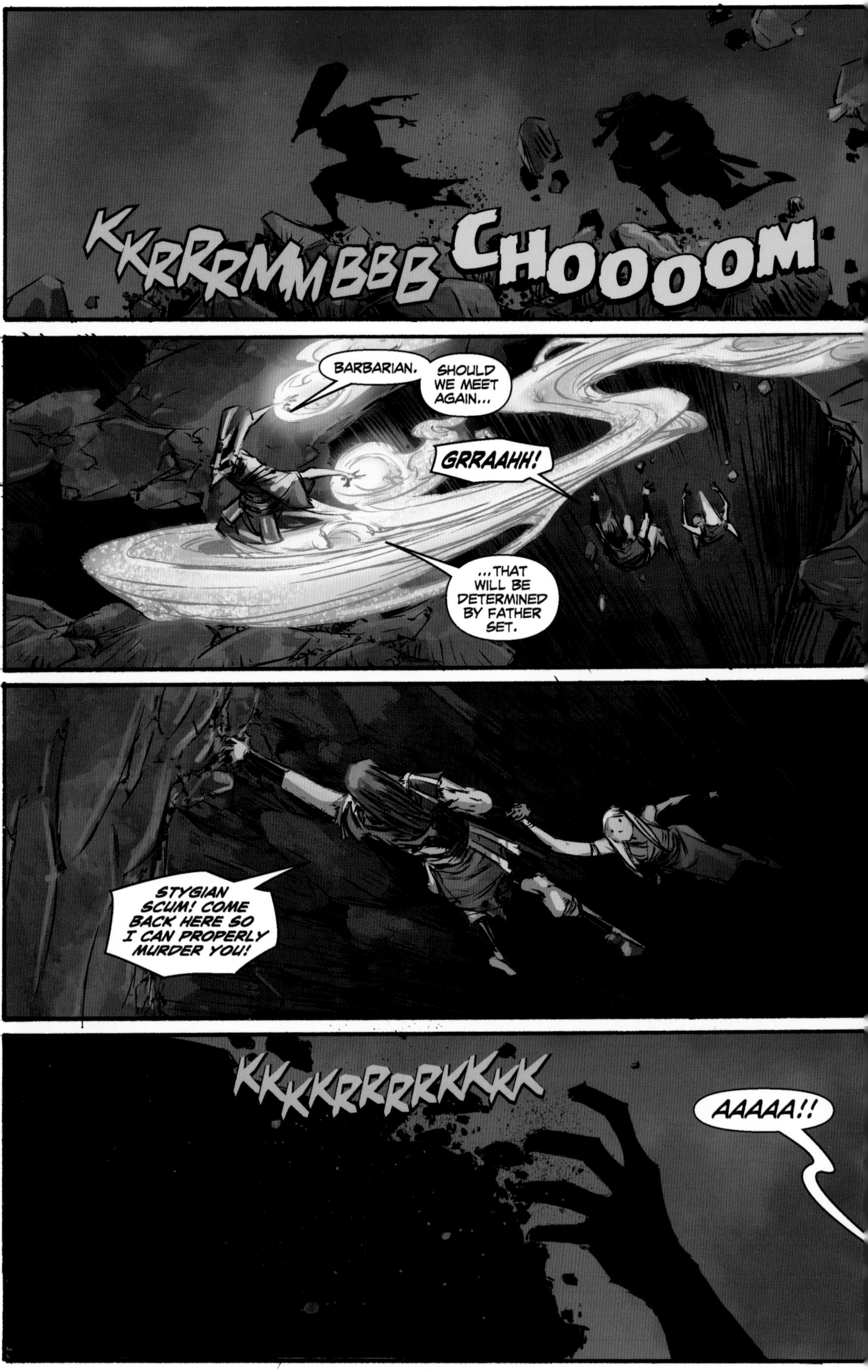
KKRRRMMBBB
CHOOOOM
BARBARIAN.
SHOULD WE MEET AGAIN...
GRRAAHH!
...THAT WILL BE DETERMINED BY FATHER SET.
STYGIAN SCUM! COME BACK HERE SO I CAN PROPERLY MURDER YOU!
KKKKRRRRKKKK
AAAAA!!

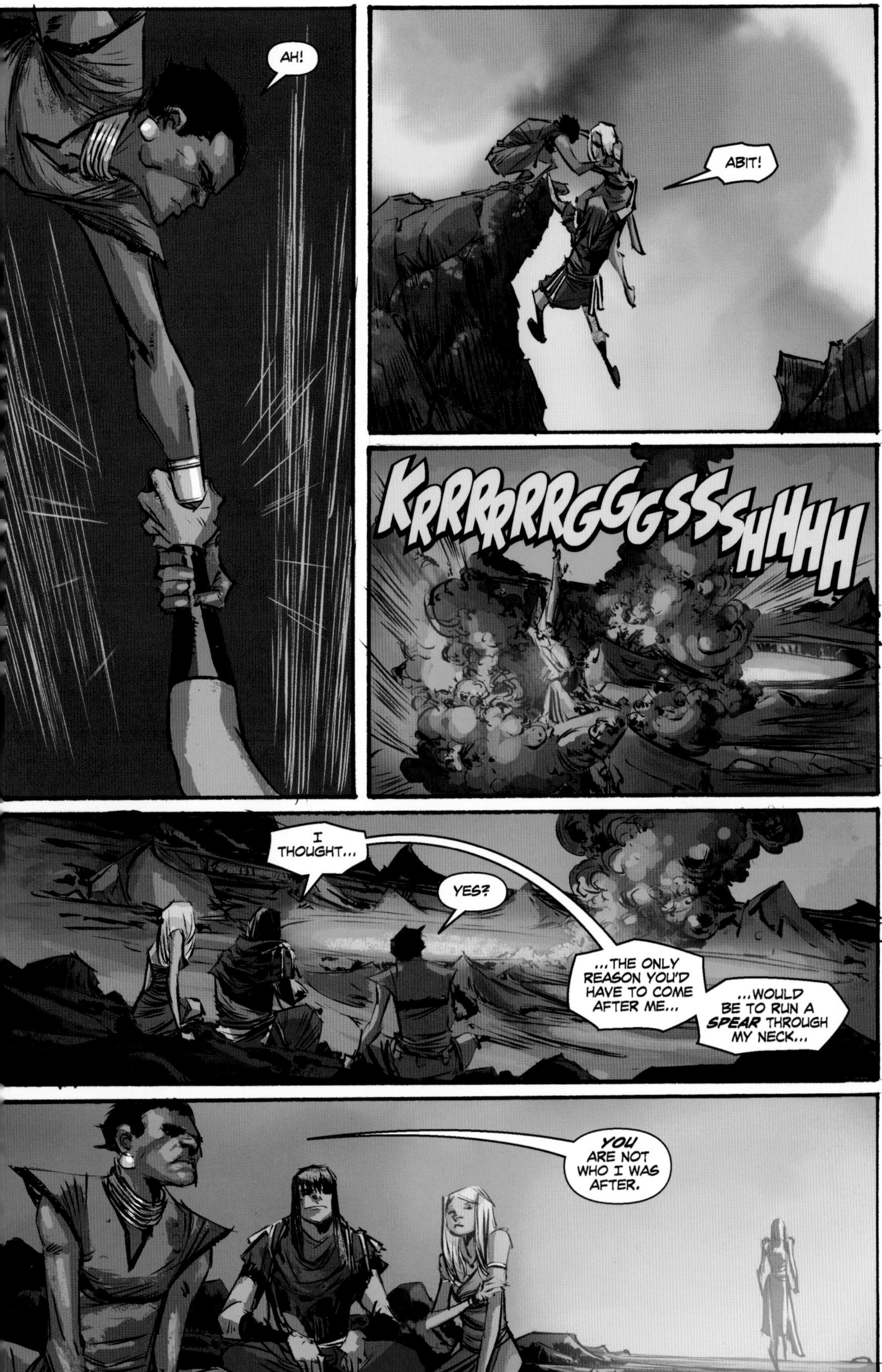
AH!
ABIT!
KRRRRRRGGGSSSHHHH
I THOUGHT...
YES?
...THE ONLY REASON YOU'D HAVE TO COME AFTER ME...
...WOULD BE TO RUN A SPEAR THROUGH MY NECK...
YOU ARE NOT WHO I WAS AFTER.

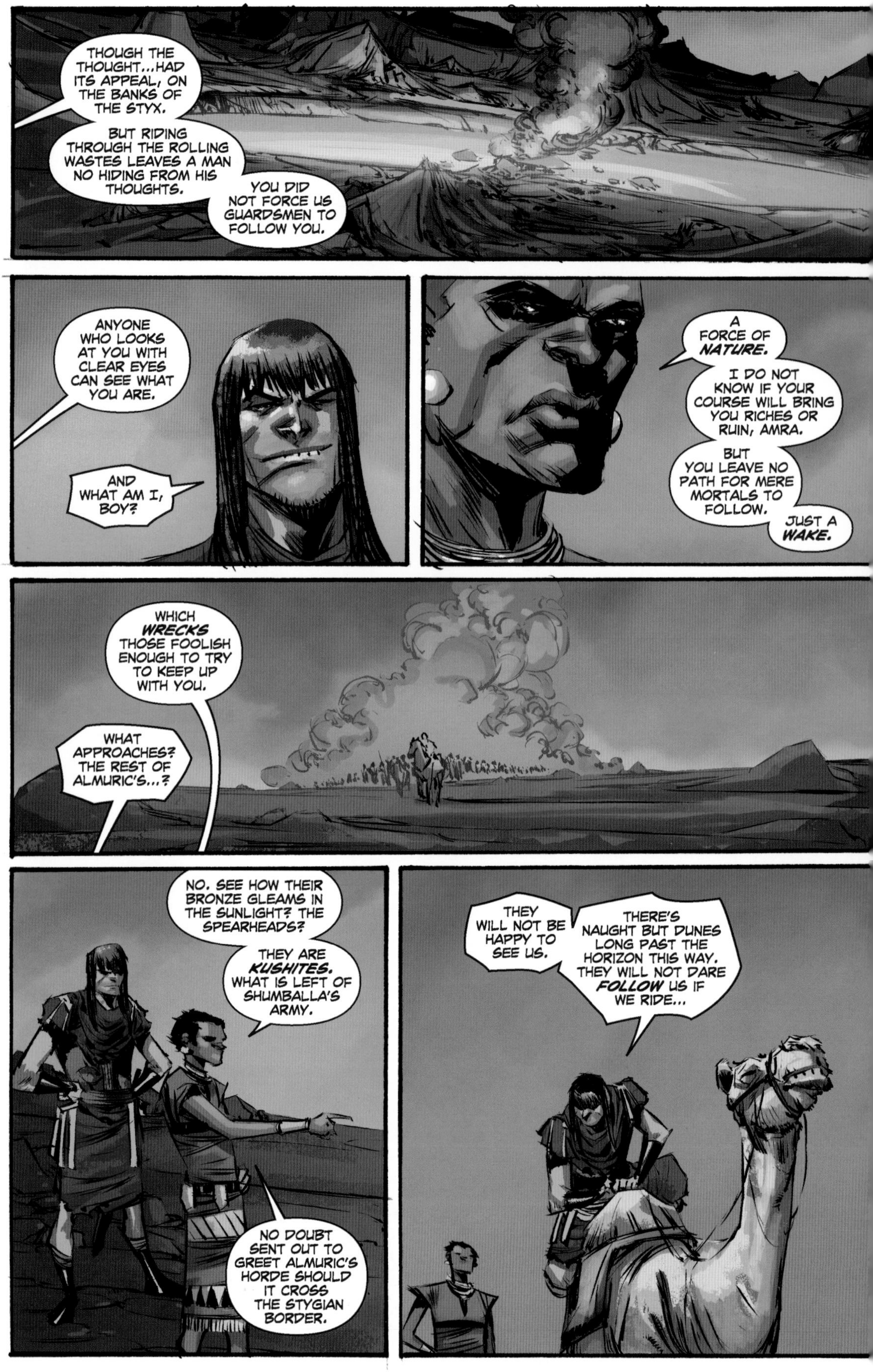
THOUGH THE THOUGHT...HAD ITS APPEAL, ON THE BANKS OF THE STYX.
BUT RIDING THROUGH THE ROLLING WASTES LEAVES A MAN NO HIDING FROM HIS THOUGHTS.
YOU DID NOT FORCE US GUARDSMEN TO FOLLOW YOU.
ANYONE WHO LOOKS AT YOU WITH CLEAR EYES CAN SEE WHAT YOU ARE.
AND WHAT AM I, BOY?
A FORCE OF NATURE.
I DO NOT KNOW IF YOUR COURSE WILL BRING YOU RICHES OR RUIN, AMRA.
BUT YOU LEAVE NO PATH FOR MERE MORTALS TO FOLLOW.
JUST A WAKE.
WHICH WRECKS THOSE FOOLISH ENOUGH TO TRY TO KEEP UP WITH YOU.
WHAT APPROACHES? THE REST OF ALMURIC'S...?
NO. SEE HOW THEIR BRONZE GLEAMS IN THE SUNLIGHT? THE SPEARHEADS?
THEY ARE KUSHITES. WHAT IS LEFT OF SHUMBALLA'S ARMY.
NO DOUBT SENT OUT TO GREET ALMURIC'S HORDE SHOULD IT CROSS THE STYGIAN BORDER.
THEY WILL NOT BE HAPPY TO SEE US.
THERE'S NAUGHT BUT DUNES LONG PAST THE HORIZON THIS WAY. THEY WILL NOT DARE FOLLOW US IF WE RIDE...

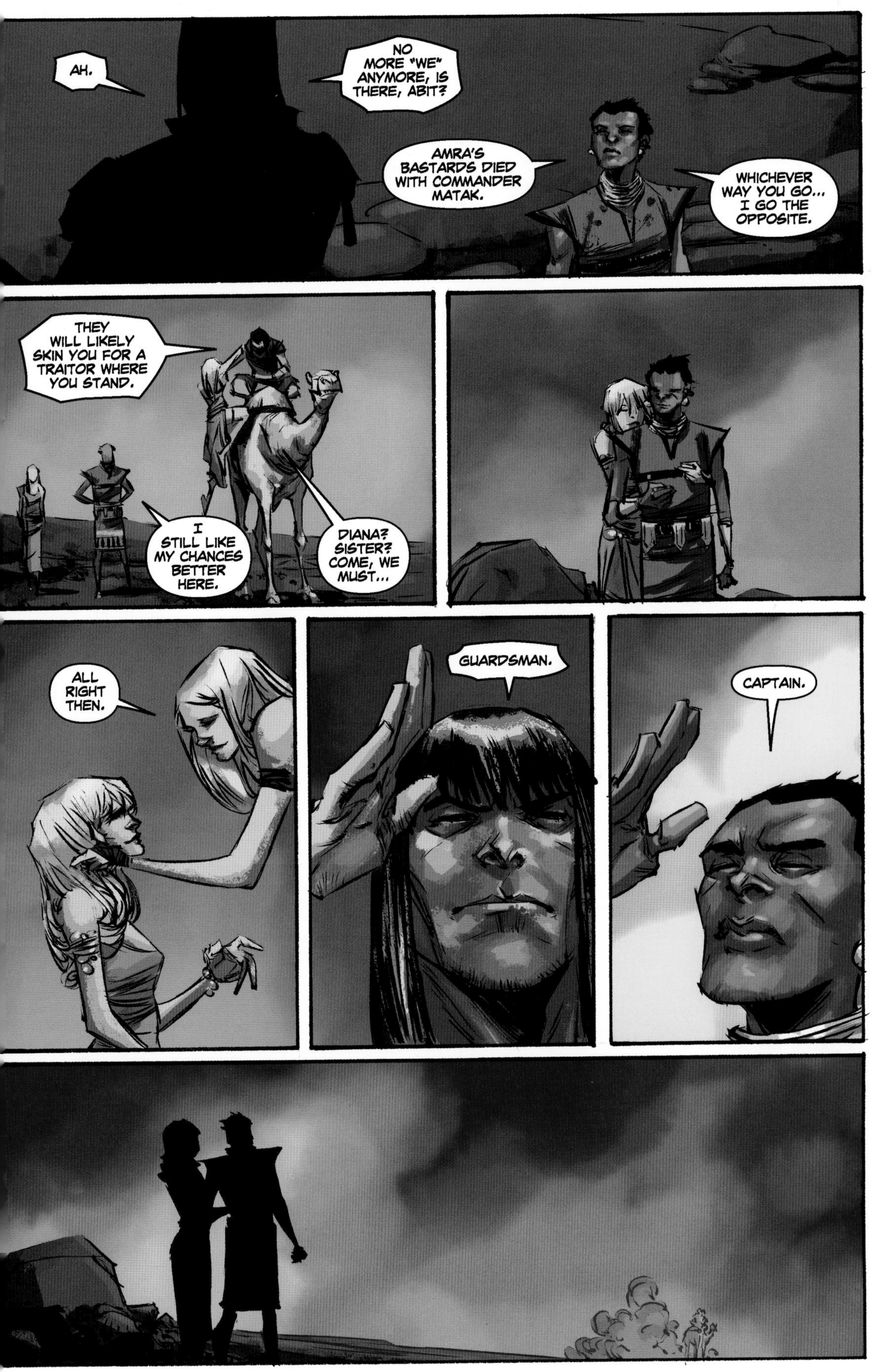
AH.
NO MORE "WE" ANYMORE, IS THERE, ABIT?
AMRA'S BASTARDS DIED WITH COMMANDER MATAK.
WHICHEVER WAY YOU GO... I GO THE OPPOSITE.
THEY WILL LIKELY SKIN YOU FOR A TRAITOR WHERE YOU STAND.
I STILL LIKE MY CHANCES BETTER HERE.
DIANA? SISTER? COME, WE MUST...
ALL RIGHT THEN.
GUARDSMAN.
CAPTAIN.

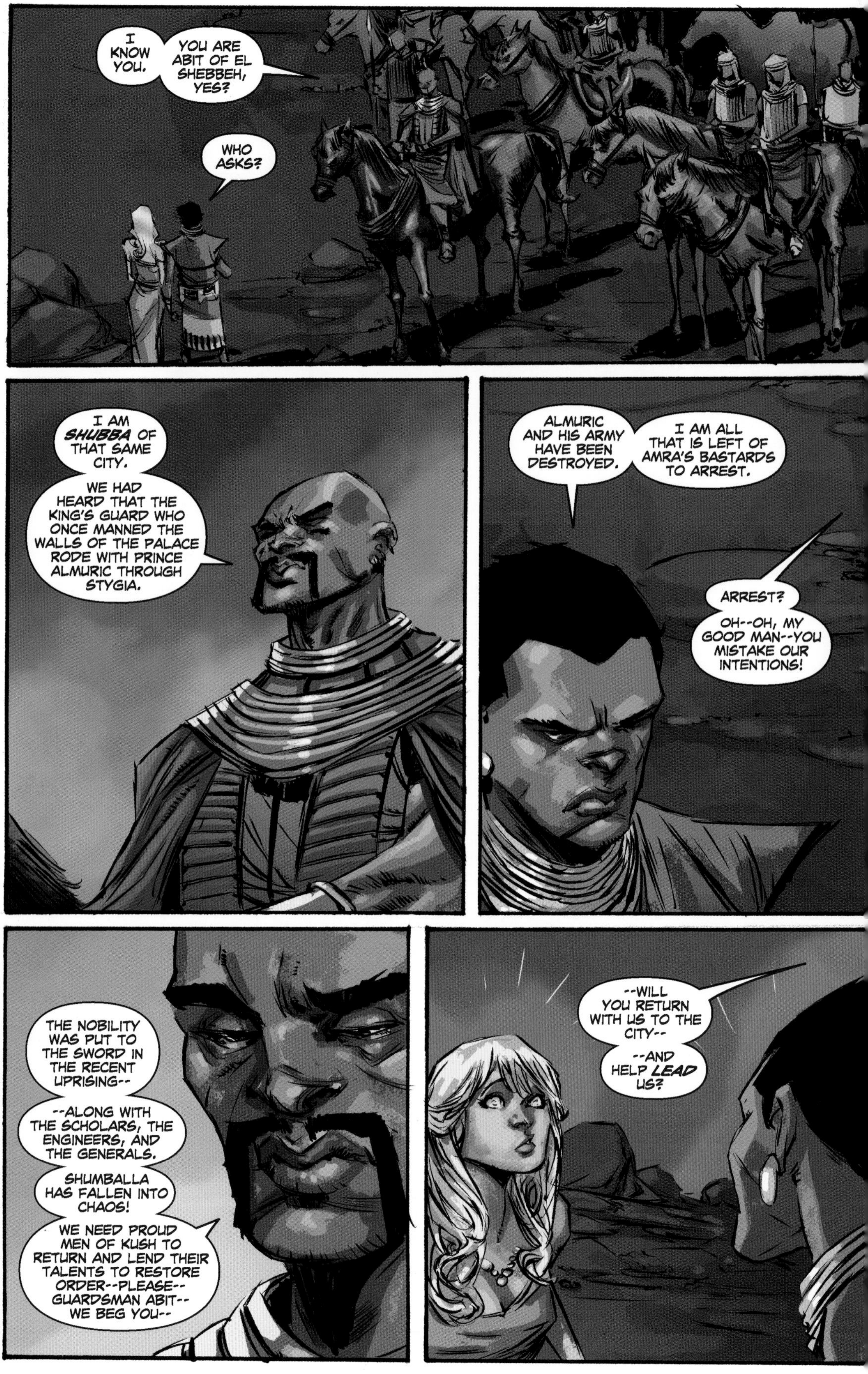
I KNOW YOU.
YOU ARE ABIT OF EL SHEBBEH, YES?
WHO ASKS?
I AM SHUBBA OF THAT SAME CITY.
WE HAD HEARD THAT THE KING'S GUARD WHO ONCE MANNED THE WALLS OF THE PALACE RODE WITH PRINCE ALMURIC THROUGH STYGIA.
ALMURIC AND HIS ARMY HAVE BEEN DESTROYED.
I AM ALL THAT IS LEFT OF AMRA'S BASTARDS TO ARREST.
ARREST?
OH--OH, MY GOOD MAN--YOU MISTAKE OUR INTENTIONS!
THE NOBILITY WAS PUT TO THE SWORD IN THE RECENT UPRISING--
--ALONG WITH THE SCHOLARS, THE ENGINEERS, AND THE GENERALS.
SHUMBALLA HAS FALLEN INTO CHAOS!
WE NEED PROUD MEN OF KUSH TO RETURN AND LEND THEIR TALENTS TO RESTORE ORDER--PLEASE--GUARDSMAN ABIT--WE BEG YOU--
--WILL YOU RETURN WITH US TO THE CITY--
--AND HELP LEAD US?

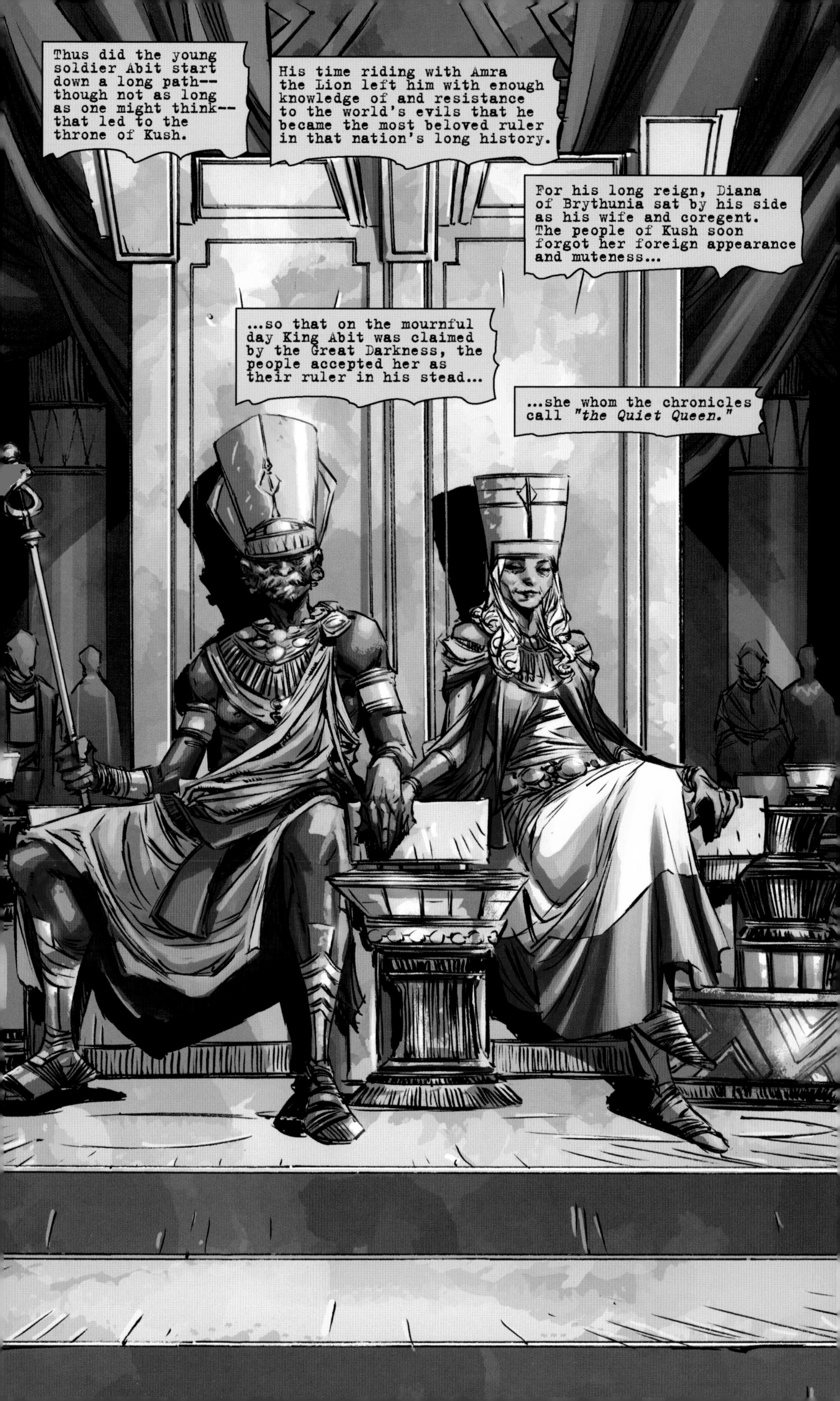
Thus did the young soldier Abit start down a long path--though not as long as one might think--that led to the throne of Kush.
His time riding with Amra the Lion left him with enough knowledge of and resistance to the world's evils that he became the most beloved ruler in that nation's long history.
For his long reign, Diana of Brythunia sat by his side as his wife and coregent. The people of Kush soon forgot her foreign appearance and muteness...
...so that on the mournful day King Abit was claimed by the Great Darkness, the people accepted her as their ruler in his stead...
...she whom the chronicles call *"the Quiet Queen."*

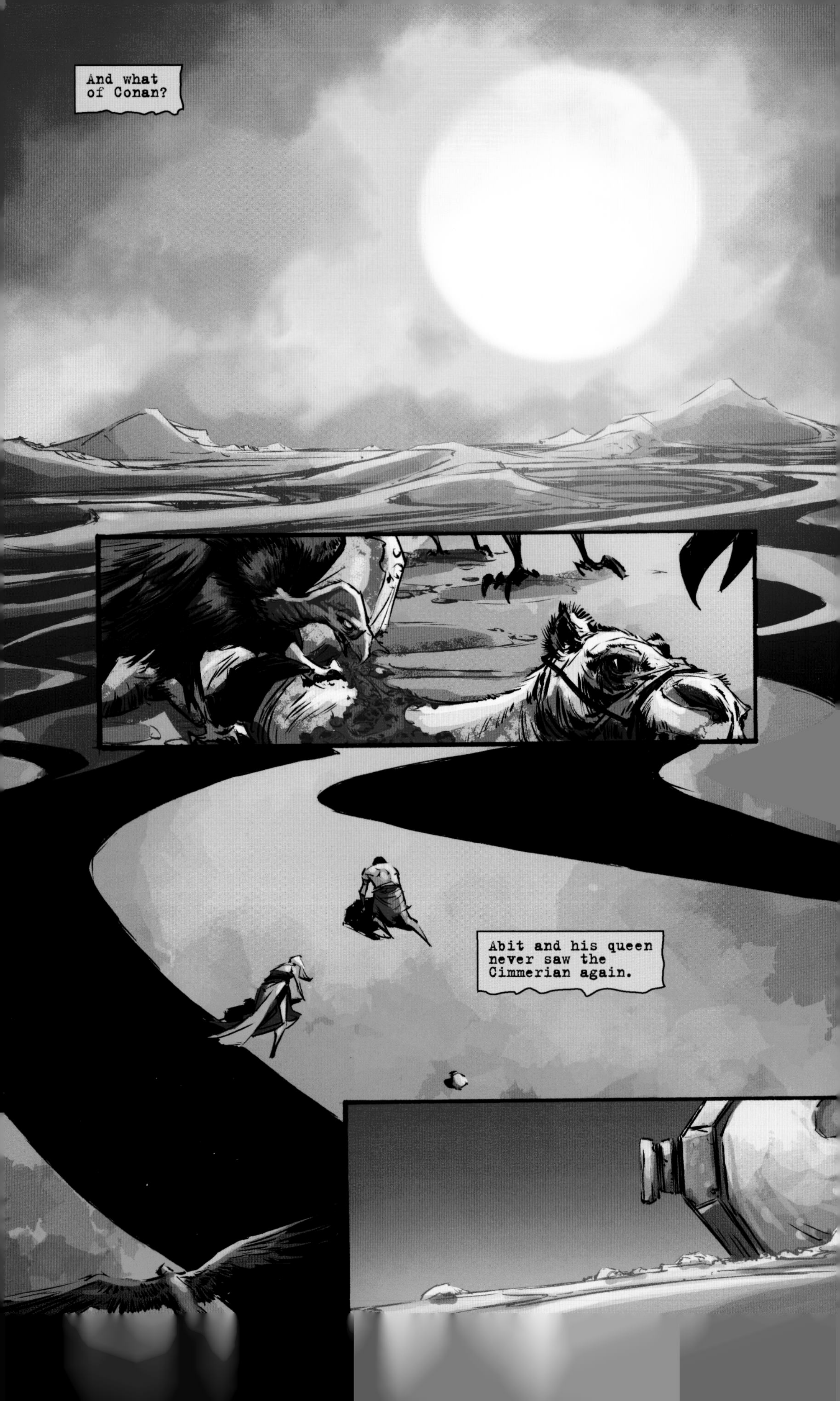
And what of Conan?
Abit and his queen never saw the Cimmerian again.

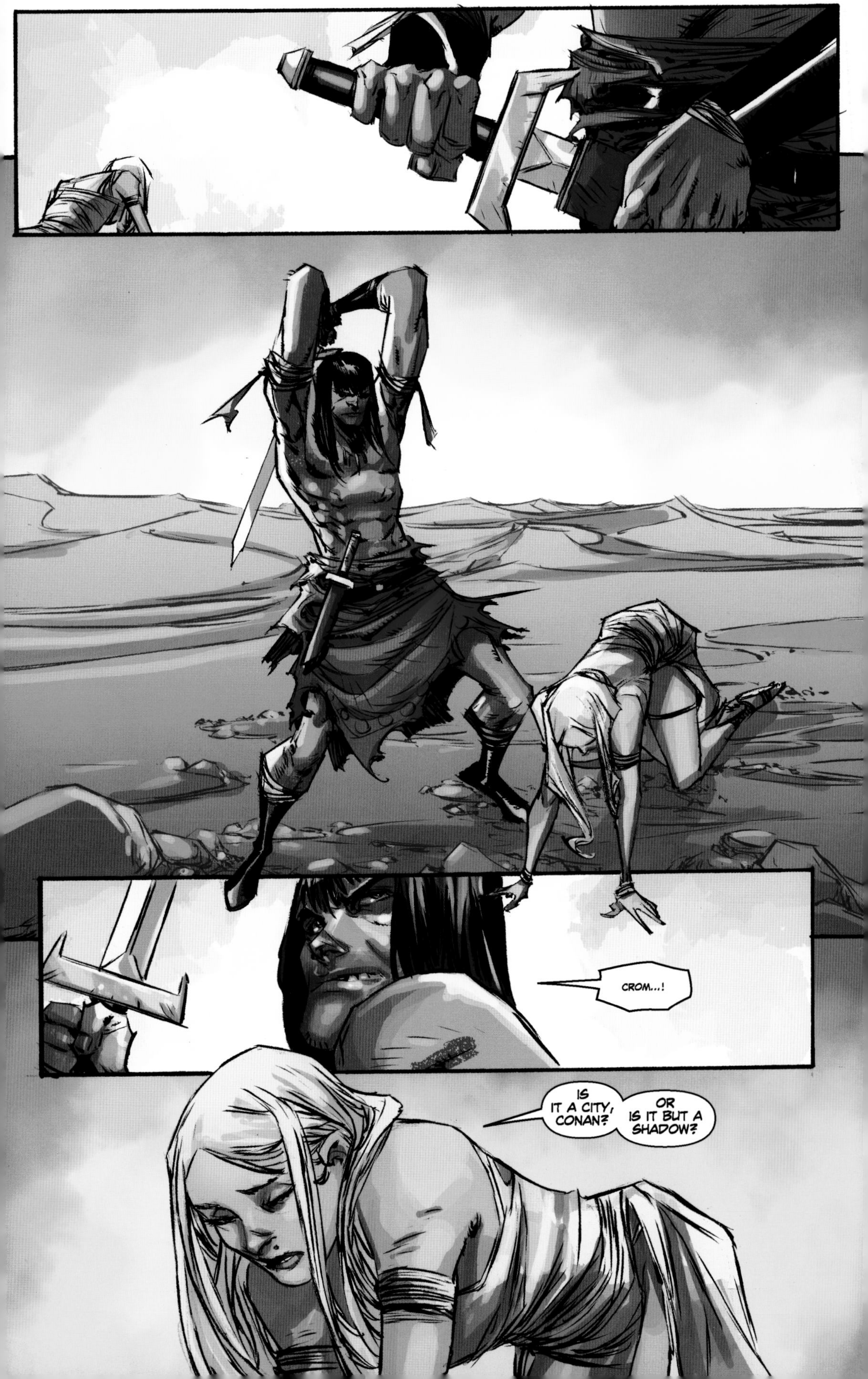
CROM...!
IS IT A CITY, CONAN?
OR IS IT BUT A SHADOW?

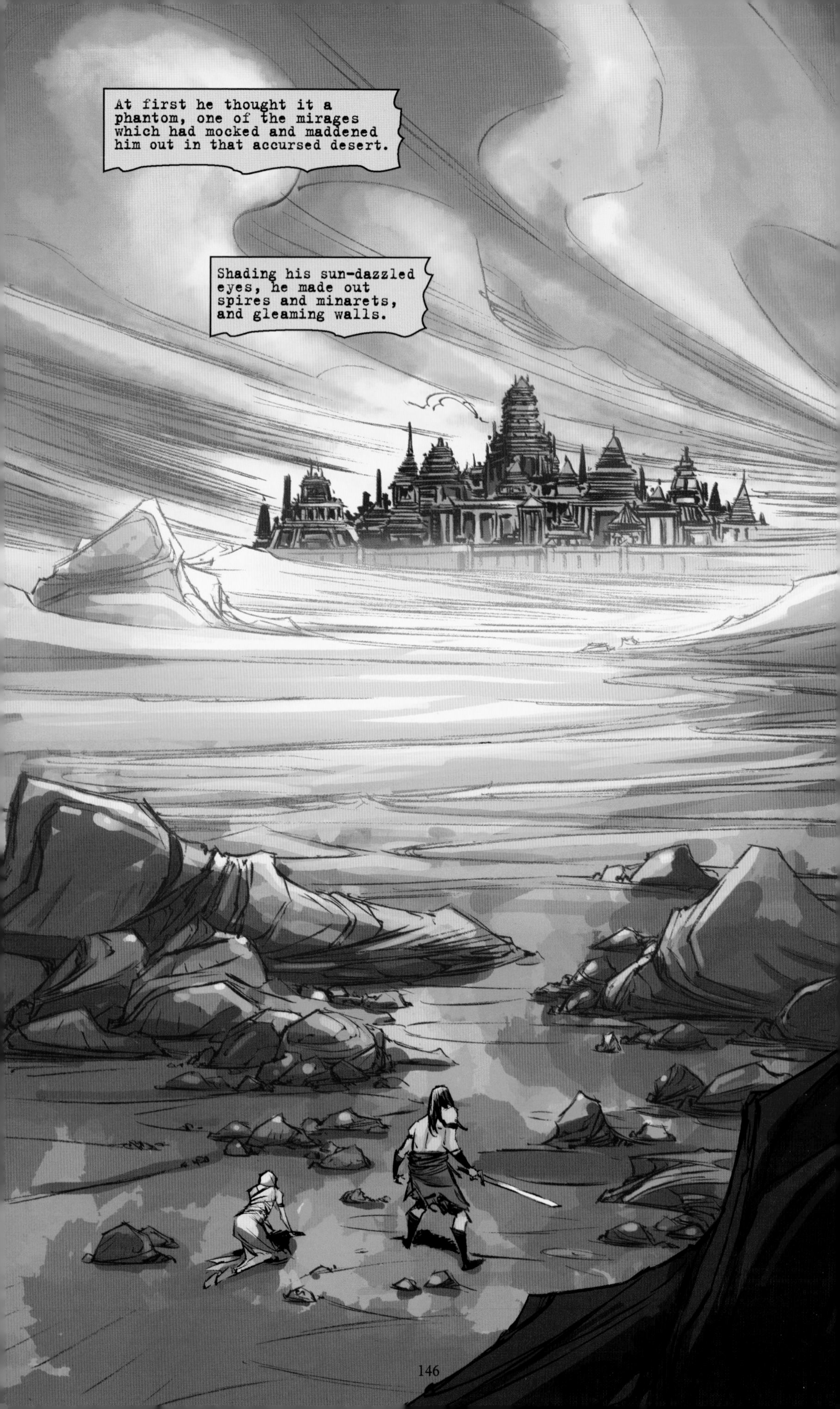
At first he thought it a phantom, one of the mirages which had mocked and maddened him out in that accursed desert.
Shading his sun-dazzled eyes, he made out spires and minarets, and gleaming walls.

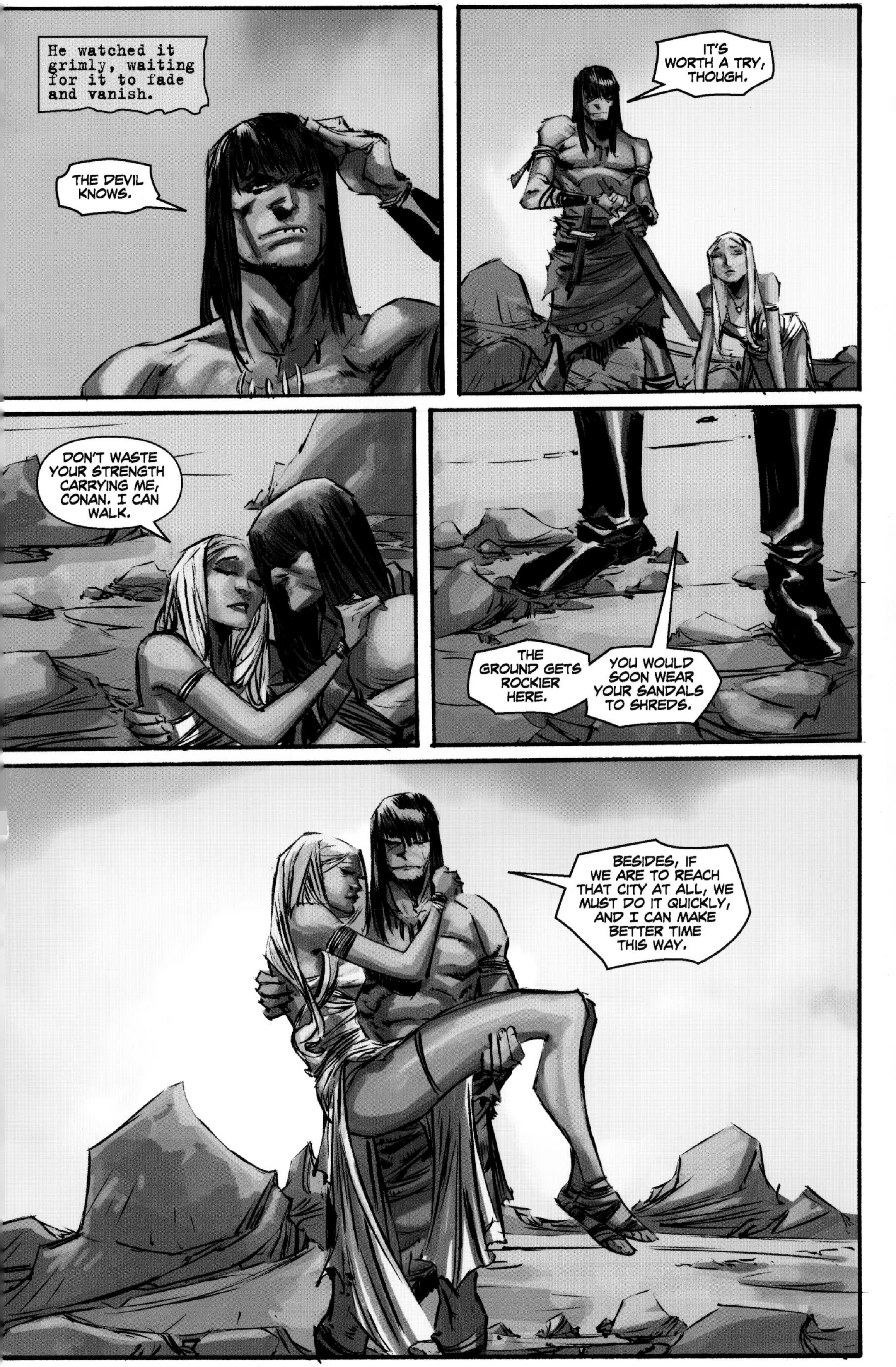
He watched it grimly, waiting for it to fade and vanish.
THE DEVIL KNOWS.
IT'S WORTH A TRY, THOUGH.
DON'T WASTE YOUR STRENGTH CARRYING ME, CONAN. I CAN WALK.
THE GROUND GETS ROCKIER HERE.
YOU WOULD SOON WEAR YOUR SANDALS TO SHREDS.
BESIDES, IF WE ARE TO REACH THAT CITY AT ALL, WE MUST DO IT QUICKLY, AND I CAN MAKE BETTER TIME THIS WAY.

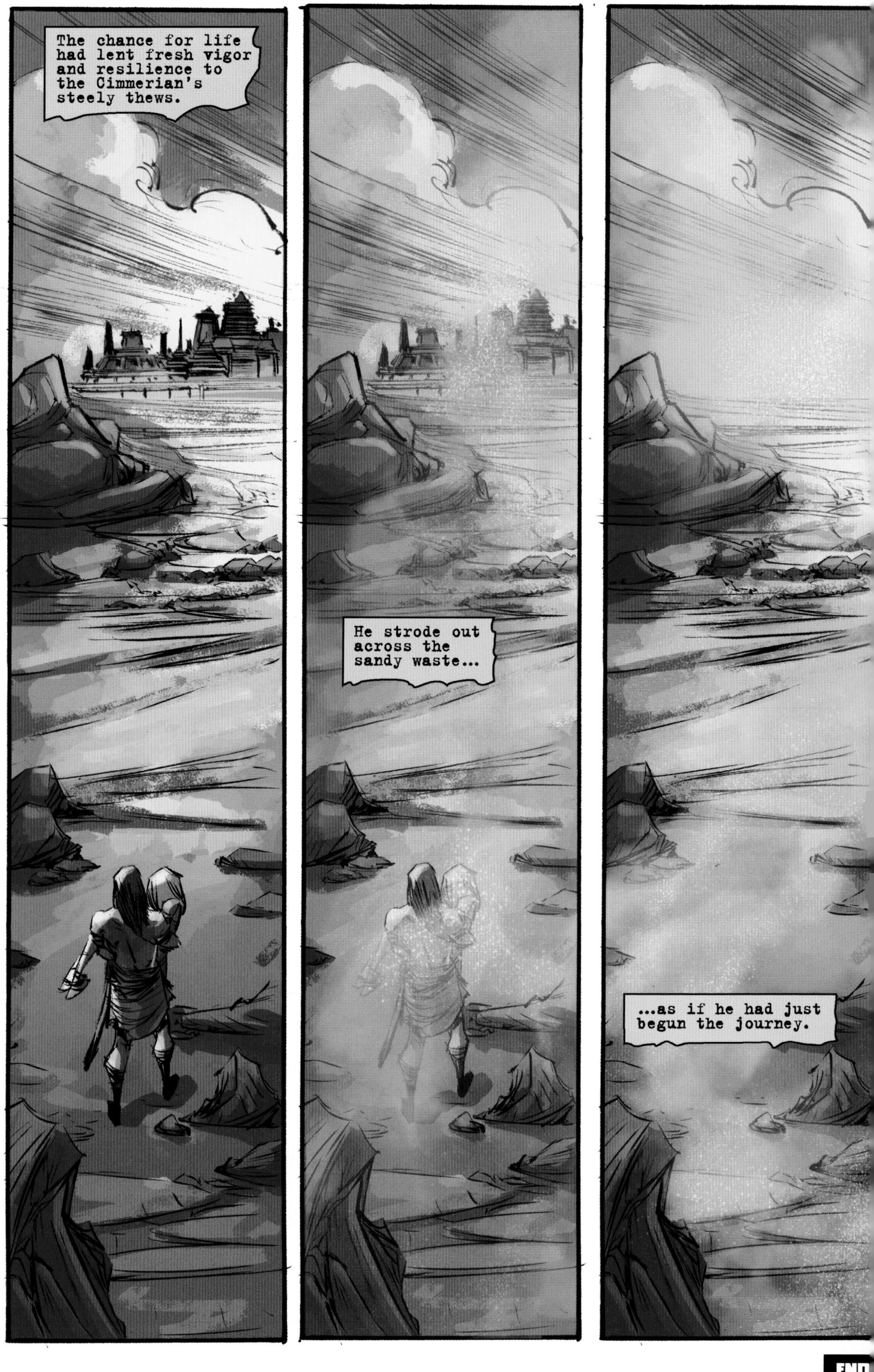
The chance for life had lent fresh vigor and resilience to the Cimmerian's steely thews.
He strode out across the sandy waste...
...as if he had just begun the journey.
END

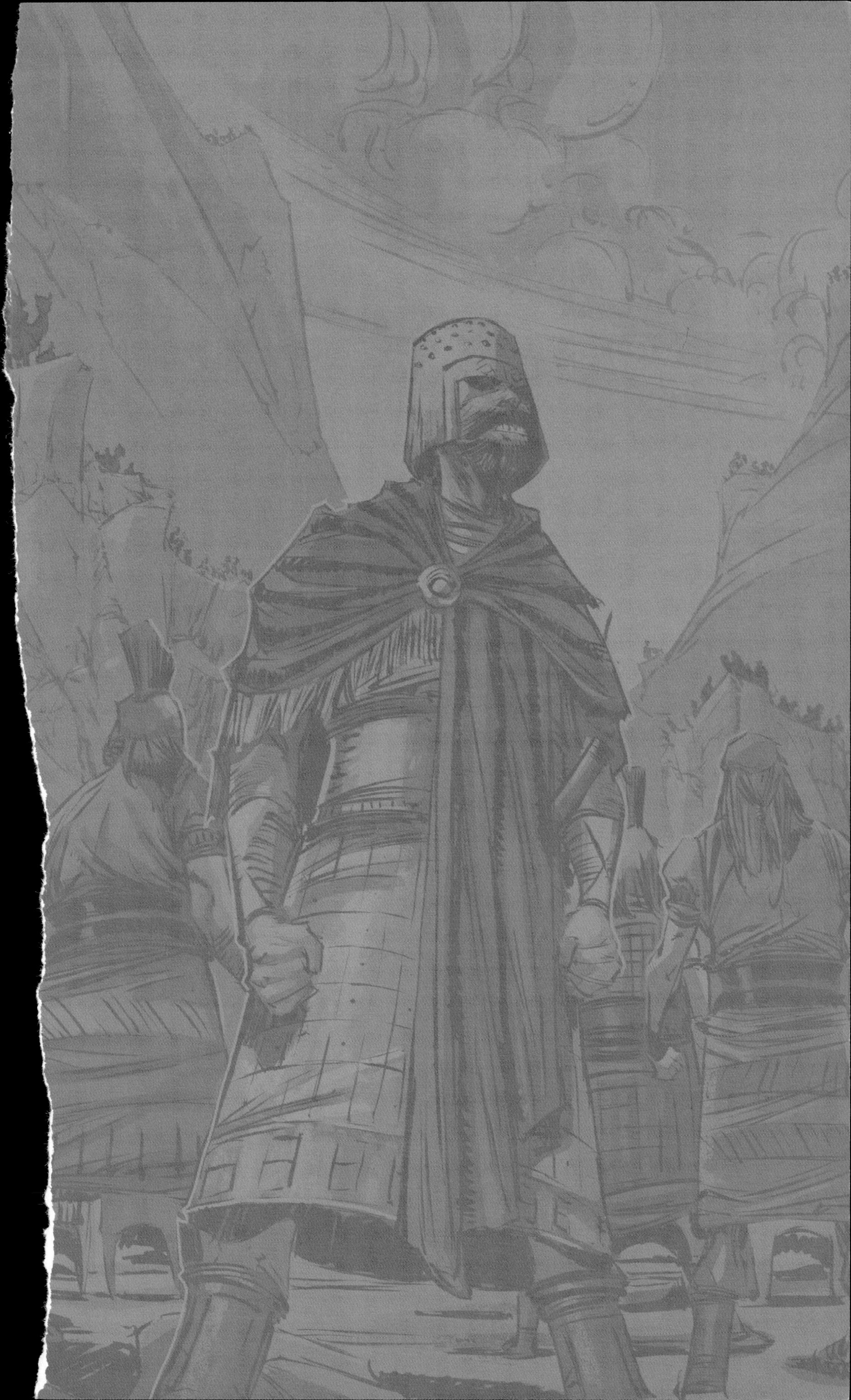

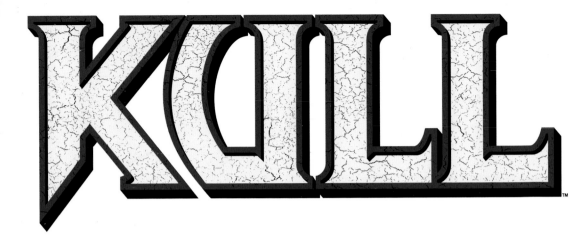